The Feminist Companion to the Bible
(Second Series)

3

Editor
Athalya Brenner

Sheffield Academic Press

Ruth and Esther

A Feminist Companion to the Bible
(Second Series)

edited by Athalya Brenner

Copyright © 1999 Sheffield Academic Press

Published by Sheffield Academic Press Ltd
Mansion House
19 Kingfield Road
Sheffield, S11 9AS
England

Printed on acid-free paper in Great Britain
by The Cromwell Press
Trowbridge, Wiltshire

British Library Cataloguing in Publication Data

A catalogue record for this book is available
from the British Library

ISBN 1-85075-978-2

To the memory of

_____

Fokkelien van Dijk-Hemmes

‫ת•נ•צ•ב•ה•‬

CONTENTS

II
RUTH AND ESTHER: MOTHERS AND DAUGHTERS

III
ESTHER

ABBREVIATIONS

AB	Anchor Bible
ABD	David Noel Freedman (ed.), *The Anchor Bible Dictionary* (New York: Doubleday, 1992)
BASOR	*Bulletin of the American Schools of Oriental Research*
BIS	Biblical Interpretation Series
BJS	Brown Judaic Studies
BK	*Bibel und Kirche*
BR	*Bible Review*
BZAW	Beihefte zur *ZAW*
CBQ	*Catholic Biblical Quarterly*
CBQMS	*Catholic Biblical Quarterly*, Monograph Series
CPB	*Christlich-pädagogische Blätter*
EncJud	*Encyclopaedia Judaica*
ErIs	*Eretz Israel*
GTBS	Gütersloher Taschenbücher Siebenstern
HAR	*Hebrew Annual Review*
HBS	Herders Biblische Studien
IB	*Interpreter's Bible*
IDB	George Arthur Buttrick (ed.), *The Interpreter's Dictionary of the Bible* (4 vols.; Nashville: Abingdon Press, 1962)
IEJ	*Israel Exploration Journal*
JAAR	*Journal of the American Academy of Religion*
JBL	*Journal of Biblical Literature*
JSOT	*Journal for the Study of the Old Testament*
JSOTSup	*Journal for the Study of the Old Testament*, Supplement Series
KT	Kaiser Taschenbücher
NEB.AT	Die Neue Echter Bibel: Altes Testament
NICOT	New International Commentary on the Old Testament
OBO	Orbis biblicus et orientalis
OEANE	Eric Meyers (ed.), *The Oxford Encyclopedia of Archaeology in the Near East* (5 vols.; Oxford: Oxford University Press, 1997)
RB	*Revue biblique*
rhs	*Religionsunterricht an höheren schulen*
TTZ	*Trierer theologische Zeitschrift*
VT	*Vetus Testamentum*
VTSup	*Vetus Testamentum*, Supplements
ZAW	*Zeitschrift für die alttestamentliche Wissenschaft*
ZBK	Zürcher Bibelkommentar

LIST OF CONTRIBUTORS

Mieke Bal, Theory of Literature, Faculty of Humanities, University of Amsterdam, Spuistraat 210, 1012 VT Amsterdam, The Netherlands

Roland Boer, United Theological College, 16 Masons Drive, North Pararamatta, NSW 2151 Australia

Athalya Brenner, Theology and Religious Studies, Faculty of Humanities, University of Amsterdam, Oude Turfmarkt 147, 1012 GC Amsterdam, The Netherlands

Leila Leah Bronner, 180 North Las Palmas Avenue, Los Angeles, CA 90004, USA

Klara Butting, Luisenstr. 54, 29525 Uelzen, Germany

Laura E. Donaldson, The Women's Studies Program, University of Iowa, 202 Jefferson Bldg, Iowa City, Iowa 52242-1418, USA

Musa W. Dube, University of Botswana, Private Bag 0022, Gaborone Botswana

Irmtraud Fischer, Catholic Faculty of Theology, University of Bonn, Germany

Carole R. Fontaine, Andover Newton Theological School, 210 Herrick Road, Newton Centre, MA 02459, USA

Bonnie Honig, Political Science Department, Northwestern University, 601 University Place, Evanston, IL 60208-1006, USA; and Senior Research Fellow, American Bar Foundation, 750 N. Lakeshore Dr., Chicago, IL 60608, USA

Cheryl A. Kirk-Duggan, Center for Women and Religion, Graduate Theological Union, 2400 Ridge Road, Berkeley, CA 94709, USA

Judith E. McKinlay, Department of Theology and Religious Studies, Post Box 56, University of Otago, Dunedin, New Zealand

Carol Meyers, Department of Religion, Duke University, PO Box 90964, Durham, NC 27708-0964, USA

Ursula Silber, Casilla 138, Potosí, Bolivia

INTRODUCTION

Athalya Brenner

This volume contains fourteen essays. Ten essays are on the book of Ruth. Two essays deal with daughters and mothers in the books of Ruth and Esther (and in other biblical texts). Two essays are on the book of Esther.

The first *Feminist Companion* for Ruth was published in 1993. It contained twelve articles, six of which were reprints or reworked versions of essays previously published elsewhere.[1] In the *Feminist Companion to Esther, Judith and Susanna* the ratio was somewhat more in favour of original essays.[2] In this volume, edited just five and three years (respectively) later, two essays are reprints[3] and one is a rewrite.[4] Three other essays are translations from recent German original publications, hence new to most English-language readers.[5] Clearly, the only two HB books that are named after female figures have continued to sustain feminist interest. If anything, this interest has grown. And, in this second series of the *Feminist Companion*, a conscious attempt will be made to bring to English-language readers as much material of other-language feminist research as possible.

But, as can be gleaned from a quick glance at the contents of the present volume, the directions of critical inquiry have shifted somewhat.

---

1. Cf. articles by Cady Stanton, Rashkow, Bal, Meyers, Brenner and Ozick in that volume (A. Brenner [ed.], *A Feminist Companion to Ruth* [Feminist Companion to the Bible, 3; Sheffield: Sheffield Academic Press, 1993]).

2. A. Brenner, *A Feminist Companion to Esther, Judith and Susanna* (Feminist Companion to the Bible, 7; Sheffield: Sheffield Academic Press, 1995).

3. 'Ruth, the Model Emigrée' by Bonnie Honig and 'Lots of Writing' by Mieke Bal.

4. ' "Women of the Neighborhood" (Ruth 4.17): Informal Female Networks in Ancient Israel' by Carol Meyers.

5. 'The Book of Ruth: A "Feminist" Commentary to the Torah?' by Irmtraud Fischer; 'Ruth and Naomi: Two Biblical Figures Revived among Rural Women in Germany' by Ursula Silber; and 'Esther: A New Interpretation of the Joseph Story in the Fight against Anti-Semitism and Sexism' by Klara Butting.

In this stage of feminist criticism, some ground has already been broken. On the one hand, interest in literary female heroes is still very much in evidence. However, so-called sex- and gender-specific (read: F[emale]/[eminine]) matters need not be justified anymore. Therefore, feminist critics can, less problematically, apply the results of their biblical criticism to contemporary life situations—as in Honig, Silber, Brenner, Donaldson, McKinlay, Dube Shomanah and Kirk-Duggan's essays. On the other hand, feminist critics have branched out to discuss issues that, until quite recently, were not considered within the realm of F interest per se. Such issues as Torah criticism (Fischer) or socio-anthropological questions (Meyers), for example, or community boundaries and identity, go beyond the definitions of F identity (for text and readers), a subject much discussed in previous feminist criticism on Ruth and Esther. Another trend discernible in at least some of the essays here collected is their links with feminist theory and praxis in general. In her 1997 essay for *A Feminist Companion to Reading the Bible: Approaches, Methods and Strategies*, Pamela Milne wrote:[6]

> The effort to make the connections with the larger feminist movement and feminist scholarship in other disciplines will have to come from feminist biblical scholars. We need to do a better job of 'selling' the relevance and importance of our subject matter to a feminist movement that has regarded our work as marginal and irrelevant.

She looked forward to

> [R]econnecting the work of feminist Bible scholars to the task of the feminist movement in making the idea of women's equality (along with the equality of other marginalized peoples) a social, political, legal and economic reality. To realize this potential it will be incumbent upon those of us who practise this kind of discourse to develop its political consciousness more fully.[7]

It seems to me that most, perhaps all, essays in this volume do connect with the theories and praxes of contemporary feminisms and, furthermore, express concern for peoples marginalized in/by various social levels and realities.

---

6. P.J. Milne, 'Toward Feminist Companionship: The Future of Feminist Biblical Studies and Feminism', in A. Brenner and C.R. Fontaine (eds.), *A Feminist Companion to Reading the Bible: Approaches, Methods and Strategies* (Sheffield: Sheffield Academic Press, 1997), pp. 39-60 (58-59).

7. Milne, 'Toward Feminist Companionship', p. 59.

Part 1: Ruth

The five articles of section A deal with various aspects of the book of Ruth. These aspects are widely different from each other. They are grouped together here precisely because they are so different from each other, thus evidencing (parts of) the current width and breadth of feminist critical interest in the HB. These essays' reader will proceed by a seesaw movement from an intertextual reading of Ruth and the Torah, to a reading of Ruth as an immigrant related to contemporary culture, then back into an examination of Ruth as an Other in past sources, back to Ruth and Naomi as inspiration for present-day women's community, then back to ancient female networks.

In 'The Book of Ruth: A "Feminist" Commentary to the Torah?', Fischer begins by a consideration of Ruth as a women's book, a book that contains such interests as female companionship, cooperation and age-free processes of learning. She then moves to ask whether Ruth is not only a women's book from the aspect of contents, but also from the aspect of composition—especially since, in addition, it supplies a female genealogy. Female composition of Ruth is thus possible. Genealogy is a prime topic in the Torah, which also contains some legal passages (redemption, levirate marriage) whose topics play a large role, this way or another, in Ruth. This motivates Fischer to consider the (possible) female author of Ruth as a Torah exegete of the highest understanding. By this intertextual reading of Ruth and the Torah, Fischer elevates the hypothetical female author into a halakhic authority—while, symmetrically, she herself shifts from a feminist critic of women's stories to the position of a Pentateuch critic.

Honig's concerns in 'Ruth, the Model Emigrée' are, overtly, with the application of the biblical Ruth to a specific time-place axis of contemporary life, from the viewpoint of political science and sociology. Honig writes directly from contemporary American experience, in which the question of how to treat the foreigner (not only the female foreigner) is of great importance. The questions of integration into a dominant local culture, or its lack, are important ones in theory as well as praxis. When integration is indeed encouraged the forms it assumes, and the price tags attached to it, are a matter of emotion as well as of policy. The book of Ruth is interpreted; then used for clarifying some of the complex issues involved. Some of these issues will return in the essays by Donaldson and Brenner (in section B, see below).

In 'Facing the Other: Ruth-the-Cat in Medieval Jewish Illuminations', Fontaine looks at Ruth illuminated as cat-headed in the

Tripartite Maḥzor. It is clear from the study of Jewish manuscripts and other ancient representations that various animal figures held particular symbolism for the communities producing these texts. Ruth's depiction marks her as both different from the illuminated Jewish *males*, who have normal human heads; and also from *Jewish* women, portrayed throughout the zoocephalic manuscripts primarily with bird's heads. Why, indeed, is she a cat? After a quick survey of cat symbolism, Fontaine concludes that Ruth-the-cat is ambiguous: a valuable domestic presence, but nevertheless an Other.

While Fontaine looks at art as commentary, Silber looks at Ruth in a completely different setting. 'Ruth and Naomi: Two Biblical Figures Revived among Rural Women in Germany' is an account of a 'confrontation' between two sets of women, ancient and contemporary (though not necessarily 'modern', not to say postmodern). As a result of this confrontational workshop, both life texts—Ruth and Naomi's on the one hand, the German rural women's on the other hand—are freshly illuminated. The contemporary women recognize themselves in Ruth and Naomi's lives and dilemmas. And, although the framework is not scholarly, some scholarly as well as experiental insights can be gleaned for the biblical text and its seemingly faraway circumstances.

And this exercise in women's networking in contemporary life leads us back, once again, to the issue of women's networking in the HB. This is the subject of Meyers' '"Women of the Neighborhood" (Ruth 4.17): Informal Female Networks in Ancient Israel'. As Meyers notes, the narrative of Ruth and Naomi's actions in Bethlehem is framed by the local women's actions (1.19 and 4.17 respectively). According to Meyers theoretical considerations based on ethnographic data from contemporary research of agrarian societies prove that women's involvement in both their marital and natal communities, although informal and often not elaborated upon in the HB, nevertheless transcended the 'private', domestic family sphere into the 'public' domain. Thus, proceeding from the book of Ruth, Meyers shows how '[t]he very informality of women's networks gave them great flexibility to respond in innovative, situation-specific ways to human needs'.

Section B contains the papers delivered at the 'Semiotics and Exegesis' session of the American Society of Biblical Literature in San Francisco, November 1997. Four short papers were presented, followed by a single response for all of them. As it happened, two of the papers—'The Sign of Orpah: Reading Ruth through Native Eyes' by Donaldson, and 'The Unpublished Letters of Orpah to Ruth' by

Dube—foreground a figure marginal to the HB Ruth narrative and largely absent from the other essays printed here, Orpah. In both, Orpah serves as a token and foil for different types of foreignness: for Donaldson it is Cherokee (Indian American), for Dube African (Botswana). Each one, in her very different style, writes from her own specific native experience as well as scholarship. By reversing the usual scholarly practice of focusing on Ruth and Naomi, as warranted by their place in the plot, these two scholars shift Orpah from the margin to the centre, together with their own concerns about native marginalization. In true feminist fashion, concern for the marginalization of women is expanded to include also non-gendered racial and cultural concerns. In McKinlay's 'A Son Is Born to Naomi: A Harvest for Israel', and in my 'Ruth as a Foreign Worker and the Politics of Exogamy', the focus goes back to Ruth and Naomi. However, these essays too are informed by social-societal concerns, especially over class and race in addition to gender. The whole session evolved into reading Ruth for today: Boer's response, titled 'Culture, Ethics and Identity in Reading Ruth', picks up the theme of reading from a specific here-and-now and takes it further.

The decision to keep the papers together, and with little if any revision asked of the participants, was motivated by the wish to maintain the atmosphere of dialogue that obtained in that SBL session. Otherwise, clearly, content considerations would have dictated other arrangements—such as having all four papers, and the response, grouped together with Honig's essay as a section about Ruth and Otherness; or grouping Donaldson's and Dube's essays together with Kirk-Duggan in a section about native/outsider and the reversal of such positions in a dominant culture; and so on.

Part II: Mothers and Daughters

Bronner's 'The Invisible Relationship Made Visible: Biblical Mothers and Daughters', and Kirk-Duggan's 'Black Mother Women and Daughters: Signifying Female–Divine Relationships in the Hebrew Bible and African-American Mother–Daughter Short Stories', are—as the titles indicate—about the biblical concepts and relations of 'mothers' and 'daughters'. None of these two essays restricts itself to a specific biblical text. However, Bronner's essay links more easily to the Ruth scroll, while Kirk-Duggan's links with both Esther and Ruth.

In the story of Naomi, Ruth and Boaz there is a mother, her daughter (or a daughter's figure) and a daughter's husband to be. The daughter has no father; there is no 'father's house'. Instead, there is a 'mother's house', a phrase that appears twice also in the Song of Songs and in Genesis 24. Bronner discusses the metaphorical use of 'daughter' in the HB, then the relationships between mothers and daughters in the few relevant HB texts, including the displacement of the absent father's role onto another narrative character, such as a woman's brothers or her lover. Bronner summarizes: 'The biblical mother–daughter relationship, as I hope I have shown, is an enduring element in the Bible well worth recovering. When the mother appears along with the daughter, love appears as well.' This essay, then, can be read as a continuation of Meyers' essay in the first *Feminist Companion to Ruth*,[8] and of Shargent's essay in the *Feminist Companion to Samuel and Kings*.[9]

Kirk-Duggan proceeds from the statement that women bond with women and with their daughters, within family, within extended family and within society. She uses mother–daughter poems and stories by contemporary African-American writers in *Memory of Kin*[10] as a lens for reading the stories of Esther and Ruth. Naomi learns wholeness from Ruth. Esther enables Israel's, her extended family's, salvation. The neighbor women, meanwhile, call the child the son of Naomi, disavowing Ruth's maternity (Ruth 4.16-17). The questions Kirk-Duggan poses for both groups of texts, ancient and contemporary, are similar: Can a positive mother–daughter relationship be developed? If so, in what way(s)? And if not, what is the price paid by women for lack of individuation, separation from, or independent cooperation with, their daughters/mothers? Kirk-Duggan's intertexts are culture-specific, as in most other essays of this volume.

Part III: Esther

The last two essays in this collection focus on the book of Esther. Bal's 'Lots of Writing' can be introduced in her own words:

> Lot(s) of writing happen(s) in the book of Esther, and writing is where
> words and images converge, where the visual and the verbal, fate and

8. C. Meyers, 'Returning Home: Ruth 1.8 and the Gendering of the Book of Ruth', in A. Brenner (ed.), *A Feminist Companion to Ruth* (Feminist Companion to the Bible, 3; Sheffield: Sheffield Academic Press, 1993), pp. 85-114.

9. Karla G. Shargent, 'Living on the Edge: The Liminality of Daughters in Genesis to 2 Samuel', in A. Brenner (ed.), *A Feminist Companion to Samuel and Kings* (Feminist Companion to the Bible, 5; Sheffield: Sheffield Academic Press, 1994), pp. 26-42.

10. Mary Helen Washington (ed.), *Memory of Kin: Stories about Family by Black Writers* (New York: Anchor; Garden City, NY: Doubleday, 1991).

agency, Providence and plotting comes together. In this article I grapple
with visual and verbal representations of self-reflexion in the story of
Esther, as depicted in the Scroll of Esther and in two paintings by
Rembrandt.[11]

The paintings are used as interpretations of the biblical texts. The
feast[12] Esther gives is presented as a 'feast of writing'. Reading Esther
as a text about reading and writing is, according to Bal, an invitation
to reflect upon, among other things, elements of history, such as
'gender, power, and the state; genocide and otherness'.

These precisely are the issues discussed in Butting's 'Esther: A New
Interpretation of the Joseph Story in the Fight against Anti-Semitism
and Sexism', the essay that closes this selection. In Butting's interpretation, the Esther Scroll presents a new interpretation of Joseph's
story. The decisive character, Joseph himself, is recreated anew in two
persons, Esther and Mordecai. They are confronted with the totalitarian, sexist power of the empire and at first adjust to it. The situation, however, demands a change of the power balance: a gender
shift occurs. Nevertheless, says Butting, Esther is *not* another total
deliverance story, after the model of the exodus from Egypt. At the
end of the book of Esther we are once again confronted with the social
context of the story: royal politics and historiography's silence concerning power and women's history.

Both Ruth and Esther are absent from the ending of the narratives
that came to bear their names. This absence and the reversal of the
silence about women's history and women's lot together with other
Others, then and now, are the main business of this collection.

---

11. From the 'Abstract' of the *Poetics Today* publication, p. 89. Bal's essay has
already been published twice: in *Semeia* 54 (1991), pp. 77-102, and in *Poetics Today*
15.1 (1994), pp. 89-114. It is reprinted here again for two reasons: one, its incredible
richness; and, two, my impression that it is hardly known to/used by feminist
critics of Esther.
12. For feasts in Esther and their opposite, hunger, in Ruth see also Kirk-
Duggan, albeit in a completely different direction than Bal's.

Part I

RUTH

A.

ASPECTS OF THE RUTH SCROLL

THE BOOK OF RUTH:
A 'FEMINIST' COMMENTARY TO THE TORAH?

Irmtraud Fischer

The book of Ruth is *the* women's book of the Hebrew Bible.[1] Of course, this is not only because of the name of the book, which in tradition has always been 'Ruth'. Yet even this is something remarkable: In the *Erzeltern* narrations,[2] where there is so much told about women, the female part of the story was passed over in silence as far as naming was concerned. One would speak of *'patriarchal* narratives', that is, narrations about the *'fathers'*. The book of Ruth was never called 'the book of Boaz' or 'the book of Elimelech'. Its title has always had a preference for female experience. Hardly any other book of the Bible manages to express the 'female voice'[3] as authentically as Ruth does. My whole understanding of the Ruth scroll results from this fact.[4]

---

1. Carol Meyers, 'Returning Home: Ruth 1.8 and the Gendering of the Book of Ruth', in A. Brenner (ed.), *A Feminist Companion to Ruth* (Feminist Companion to the Bible, 3; Sheffield: Sheffield Academic Press, 1993), pp. 85-114: 'the dominant androcentricity of Scripture is interrupted by the gynocentricity of Ruth' (p. 86).

2. As far as the term 'Erzeltern-Erzählungen' is concerned, see I. Fischer, *Die Erzeltern Israels* (BZAW, 222; Berlin: W. de Gruyter, 1994).

3. For fundamentals in theory see A. Brenner and F. van Dijk-Hemmes, *On Gendering Texts: Female and Male Voices in the Hebrew Bible* (BIS, 1; Leiden: E.J. Brill, 1993), pp. 1-32; also F. van Dijk-Hemmes, 'Ruth: A Product of Women's Culture?', in A. Brenner (ed.), *A Feminist Companion to Ruth* (Feminist Companion to the Bible, 3; Sheffield: Sheffield Academic Press, 1993), pp. 134-39. Several articles in the first volume of *A Feminist Companion to Ruth* already adopt this basic approach.

4. The concept of the book of Ruth presented in the following originated in a guest lecture on 12 December 1995 at the Evangelisch-theologische Fakultät of Marburg an der Lahn. The first part has been published in the meantime: I. Fischer, 'Rut—*Das* Frauenbuch der Hebräischen Bibel', *rhs* 39 (1996), pp. 1-6.

1. *The Book's Worldview* Is *Female*[5]

a. *Exposition of a Women's Story*

The first verse of the book of Ruth introduces a woman, together with three men: A man leaves Bethlehem with his wife and both of his sons because of a famine and seeks shelter in Moab (1.1). The wife, Naomi, is first of all characterized as Elimelech's wife (v. 2)—a common definition of women's identity in patriarchal society. Already in the next verse, however, all three men are defined by the woman (1.3):

> Elimelech, *Naomi's husband*, died, and she was left with both of *her* sons.

In v. 4 two more persons appear: Both sons marry Moabite women, Ruth and Orpah. About ten years later the two young men die as well.

> And the woman was left—without both of *her* sons and without *her* husband (v. 5).

The story began with a man, *his* wife, *his* two sons, that is, with three men and one woman. After the exposition there are three women left without *their* husbands[6]—indeed, a programmatic exposition for a women's book!

b. *Women's Different Plans of Life*

Because of the husband's (v. 3) and the sons' (v. 5) death, the story focuses on Naomi. Having heard that the famine had ended at home (v. 6), she and her daughters-in-law set out for Bethlehem. The following dialogue between the mother-in-law and her two daughters-in-law takes place on their way to Judah (vv. 6-22). While walking, the older woman is obviously beginning to realize that she cannot care for the two young women. She wants to send both back home. She defines the women's home from a female viewpoint—contrary to the expression 'father's house',[7] which is common in patriarchal societies.

---

5.   For further arguments cf. my previously published articles: 'Affidamento in einer patriarchalen Gesellschaft: Frauenbeziehungen im Buch Rut', in Grazer Interdisziplinäre Frauengruppe (ed.), *Paris-Milano-Graz* (Vienna: Wiener Frauenverlag, 1991), pp. 111-25; 'Eine Schwiegertochter—mehr wert als sieben Söhne! (Rut 4.15)', in H. Pissarek-Hudelist and L. Schottroff (eds.), *Mit allen Sinnen glauben: Für Elisabeth Moltmann-Wendel zum 65. Geburtstag* (GTBS, 532; Gütersloh: Gütersloher Verlagshaus, 1991), pp. 30-44; *Gottesstreiterinnen* (Stuttgart: W. Kohlhammer, 1995), pp. 175-94.

6.   Cf. A. Berlin, *Poetics and Interpretation of Biblical Narrative* (Winona Lake, IN: Eisenbrauns, 1994), pp. 83-84.

7.   Meyers, 'Returning Home', pp. 91-114. She shows that the expression

Go back, each of you, to *your mother's house* (v. 8).

Her farewell words are blessings in order to thank the women. Naomi wishes her daughters-in-law a happy and safe life. According to her they will find such a life 'each in *her husband's house*'. Although Naomi defines the two fictitious, potential husbands of her daughters-in-law through their wives, her desired concept of life is traditional: a woman gains fulfillment and social security only in her husband's house. Naomi realistically judges that the two widows have more chances of marrying among their own people than away from home.

Ruth as well as Orpah are attached to their mother-in-law and will not let themselves be sent back. Both decide to go with the mother-in-law to 'your people', to the *mother-in-law's people*. With that, the women define the people not in terms of their deceased husbands but again by means of a woman, Naomi.

In a second attempt of persuasion, Naomi drastically reduces the possibility of a levirate marriage for the younger women.[8] Orpah is now persuaded by her mother-in-law, listens to her advice and goes back. Ruth, however, refuses (v. 14). Therefore, Naomi presents Orpah as an appropriate model to her second daughter-in-law (v. 15).

Ruth has an alternative plan for her life. Ruth's oath (vv. 16-17), which is often used as a marriage vow in churches, does not tie her to a *man* but to a *woman*. She swears faithfulness until death to her mother-in-law. She wants to go to the people and to the God[9] she has met through the female tradition of Naomi. In order to live together with the older woman, Ruth is willing to leave her own life context and to integrate herself into foreign situations (people, religion, grave). In a patriarchal society, where social structures are arranged from an androcentric viewpoint, women are discriminated against when surviving without men's companionship.[10] Therefore Ruth's

---

'house of the mother' is used mostly in women's texts that point to a 'female voice', as an alternative to the patriarchal 'father's house'. She correctly rejects the division that would assign the private domain to the female and the public to the male. See also I. Fischer, 'Den Frauen der Kochtopf—den Männern die hohe Politik?', *CPB* 108 (1995), pp. 134-38.

8.   See pp. 37-41.

9.   I. Rashkow, 'Ruth: The Discourse of Power and the Power of Discourse', in A. Brenner (ed.), *A Feminist Companion to Ruth* (Feminist Companion to the Bible, 3; Sheffield: Sheffield Academic Press, 1993), pp. 26-41; p. 30 points out that the formulation of Ruth's speech is the opposite of Naomi's in 1.15, where she speaks highly of Orpah and her return to *her* people and *her* God.

10.   See W. Schottroff, 'Die Armut der Witwen', in M. Crüsemann and W. Schot-

oath to be inseparably tied to her mother-in-law depicts an alternative, seemingly unsuitable concept of living.

c. *Ruth in Female Companionship*

The mother-in-law accepts Ruth's decision but does not react to it (v. 18). As Naomi returns to Bethlehem, the women of the place recognize her again. They have not forgotten the emigrant and kindly receive the childless widow (vv. 19-22). Naomi tells them about her bitter fate, which she thinks was caused by YHWH. Ruth's faithful company, however, is not appreciated as a remedy against her blow either by the women of Bethlehem or by Naomi herself. For a life of fulfillment it is obviously only men who count. Ruth does not appear in Naomi's or the other women's speech. Only the narrator corrects Naomi's view, having returned in emptiness: Ruth did come to Bethlehem with her (vv. 19, 22).

Ruth followed her mother-in-law (1.16-18) and swore to her faithfulness beyond death. This voluntary undertaking makes it clear that Ruth cannot look for a place of social security on her own. A new marriage would mean leaving her mother-in-law on her own, because the mother of a deceased husband would not be taken into the house of a future husband. Thus Ruth has to find a solution both for herself *and* for Naomi.

After arriving at Bethlehem Naomi remains passive,[11] although the women receive her and she still has a kinsman there. He is descended from Naomi's deceased husband, a socially distinguished landowner named Boaz. This information, however, is given only to the readers of the book of Ruth. Naomi does not inform her daughter-in-law about this (2.1, 3).[12]

---

troff (eds.), *Schuld und Schulden* (KT, 121; Munich: Chr. Kaiser Verlag, 1992), pp. 54-89.

11. In chs. 1 and 4 Naomi is represented as the main character; in chs. 2 and 3, however, Ruth is the main character. A. Brenner, 'Naomi and Ruth', in *idem* (ed.), *A Feminist Companion to Ruth*, pp. 70-84, presumes two strands for the book of Ruth: '…the book of Ruth is composed of two still-distinct strands, a Naomi story and a Ruth story' (p. 70).

12. D.N. Fewell and D.M. Gunn, ' "A Son Is Born to Naomi!": Literary Allusions and Interpretation in the Book of Ruth', *JSOT* 40 (1988), pp. 99-108, doubt the commonly drawn picture of Naomi (i.e. being a perfectly unselfish woman, without having any interests of her own, only acting for her daughter-in-law). The article has not remained unchallenged; cf. P.W. Coxon, 'Was Naomi a Scold? A Response to Fewell and Gunn', *JSOT* 45 (1989), pp. 25-37, and their very reply: D.N. Fewell and D. Gunn, 'Is Coxon a Scold? On Responding to the Book of Ruth', *JSOT* 45 (1989), pp. 39-43.

Yet Ruth is becoming active in order to make her and Naomi's livelihood. The young woman discusses her intentions beforehand with the older one. It is the first time Naomi speaks to her daughter-in-law since the command for her to return to Moab in 1.15. Naomi answers Ruth without enthusiasm but not heartlessly, saying, 'Yes, go, my daughter!' (2.2b). Being a stranger and a widow, Ruth claims the right to legal aid, namely to glean (cf. Deut. 24.19-22). In doing so she finds herself in the field that belongs to Naomi's kinsman, who has been introduced to the reader in 2.1. Having arrived at the field, Boaz inquires after the young woman who is gleaning. Obviously the kinsman has not properly cared for the poor widows, otherwise he would have to have known Ruth. The foreman of the harvesters tells Boaz who Ruth is. She is the Moabite woman who came to Bethlehem with Naomi, has explicitly asked for permission to glean and distinguishes herself by remarkable diligence (2.6-7).

Boaz takes pleasure in being the generous benefactor of the young widow. Not only does he provide food, drink and a supply of grain but he also saves her from the harvest workers' (sexual?) molestation. The man obviously knows what young women have to face in the fields (2.8-9, 15-16)—a drastically realistic judgment of male behavior in patriarchal society!

In her answer to the landowner's generous offer, Ruth points out the fact that she is a stranger. She accepts Boaz's offer with pleasure and does not take his generosity for granted. Ruth responds with exquisite courtesy that would not blur the social differences between the destitute foreign widow and the well-off native. It then becomes obvious by the man's second speech that he is well informed about the two women. He was not aware of the obligation of kin solidarity to Naomi (2.11-12). Yet Boaz, in his speech, represents himself as a sensitive man. He is aware of the fact that Ruth is acting for her mother-in-law:

> Indeed, they have told me *all that you have done for your mother-in-law* since your husband's death. You have left your father and your mother, the land of your birth and your kinship in order to come to a people you did not know before! (2.11).

Even *he* does not define the parental house as exclusively male; Ruth had left father *and mother*. Ruth acted for the sake of her mother-in-law. From the beginning Boaz accepts the companionship of the two women and gives Ruth the blessing of the God of Israel. At noon he gives her so much that there is enough left over to take home, so that Naomi too has enough. For the afternoon, he strictly orders his servants to let fall some barley so that her gleaning should not turn out poorly, and that Ruth should even be allowed to glean among the sheaves (2.15-16). In the evening, as Ruth takes the harvest to her mother-in-law, the wages from her effort are about 1 efa of barley (2.17). What a yield, what a blessing!

d. *The Older Woman's Learning Process*

Ruth supplies Naomi with the leftover part of lunch for that day. With the barley harvest she secures their sustenance for some time. Naomi, however, does not bless Ruth, who brought home the bread, but the landowner who permitted Ruth's work (2.19). As Ruth mentions his name, Naomi blesses him again (2.20) and, for the first time, revises the interpretation of her fate she pronounced in 1.20-21. There she blamed YHWH for her misery. Yet now she realizes that YHWH withdraws his goodness neither from the living nor from the dead. The interpretation of her situation as having returned empty and alone will, later on, also be revised by Naomi.

Not until after the blessings does Naomi tell her daughter-in-law something that the readers of the book of Ruth already know: Boaz is related to them as *'one of our next of kin'* (2.20). Indeed, Naomi undergoes a learning process. She does not refer only to herself, but to Ruth and her in terms of a communal 'we'. She realizes that there will be a solution only together with the faithful woman at her side.

Similarly to Boaz, Naomi too wants to protect her daughter-in-law from the harvest laborers' sexual molestation. She recommends the young woman to stay near to the working women in Boaz's field. Verse 2.23 emphasizes that Ruth spent the whole harvest time in female company: with the female workers during work, and with Naomi in the evenings. The position of this passing remark is not by pure chance. From this viewpoint, one has to read ch. 3!

e. *In Unconventional Life-Partnership, Women Do Go Unconventional Ways*

Naomi is grateful to Ruth for her support, yet she is still looking for a new marriage for her daughter-in-law (cf. 1.8-13)—which, for the older woman, is still the only way of finding fulfillment and happiness in life (3.1). Thus, she suggests that Ruth visits Boaz at night at the threshing floor, where he is winnowing barley. This is an ambiguous proposal through and through. This time, Ruth shall not go in her working clothes but bathed and anointed, in her cloak. She should wait until he has finished eating and drinking and has laid down. Then she shall uncover his legs, lie down (3.4) and do as Boaz tells her. This instruction of the mother-in-law, who shortly before has been worried that Ruth could have been molested by men, is an unreasonable demand for the young widow. If Ruth did this she would risk her good reputation, the supreme asset of women in patriarchal society. If this is not an instruction to seduce the man, it is at least a plan to give Boaz the opportunity to seduce Ruth. Athalya Brenner[13] points out that texts presenting a female voice can be identified by not making female sexuality invisible but by recognizing it and dealing with it.

Ruth listens to her mother-in-law's advice. She goes to the threshing floor, waits until the man has fallen asleep and then follows Naomi's instructions. When Boaz awakes at midnight, trembling, he finds a woman lying at his legs (3.8).[14] But Ruth does not wait for Boaz to tell *her* what *she* has to do; instead, *she* tells *him*.[15] She asks for marriage and for 'redemption', that is, fulfilling the duty of solidarity for relatives in poverty. With her request Ruth fulfills the promise she had given Naomi, namely to be faithful. She creates a plan in which Naomi could be a part of the new husband's home.

Instead of seducing Boaz, Ruth made an appeal to the man's ethics.[16] She tells him what he has to do and he promises to do everything she wants (3.11; cf. 3.4). Being pleased with himself as a benefactor, he is now willing to put the woman on his level: the 'strong man' (אִישׁ חַיִל, 2.1) accepts the socially weak, alien widow as a 'strong woman' (אֵשֶׁת חַיִל, 3.11b). Beyond any bashful embarrassment he then invites the woman to spend the night with him and the following morning he is immediately willing to keep his promise (3.13). They get up well before dawn, neither wishing their meeting during the night to become public knowledge. They separate. Boaz gives Ruth a full part of his plentiful harvest and goes up to the city gate in order to legalize his promise of the night.

13. Brenner, 'Naomi and Ruth: Further Reflections', in *idem* (ed.), *A Feminist Companion to Ruth*, pp. 140-45, thinks that, based on the fact that the book of Ruth includes a story about Ruth and a story about Naomi, both sides of femininity— sexuality and motherhood—are divided among Ruth and Naomi. Together, both establish one whole female personality (p. 144).

14. For erotic connotations in speech in this chapter see Rashkow, 'Ruth', pp. 37-39; also M.J. Bernstein, 'Two Multivalent Readings in the Ruth Narrative', *JSOT* 50 (1991), pp. 15-26, esp. pp. 16-20.

15. J.W.H. Bos, 'Out of the Shadows', *Semeia* 42 (1988), pp. 37-67 (62).

16. Berlin, *Poetics*, p. 88, fails to see the intention here, saying, 'Ruth has misunderstood. Naomi sent her on a romantic mission but she turned it into a quest for a redeemer.'

When Ruth returns home in the morning (3.16-18), Naomi immediately asks how things went. Ruth declares that Boaz's gift is for her mother-in-law. She says nothing about her own activity and tells only what the man has done (3.16). Naomi still places her hopes in men and not in women (3.18). Ruth, on the other hand, has tied her life to her mother-in-law and will not separate from her. Her life fulfillment is not to be found on the side of a man but in the solid companionship with Naomi.

f. *Marriage as a Means to an End*

Boaz does as he promised and presents the matter at the local court— just as Ruth wanted him to do. The levirate and the act of redemption must be carried out together. Each on its own would only help one of the women. Boaz argues in a tactically subtle way in the presence of the elders of the town, taking the androcentric view of law. He interprets the levirate not for the benefit of the woman but for the benefit of the deceased.[17] The name of the dead man shall be perpetuated by his patrimony (4.5, 10). The next of kin wants to fulfill his duty of redemption but refuses to carry out the duty of the levirate.[18] Therefore, Boaz is free to marry Ruth. He is willing to carry out both duties legally. By developing a solid relationship with Boaz, without the help of Naomi, Ruth has brought the man to care for both of them. He adequately helps her to fulfill her vow of faithfulness. Marrying Boaz is a means to an end for her to become socially integrated and properly cared for, along with her mother-in-law.

g. *Realization and Social Acceptance of a Woman's Concept of Life*

Boaz has learnt from Ruth what human kindness, similar to that of YHWH's, is. Through her guidance he attains the ability to act with solidarity too. Ruth's mother-in-law has learnt that female companionship is stronger than male companionship, of more worth than the sons and male relatives who know about women's misery (cf. 2.11)

---

17. See pp. 37-41.

18. In 4.5, according to the MT, one has to read the *qere* קָנִיתָ ('you shall purchase') instead of the *ketib* קָנִיתִי ('I shall purchase'), because the halakhah given by Ruth combines levirate and redemption. The *ketib* would imply that Boaz has already gained Ruth and that the next of kin could have bought only the field that would later return to Ruth's descendants. A.J. Bledstein, 'Female Companionships: If the Book of Ruth Were Written by a Woman', in A. Brenner (ed.), *A Feminist Companion to Ruth* (Feminist Companion to the Bible, 3; Sheffield: Sheffield Academic Press, 1993), pp. 116-33 (127-28), however, pleads for the *ketib*, because she sees the nightly scene on the threshing floor as a consummation of marriage.

but do not take any initiative to help. A daughter-in-law like Ruth is not only better than *both* her deceased sons but even better than *seven* sons.[19] That is what the women of Bethlehem have learnt from Ruth (4.15). They call Ruth's son, who enables Naomi's social reintegration, *gô'ēl* (redeemer) because Ruth has born him.

Ruth neither gives birth to a child for her deceased husband, as the levirate law would provide, nor for her husband Boaz, as patriarchal societies would normally have it.[20] Ruth gives birth to a child for a woman, namely Naomi (4.15).[21] This is confirmed by the women of Bethlehem, and in doing so they appreciate Ruth's approach to life— solidarity not with her husband but with Naomi. The child is a son for *both* women. He brings back hope. Thus the final outcome of the book of Ruth is not simply the patriarchal ideal of a mother having a male child on her lap, but the realization of the only way of socially integrating two childless widows into a patriarchal society. Such societies define women by means of men and tie material resources in such a way as to guarantee survival to the patrimony. The book of Ruth breaks this structure. Yet it does not offer a revolutionary counterpart for women but a politically realizable one.

Ruth is accepted as the active one, even by the elders and the whole people. According to them, she is not being 'taken' by Boaz, as getting married is usually called in male speech. Ruth 'comes' (בוא, 4.11)— independently and on her own initiative[22]—to the house of Boaz.

h. *Israel's Female Genealogy*
After Ruth arranges her own integration in Bethlehem not only the women of Bethlehem, who had ignored her on her arrival, but also the whole people and the elders accept the 'foreign' woman (4.11-12,

19. With that Ruth serves as a substitute for seven members of the male genealogy. Cf. I. Fischer, 'Der Männerstammbaum im Frauenbuch', in R. Kessler *et al.* (eds.), *'Ihr Völker alle, klatscht in die Hände!': Festschrift für Erhard S. Gerstenberger zum 65. Geburtstag* (Exegese in unserer Zeit, 3; Münster: LIT-Verlag, 1997), pp. 195-213.

20. For notes of childbearing, with or without mentioning the father, see Fischer, *Erzeltern*, pp. 61-70.

21. Cf. K. Butting, *Die Buchstaben werden sich noch wundern* (Alektor-Hochschulschriften; Berlin: Alektor-Verlag, 1994), pp. 43-44, who quite correctly distinguishes between that and the substitutional childbearing of a slave for a free woman. M. Bal, 'Heroism and Proper Names, or the Fruits of Analogy', in Brenner (ed.), *A Feminist Companion to Ruth*, pp. 42-69 (61), points out that irregularly relating the son to Naomi and not to the father is a 'lapsus'.

22. Cf. R. Jost, *Freundin in der Fremde* (Stuttgart: Quell, 1992), p. 68.

14-15). In the blessing to the couple Ruth is not only on the *same* level with the women of her *own* people, but is even put on the side of Israel's ancestresses.

In the presence of a woman with that strength, the elders and the whole people define the people's genealogy as female. It is not Israel/ Jacob who has built up the people but both women, Rachel and Leah. Ruth is being compared to the unconventional ancestress of the house of Judah, Tamar, who founded the house of Judah against her father-in-law's will (cf. Gen. 38). The fact that the people do not talk about the 'seed' of the man, as usual, but about the 'seed of the young woman' (4.12) strengthens the view of the foundation of a genealogy through a woman.

The worldview in the book of Ruth is thoroughly female,[23] even if it does not get beyond the scope of patriarchal social order. Marriage is at the end, which, however, does not separate Ruth from Naomi. The final outcome is the traditional patriarchal ideal of a mother with a *son* on her lap, not perhaps with a *daughter*. The book of Ruth shows how to take seriously the real social system as well as the women's independent concept of living.

2. Who Wrote the Book of Ruth?

Since the beginning of the seventies, more and more exegetes (even male ones) have accepted that Ruth could have been composed by a woman.[24] As Fokkelien van Dijk-Hemmes and Athalya Brenner[25] have worked out, while it is not that relevant whether the author was male or female; the viewpoint from which the texts have been composed is. Do the biblical texts exclusively reflect a male viewpoint, even where the author is narrating about women? Or does a text represent an authentic female voice, perhaps even through the formulations of a male author? The latter option is highly likely to be valid in the book of Ruth. Inasmuch as we expect that some Hebrew Bible texts might have been composed by women—for example, the songs of Miriam, Deborah and Hannah—the assumption that Ruth could

23. J. Ebach, 'Fremde in Moab—Fremde aus Moab', in J. Ebach and R. Faber (eds.), *Bibel und Literatur* (Munich: Fink, 1995), pp. 277-304: 'Als Literatur ist das Rutbuch Anwalt des einzelnen gegen das Allgemeine, *eine* Geschichte (story) gegen *die* Geschichte (history)—und allemal "herstory" gegen "history" ' (p. 291).

24. See E.F. Campbell, *Ruth* (AB, 7; Garden City, NY: Doubleday, 1975), pp. 21-23; also N.K. Gottwald, *The Hebrew Bible: A Socio-literary Introduction* (Philadelphia: Fortress Press, 1985), p. 557.

25. Brenner in Brenner and van Dijk-Hemmes, *On Gendering Texts*, pp. 4-10.

have been written by a woman is quite realistic. As far as biblical literature is concerned, one can never find out for sure who the author
was. At least Ruth has not been ascribed to a male author by its super-
scription, as it happened to other *Megillot*—for example, The Song of
Songs (1.1) and Ecclesiastes (1.1), as well as Lamentations in the Septuagint version. That is why I am talking about a female author of the
book of Ruth: in case this author was not a woman, it was a 'women-
identified'[26] man, a man who saw women's interests and took them
seriously.

The fact that Ruth was written after the exile seems quite peremp-
tory to me.[27] The narrated time sets the story between Judges and
Kings, although the book can be found in the third part of the canon,
namely the *Ketûbîm* (Writings). This indicates that the book was written at a time when the Pentateuch[28] and a great deal of the Deuteronomic History were probably already completed. I agree with those
exegetes[29] who think that the book of Ruth is a tendentious, if not a
polemic, piece of work against the attempts of the books of Ezra and
Nehemiah to reject mixed marriages.

3. *Women Are Better Exegetes*

In research, it has always been clear that the book of Ruth tackles *legal
texts* of the Torah. But Ruth obviously also deals with *narrative texts* of
the Pentateuch. This brings in themes and traditions that offer instruction for interpretations that show how to read the book. In her representation, the author[30] refers to the older traditions that already exist

26. E. Schüssler Fiorenza, *Brot statt Steine* (Fribourg: Exodus-Verlag, 1988),
p. 15.

27. For the discussion about early or late dating see R.L. Hubbard, *The Book of
Ruth* (NICOT; Grand Rapids: Eerdmans, 1988), pp. 23-35, who pleads for a pre-
exilic dating.

28. Butting, *Buchstaben*, p. 24, assumes that the book of Ruth 'mit einer
nachexilischen Bearbeitung des ersten Buches der Tora im Gespräch ist'.

29. As R. Bohlen, 'Die Rutrolle', *TTZ* 101 (1992), pp. 1-19 (4 n. 17), has found
out, this viewpoint was already held by Thaddaeus Antonius Dereser at the
beginning of the previous century.

30. From my viewpoint, an originally oral tradition (cf. van Dijk-Hemmes,
'Ruth', p. 138) is not to be presumed. But the social-cultural context of the book of
Ruth is that of the wise women (cf. pp. 138-39). It can be assumed that the author
was past the middle of her life. This becomes clear through Naomi, who is the
main figure (although not the hero) of the story. Most of the things happening are
being watched from her viewpoint and almost all persons concerned in the book
are related to her (see Berlin, *Poetics*, p. 84).

in writing. She anchors her characters in Israelite history and offers a new interpretation of the tradition, from a woman's viewpoint. I would like to add at this point that works (see references in the notes) by Mieke Bal, Klara Butting, Jürgen Ebach, Jean-Luc Vesco, Georg Braulik and Michael Goulder were particularly stimulating for formulating my views (see below).

a. The Book of Ruth as Exegesis of Torah Legal Texts

I would like to focus on three essential points here: (1) the law of Deuteronomy stating that no Moabite shall become a member of the congregation of Israel; (2) the legal institution of levirate marriage; and (3) the duty of redemption. The last two issues appear intertwined in the book of Ruth.

The manifold references in Ruth to Deuteronomy have recently been dealt with by Georg Braulik.[31] Michael D. Goulder[32] has, above all, pointed out the references to Deuteronomy 22–25—to the commandment of gleaning, to the law concerning incest (cf. Deut. 23.1 and the wording in Ruth 3.4-9), and to levirate marriage.

1. *A Moabite woman is not only admitted to the congregation, but also to the people's genealogy.* Exegetes have always wondered how it was possible that a Moabite woman was tolerated in David's genealogical tree, although it says in Deut. 23.4-5:

> No Ammonite or Moabite, even down to the tenth generation, shall become a member of the assembly of YHWH. They shall never become members of the assembly of YHWH because they did not meet you with bread and water on your way out of Egypt...

Those who think that the book of Ruth was composed in the period of the monarchy argue that the Moabite great-grandmother of David was firmly linked to the tradition, thus she could not be left out.[33] If,

---

31. G. Braulik, 'Das Deuteronomium und die Bücher Ijob, Sprichwörter, Rut', in E. Zenger (ed.), *Die Tora als Kanon für Juden und Christen* (HBS, 10; Freiburg: Herder, 1996), pp. 61-138 (105-27), intensively tackles the structures of 'seven' which can be found in both books.

32. M.D. Goulder, 'Ruth: A Homily on Deuteronomy 22–25?', in H.A. McKay and D.J.A. Clines (eds.), *Of Prophets' Visions and the Wisdom of Sages: Essays in Honour of R. Norman Whybray on his Seventieth Birthday* (JSOTSup, 162; Sheffield: Sheffield Academic Press, 1993), pp. 307-19.

33. See, e.g., G. Gerleman, *Ruth: Das Hohelied* (BK, 18; Neukirchen–Vluyn: Neukirchener Verlag, 1965), p. 8: 'Eine moabitische Herkunft wäre für den Gesalbten Israels keine harmlose Arabeske gewesen ... Im Gegenteil, diese scheinbar bei-

however, the book is supposed to have been formed at the same time or later than Deut. 23.4-7, one gets into trouble. How is it possible that—against the injunction of the Torah—a Moabite ancestress is inserted in the Judah genealogy at such a prominent place?

The author of Ruth reverses the order of Deut. 23.4-7 as well as its foundations.[34] The prohibition is based on the fact that Moab did not support Israel on its way to the promised land. Yet in the book of Ruth a starving family of Judah is accommodated in Moab. Yes, the Moabite woman provides for bread even in Bethlehem. In gleaning, Ruth provides for bread for her mother-in-law and herself. She does this even though the older woman still has social contacts in Bethlehem (cf. 2.1, 20). The alien Moabite woman does not have any contacts that would supply solidarity and support. She depends on her own strength, her efficiency—and her willingness to live her life with her mother-in-law. She claims the right to legal aid, namely to glean, which, according to Deut. 24.19, widows and orphans are entitled to.[35] Until the end of the harvest, the foreigner who is a widow brings home the daily bread. Then she permanently cares for Naomi in urging Boaz also to supply for the mother of her deceased husband through her marriage. The halakhah, the interpretation of law used by the author of Ruth for Deut. 23.4-7, says: If the reason no longer applies, the prohibition is no longer justified.[36]

Therefore the book of Ruth pleads for differentiated judging of the criterion for admission to the congregation, which also includes a differentiated view of integrating alien women by marriage. The female exegete is critical of her male colleagues who, in the books of Ezra and

---

läufige Notiz ist als der ursprüngliche Kern zu betrachten, um dessentwillen die Rutherzählung entstanden ist.'

34. On reasons for excluding from the congregation and its refutation in Ruth see Braulik, 'Deuteronomium und Rut', pp. 116-17.

35. Concerning the connections between Ruth 2 and the gleaning laws of the Torah (Lev. 19.19; 23.22) and above all Deut. 24.19, see Braulik, 'Deuteronomium und Rut', pp. 118-19.

36. Braulik, 'Deuteronomium und Rut', p. 116. He also includes the second reason for prohibiting admission, that is, the malediction of Israel through Balaam (Deut. 23.5b-6), in his arguing that Ruth is 'eine *Gegengeschichte vor allem zum sogenannten Gemeindegesetz des Deuteronomiums (23.4-7)'* (p. 115). As YHWH blessed Israel in spite of the malediction, the Moabite woman Ruth is blessed as well, because she took refuge under his wings (2.12). As Ebach, 'Fremde', p. 294, points out, in the book of Ruth the laws concerning membership in the congregation according to Deuteronomy are 'nicht universal überboten, sondern partikular unterlaufen—und darin ihres Scheins entkleidet. Eben darin zielt die einzelne Geschichte auf eine universale (nicht universelle!) Ethik.'

Nehemiah, take an altogether disapproving view of mixed marriages (Ezra 9–10; Neh. 13.23-27), with an explicit reference to the Moabite passage of Deut. 23.4-7 in Neh. 13.1-3.

2. *The creative halakhah of the levirate duty and of the duty of redemption.*[37] The book of Ruth echoes two legal institutions of Israel, the levirate marriage and the duty of redemption.

In three different contexts the Hebrew Bible refers to the regulation for the case of a childless man's death which states that his brother[38] is to beget a child with the widow:

Deut. 25.5-10 presents the legal text. It is formed casuistically and indicates the procedure. This law favors the deceased man, whose name is not to be erased. The first son the widow gives birth to is regarded as the son of the deceased. Verses 7-10 lay down the rules in case the brother refuses. The woman is the one who presents herself as the plaintiff at the town gate, not the male members of the family, as one would expect. Favored is the deceased, who is in need of justice (v. 7).[39] If the woman's brother-in-law still refuses to fulfill his duty, in spite of having justified himself before the legal court, the widow humiliates him in public and carries out the shoe rite.[40] That is obviously how the widow is released from the levirate duty and is able to marry a man outside the family.

The only narrative text referring to the levirate marriage apart from Ruth is Genesis 38.[41] It is about Tamar, whose father-in-law, Judah,

---

37. See Fischer, *Gottesstreiterinnen*, pp. 184-87.

38. G. Braulik, *Deuteronomium II* (NEB.AT, 28; Würzburg: Echter Verlag, 1992), p. 187, presupposes concerning the legal family situation that the father's patrimony is still undivided. By the way, the Septuagint makes the law accessible even for daughters by using gender-neutral language.

39. The legal text of Deut. 25.5-10 is clearly androcentric. It certainly does not intend to support the widows, as pointed out by Campbell, *Ruth*, p. 136, and recently again by E. Otto, 'Biblische Altersversorgung im altorientalischen Rechtsvergleich', *Zeitschrift für altorientalische und biblische Rechtsgeschichte* 1 (1995), pp. 83-110 (109-110).

40. In Ruth 4 the shoe rite does but visualize a release from the levirate through the next of kin as well, yet it does not correspond with the regulations in Deuteronomy. As far as the shoe rite as a renunciation of a legal act is concerned, see Otto, 'Altersversorgung', p. 109.

41. T. Krüger, 'Genesis 38—ein "Lehrstück" alttestamentlicher Ethik', in R. Bartelmus *et al.* (eds.), *Konsequente Traditionsgeschichte: Festschrift für Klaus Baltzer zum 65. Geburtstag* (OBO, 126; Freiburg: Universitätsverlag; Göttingen: Vandenhoeck & Ruprecht, 1993), pp. 205-26 (225-26), considers Gen. 38, like Ruth, a biased

initiates the levirate for Tamar with his second son, Onan, after the
death of his eldest son. Onan obeys, yet refuses to grant issue to the
deceased brother (38.6-10). He also dies but Judah does not release his
daughter-in-law from the state of levirate. He promises her a brother-
in-law marriage to his third son, Shelah. He blames the woman for the
death of his two sons and does not provide for her in his own house
but sends her back to her parents' house (v. 11).Yet when Shelah
becomes an adult, Tamar is not given to him as a wife. Thus Tamar
goes and fetches from the father what he refuses to give her through
his son, that is, the posterity that he refused to give to her because he
did not release her from the state of levirate, at the same time not
allowing her to consummate the levirate marriage. The various references to and similarities between Genesis 38 and the book of Ruth
have already been shown by Ramona Faye West.[42]

The book of Ruth refers to the levirate twice: Naomi wants to separate from both her daughters-in-law, saying that she is too old to
have sons who could get married to the young widows (1.11-13).
Although there is no verbal suggestion of the legal text of Deuteronomy, Naomi clearly hints at levirate marriage. Yet she does not see it
as a duty of solidarity towards her deceased sons, as it is in Deuteronomy, but as a legal institution for providing for her widowed daughters-in-law. That is how she breaks up the androcentricity of the legal
text.

Ruth 4.1-10 clearly refers to the legal text in Deut. 25.5-10.[43] But
Boaz is neither the full brother of Mahlon, nor have they dwelled
together (cf. v. 5). Therefore, he is not obliged to perform the levirate
according to the law in Deuteronomy.[44] Nevertheless is he introduced

---

narration against a strict rejection of mixed marriages. Such a view can be proved
through the interpretation of Gen. 38 in the book of Ruth. Another indication for
that might be that both narrations are determined by crucial theological words,
that is, חסד in the book of Ruth and צדקה in Gen. 38.26.

42. R.F. West, *Ruth: A Retelling of Genesis 38?* (Ann Arbor: UMI, 1987), p. 169:
'...from a reader's perspective, elements in the book of Ruth lead the reader to
associate its story with Genesis 38.' She is talking of Ruth as 'the focused text and
Genesis 38 as the intertext'.

43. Cf. Braulik, 'Deuteronomium und Rut', pp. 121-25, as well as the synopsis
of both texts in pp. 114-15.

44. Assuming that the legal regulation of Deut. 25.5-10 refers to an exceptional
case of the levirate (cf. Otto, 'Altersversorgung', p. 110) and that the essential, more
extensive regulations in codified law have not been passed on (cf. Campbell, *Ruth*,
p. 137), it is inexplicable why the book of Ruth should quote the text of Deuteronomy, even if it is actually inappropriate for its situation.

by the term *gô'ēl* (redeemer), which refers to a different kind of a next of kin obligation.

It is difficult to reconstruct the concept of redemption in the book of Ruth. In buying Naomi's strip of field (4.3-9), Boaz is obviously referring to the regulation of Lev. 25.23-34[45] that aims at preserving the share of land for impoverished landowners. The redemption (Lev. 25; cf. Jer. 32, from v. 8)[46] is nowhere connected with the levirate in the Torah. Both laws relate to each other by referring to the inalienable claim to an estate[47] in the promised land, which is to be guaranteed through kin solidarity.[48] Mieke Bal[49] has realized that both legal institutions—that of redemption, and that of the levirate—concern the two constitutive aspects of Israel's history, namely possession of land and posterity.

The harmonization of both institutions in the book of Ruth is to be explained.[50] Research has tried again and again to ascertain different legal backgrounds for both institutions, in the book of Ruth and in the Torah. There even exists the opinion that the book of Ruth has nothing to do with these two laws. This depends primarily on when the book of Ruth is dated. An earlier date would imply that both

45. R. Kessler, 'Zur israelitischen Löserinstitution', in M. Crüsemann and W. Schottroff (eds.), *Schuld und Schulden* (KT, 121; Munich: Chr. Kaiser Verlag, 1992), pp. 40-53 (46), shows that the kin degree is important in Lev. 25.25 as well as in Ruth 3.12. Kessler dissociates himself from the social-romantic idea that the next of kin who appears as a purchaser would have returned the piece of land to the owner without anything in return.

46. The redemption of vows and obligations is found in Lev. 27. Only these two texts refer to an exchange (תְּמוּרָה, Ruth 4.7; Lev. 27.10, 33) in the context of redemption (גְּאוּלָה). See A. LaCocque, *The Feminine Unconventional* (Minneapolis: Fortress Press, 1990), p. 97 n. 34.

47. R. Westbrook, *Property and the Family in Biblical Law* (JSOTSup, 113; Sheffield: Sheffield Academic Press, 1991), p. 75, interprets the receipt of the name as keeping the legal title of the deceased on his property. In his view the levirate does not function as a provision for widows but is to be realized as a special regulation of the inheritence law. D. Thompson and T. Thompson, 'Some Legal Problems in the Book of Ruth', *VT* 18 (1968), pp. 79-99 (87-88), support their opinion that name preservation means preserving the inheritance within the family, quite sensibly by referring to the daughters of Zelophehad (Num. 27.1-11).

48. Kessler, 'Löserinstitution', p. 51: 'Zusammenfassend läßt sich sagen, daß die israelitische Löserinstitution von Grund auf und in allen Einzelzügen von der Sippe und ihrem Besitz her konstruiert ist.'

49. Bal, 'Heroism', p. 59.

50. LaCocque, *Feminine*, p. 99, solves the problem regarding Ruth as a substitute for Naomi, who is already beyond her fertile period of life: 'Boaz has become the *go'el* and *levir* of Ruth representing Naomi.'

institutions had not been separated yet. In case Ruth is dated later than the laws of the Torah, it is assumed that the instructions of the Torah had already faded and levirate and redemption were therefore falsely connected.[51]

Basically, narrative texts hardly ever fully agree with legal texts—as 'real' life does not always correspond with law. Besides, narratives in the Hebrew Bible that illustrate the law are almost always of halakhic nature. This means that such narrations have the *intention* to adapt the law to specific situations and to apply them adequately.

Such an intention is to be proved, especially for the book of Ruth. The link between levirate and redemption is created by the Moabite, Ruth. She is sent onto the threshing floor during the night by her mother-in-law, who claims redemption, in order to move Boaz, the kinsman (3.2) to marry her. But Ruth explains her request for marriage on the grounds *that he is a gô'ēl* (3.9). Here, Ruth's author lets her protagonist become an exegete: Ruth is creating a new halakhah from the two legal institutions that guarantee the solidarity of kinship. In combining the levirate marriage and the duty of redemption,[52] she presents an interpretation of the Torah, a halakhah that is adequate for her and for Naomi's situation. The associative exegesis of both laws shows that Ruth does not only have herself in mind, but Naomi as well. She makes use of the relations and obligations of her mother-in-law, *although* she has already established an independent, reliable contact with Boaz. However, if she wants to keep the vow she had made to her mother-in-law (1.16-17), she will have to find a way that enables her to provide for Naomi and herself. The halakhah, which the Torah exegete who composed the book of Ruth puts into the mouth of her exegete Ruth, aims at the secure living of women who

51. For a survey of research see: J.A. Loader, 'Of Barley, Bulls, Land and Levirate', in F. García Martínez *et al.* (eds.), *Studies in Deuteronomy: In Honour of C.J. Labuschagne on the Occasion of his 65th Birthday* (VTSup, 53; Leiden: E.J. Brill, 1994), pp. 123-38.

52. E. Zenger, *Das Buch Ruth* (ZBK, 8; Zürich: Theologischer Verlag, 1986), p. 88: 'Der Erzähler will durch diese von ihm selbst narrativ geschaffene Verbindung von Levirat und "Lösung", die sonst im AT nicht bezeugt ist, eine originelle Neuinterpretation des Ethos der verwandtschaftlichen Solidarität geben.' Braulik, 'Deuteronomium und Rut', p. 121, doubts that the connection of both legal institutions is original in the book of Ruth, referring to A. Lemaire, 'Une inscription phénicienne découverte récemment et le mariage de Ruth la Moabite', *ErIs* 20 (1989), pp. 124*-29*, who, with a new interpretation of a Phoenician inscription, manages to show that a similar connection of both legal institutions has already been ascertained. It is a fact, however, that the Torah does not know such a connection and that Ruth obviously seeks to interpret the Torah.

are only granted a marginal position in a patriarchal society. The halakhah given by Ruth interprets both laws for the benefit of *women* and thus can be called 'feminist'. Ruth contradicts the androcentricity of the levirate, which does not focus on the widow but only on the deceased *husband*. She also contradicts the androcentricity of the concept of redemption that primarily deals with the man who owns land and the patriarchal family.

In Boaz Ruth has found a man who is open for such a halakhah. He is a God-fearing man and recognizes Ruth's kindness, which is similar to that of his God (3.10).[53] The following morning he waits at the gate for the kinsman who is even closer than him, who might claim the right of redemption. The fact that this man has no name, but is called 'so and so', is significant for the expressive names in the book of Ruth. He does not want to marry Ruth but only to buy Naomi's field. Thus 'Mr. So and so' closes his mind to the halakhah initiated by Ruth. As Boaz wants both, he presents the legal position as if one would not be possible without the other, that is, the duty of redemption is inseparably connected with the levirate marriage (4.5). At the town gate, in the presence of the elders (4.2 onwards; cf. Deut. 25.5-10) and the whole people, he undertakes the duty of redemption for Naomi and contracts the levirate marriage with Ruth. They marry the same day, as he promised.

The 'feminist' exegete who has written Ruth lets the elders confirm her halakhah. She emphasizes that the whole people and the elders are witnesses to the legal matter that connects levirate and redemption (4.10-12).[54] That is how a distinguished Israelite man marries a Moabite woman in full obedience to the Torah!

The author regards levirate marriage and redemption as a duty of solidarity for women, even for foreign women. In her eyes it is not a legal institution beneficial only for men, even if they are already deceased. Therefore it is not at all reasonable to assume that the author had not known the legal regulations of Deuteronomy, or that she had simply forgotten a notice of birth for Mahlon. From her viewpoint the law favors the living women, not the dead men.[55]

---

53. For 'kindness' (חסד) as a leading word and a word of interpretation in Ruth see Zenger, *Ruth*, pp. 19-20.

54. LaCocque, *Feminine*, p. 101, assumes that in postexilic times there was an opposition to levirate marriages, as neither P nor H talk about it and sexual contacts with relatives, even with those who married into the family, were considered incestuous (cf. Lev. 18.16; 20.21).

55. Cf. P. Trible, *Gott und Sexualität im Alten Testament* (GTBS, 539; Gütersloh: Gütersloher Verlagshaus, 1993), p. 224.

b. *The Book of Ruth as Exegesis of Torah Narrative Texts*[56]

The date at the book's beginning places it as a prehistory of David, in the period of the judges: Ruth 1.1 starts: There was a famine in the land and a man and his wife went to live in a foreign country in order to escape the famine. Such language refers to the narration in Gen. 12.10, and even more—through the usage of specific words—to Gen. 26.1. That is how stories begin when it becomes dangerous for the emigrant couple, especially for the ancestress. In fact, the book of Ruth states shortly afterwards that a misfortune has happened, but this time to the men. All of them die. In Genesis such expositions opened stories that endangered Israel's ancestresses by denying their married status. They were in danger of being integrated into the genealogy of a foreign king (Gen. 12, 20, 26). In Ruth, however, the author starts her narration in telling about the integration of a foreign woman into the genealogy of the Judahite kingdom. The author's view is that of Israel: to be integrated into Israel means to enter into a salutary communion with YHWH.

The famine is the reason for emigration. This is also hinted at in the preface of the Exodus. Jacob–Israel leaves the promised land because of famine (cf. Gen. 41.53-57; 43.1) and goes to Egypt in order to live there as a foreigner (לָגוּר, Gen. 47.4; Ruth 1.1). A return on their own initiative is not possible, because the people have been enslaved (Exod. 1). Only when YHWH cares for his people (Gen. 50.24; Exod. 3.16; 4.31; cf. Ruth 1.6)[57] is the Exodus possible.

Mieke Bal and Klara Butting have already pointed out that the terms 'cleave unto' (דבק, 1.14; 2.8, 23) and 'leaving' father and mother (עזב, 1.16; 2.11) definitely refer to Gen. 2.24.[58] There it says that a man leaves (עזב) his father and mother[59] and cleaves (דבק) unto his wife. Ruth presents an alternative concept of living. She leaves father

---

56. A survey of parallels to the narrative texts of Genesis is supplied by Hubbard, *Ruth*, 40; for the Hebrew Bible see Jean-Luc Vesco, 'La date du livre de Ruth', *RB* 74 (1967), pp. 237-40.

57. Zenger, *Ruth*, p. 38, shows that the phrase 'YHWH encounters' can be found in two contexts, namely in the exodus tradition and in the narrations of a God-given birth.

58. Cf. Bal, 'Heroism', p. 48; as well as Butting, *Buchstaben*, p. 41 who in nn. 52, 53 sets the parallel quotations of Gen. 2.24 and 12.1.

59. It is possible that the terms 'father and mother' are referring to Deut. 21.13 as well. This law explicitly enables—quite contrary to the Moabite paragraph—the integration of alien women, namely captives. These women first of all are to weep over 'father and mother' before an Israelite is allowed to marry them.

and mother in order to cleave to her mother-in-law, not to a husband.

In Ruth 2.11 the author mixes the quotations of Gen. 2.24 with another quotation in a very subtle way: Ruth's decision to leave her people and her land and to join the God of Israel means comparing Ruth to Abraham[60] and Rebekah. Abraham followed the call of YHWH and became ancestor of Israel (Gen. 12.1-4). Rebekah followed the call and became ancestress of Israel (Gen. 24.58). Ruth does not follow any call. She leaves on her own initiative, irrespective of the advice of an Israelite woman not to do so.[61]

> Wherever you go, I will go, and wherever you stay, I will stay. Your people is my people, and your God is my God. Wherever you will die, I will die and there I will be buried (1.16-17a).

In Boaz's speech of Ruth 2.11 the author lets the God-fearing man express that Ruth's decision is equal to Abraham's and Rebekah's:

> They have told me all you have done for your mother-in-law since your husband's death. You *left* your *father* and your mother and *your kindred* and you *went* to a people you did not know before.[62]

In Gen. 12.1 God speaks to Abraham:

> *Leave* your own country, your *kindred* and *your father's house* and *go* to a country that I will show you!

This order of God appears again in 24.7. There Abraham is just about to tell his servant to go to his kin in order to look for a wife for his son, a wife willing to leave her country (24.4-9). The servant finds this wife in Rebekah, who leaves her parents' house saying, 'Yes, I *will go!'* (Gen. 24.58), as Abraham *did go* (12.4).[63]

In using a well-aimed language to express Ruth's decision, the narrator is referring to the decision of the patriarch of the first generation and to that of the ancestress of the second generation of the *Erzeltern* (2.11). Naomi blesses Boaz after having heard of his meeting with

---

60. See Trible, *Gott und Sexualität*, p. 198.

61. LaCocque, *Feminine*, pp. 111-12, has referred to the parallel story of Ittai the Gittite, who has also been sent back by David, but refuses to do so (2 Sam. 15.19-22). The Jewish tradition interprets Ruth's words in 1.16-17 as a conversion of the Moabite woman. See L.L. Bronner, 'A Thematic Approach to Ruth in Rabbinic Literature', in Brenner (ed.), *A Feminist Companion to Ruth*, pp. 146-69 (148-51).

62. The passages underlined quote Gen. 2.24, the one in italics Gen. 12.1 and 24.4-8.

63. For Abraham's succession through Rebecca, see Fischer, *Gottesstreiterinnen*, pp. 72-80.

Ruth (2.20). This quite clearly parallels the servant's praise after hav-ing met Rebekah.[64]

> Blessed be YHWH [ברוך ה יהוה'], the God of my master Abraham, who has not failed to keep kindness … [חסדו; Gen. 24.27].

> Blessed be he by YHWH [ברוך הוא לה יהוה'], who has not failed to keep kindness … (חסדו, Ruth 2.20).

Another peculiarity of the Rebekah narration is taken up by the Ruth author too. Contrary to the usual terminology that relates 'seed' to men, the wedding wishes to Rebekah (Gen. 24.60) relate to her own 'seed' (זרע). In the wish that Boaz's house might be like the house of Perez, the congratulations are about 'the seed [זרע] the Lord will give you by this young woman' (Ruth 4.12).[65] Thus Ruth succeeds Rebekah, the ancestress of the second generation of the *Erzeltern*, through repeated references to Genesis 24.

The author continues this line of reference. The wedding wishes she has put into the mouths of 'the whole people at the gate and the elders' (4.11) say that Ruth might become the same as Rachel, Leah and Tamar, the ancestresses of the third and fourth generations. By mentioning Rachel and Leah, the exegete of the Genesis texts, who wrote Ruth, refers to the foundation of the house of Israel. Tamar[66] is the one who—like Ruth—has enrolled herself in the genealogical line of Judah, which she has founded as ancestress in unconventionally demanding the levirate marriage. The people and the elders think that the Moabite woman[67] is not only equal to the women of their own people but that she also belongs to the same category as the people's ancestresses.

The story about Lot's daughters, one of whom is the ancestress of Ruth the Moabite, is not really dealt with by the exegete who wrote the book.[68] She only refers to the offensive story about the incestuous relationship between both daughters and their father that was

64. Vesco, 'Ruth', p. 238, has already referred to this parallel.

65. Bal, 'Heroism', p. 64, has shown that 'Perez is presented as the object of a female subject'.

66. Bal, 'Heroism', p. 55, also sees Rachel and Leah standing in this line: 'They [= the elders] evoke by analogy three other women, subjects of the building of the house of Israel, thus sanctioning a sexual practice in which the power of the male is overruled by the female subject.'

67. As in Boaz's declaration in 4.10, Ruth is defined as Mahlon's wife and explicitly as a Moabite woman, a reference to Deut. 23.4 is inevitable. In marrying Boaz, Ruth agrees to the second 'mixed marriage' with a Judahite.

68. This reference has been pointed out by Ebach, 'Fremde', pp. 281-82, too.

probably read pejoratively when the book of Ruth was composed. The two stories have many similarities, though. Just as Lot's daughters went to their father during the night, Ruth went down to the threshing floor during the night (בלילה, Gen. 19.33, 34, 35; Ruth 3.2, 8, 13). Both men, Lot and Boaz, had drunk before (Gen. 19.33-35; Ruth 3.3, 7). Both women lay (שכב is the leading word in both passages: Gen. 19.32-35; Ruth 3.4, 7, 8, 13-14) with the man but (at first) he does not realize it (Gen. 19.33, 35; Ruth 3.7 onwards). The result of these meetings in each case is the reintegration of the women into the stream of life, from which they had been cut off. All three women give birth to a child. The deed of Lot's daughters is described as the vital force of the women. The atmosphere on the threshing floor described by the book of Ruth is highly erotic, but is interrupted abruptly through Ruth's request, which appeals to ethics. In doing so, the Moabite woman redeems the incestuous deed of her ancestress.[69] She does it for Naomi's sake and because Naomi advises her to do so.

As a true daughter-in-law, Ruth has proved to be better than *seven* sons of Israel (4.15). Compared with the ten-member genealogy in 4.18-22, the rather short genealogy in 4.17b[70] mentions Obed, Jesse and David. In 4.17 the first seven parts are left out. They are replaced by Ruth! Later on David will be like his great-grandmother: anointed by Samuel, he, too, is the one who is better qualified for the kingship than the *seven* older sons of Jesse, Ruth's grandson (cf. 1 Sam. 16.1-13).

4. *The Book of Ruth as a 'Feminist' Exegesis of the Torah, in Opposition to Contemporary Interpretation and Actualization of Tradition*

The contemporary male colleagues of the exegete who wrote the book of Ruth argue about the same time in the 'Chronicler's History' that it is not recommended to marry a Moabite woman.[71] They even want to

---

69. H. Fisch, 'Ruth and the Structure of Covenant History', *VT* 32 (1982), pp. 425-37 (435-36), interprets the leading word, 'to redeem', with regard to the stories around Lot's daughters and Tamar. The story of Ruth redeems both stories: he recognizes in Boaz, who contracts the levirate marriage, the redemptor of the one who refuses the levirate, namely Judah. Fisch, pp. 430-31, makes a table of the structural similarities between the stories of Lot, Gen. 38 and the book of Ruth. Abraham's separation from Lot (Gen. 13.9) is cancelled through the union of Ruth and Naomi (1.17; cf. p. 435).

70. For greater detail see Fischer, 'Männerstammbaum'.

71. In addition to this cf. Num. 25.1-5: the Israelites are seduced and tempted to idolatry by Moabite women (cf. Bal, 'Heroism', p. 57; mentioning 24.1, however, is incorrect). The example that is given in 25.6-18, however, speaks of a Midianite woman.

promulgate that existing marriages have to be dissolved (cf. Neh. 13.23-27). These exegetes even let their protagonist Nehemiah beat the offenders and tear out their hair (13.25). They give reasons for their severe prohibition against marrying foreign women by referring to Solomon, David's son. Even the wise king was led astray by foreign women and into sin (13.26)—how much more risk do common people run!

In her arguing, the author of Ruth refers to the Deuteronomic History as well (cf. already 1.1a). Yet she does not refer to Solomon, who is corrupted by mixed marriages (cf. 1 Kgs 11.1-8), but to his father David, whose great-grandmother was a Moabite. Even she, the author, goes back to earlier sources. She beats her male colleagues at their own game: in order to remedy abuses in the postexilic community, the people are bound to the Torah by those who work on the book of Nehemiah (Neh. 8). The exegete who wrote the book of Ruth does this too. She consciously refers to different kinds of texts of the Torah[72] in order to legitimate her counter-position. Thus she quotes texts from Genesis in order to tell her new story.[73] She consciously refers to the commandments of the Torah, treating them in an unusual way in order to point out a new view of legal regulations. In her arguments she refers to the tradition, yet she actualizes it[74]—and especially in favor of women.

With the approval of the people and the elders who have the competence of jurisdiction, she lets the Moabite woman who has settled in

72. What Vesco, 'Ruth', p. 247, concludes from the reference to other presumed texts in fact corresponds with my thesis: the book of Ruth is an example of a 'style anthologique' dated after the exile, which refers to old texts through 'un style d'imitation'. He also thinks that Ruth is an unpolemic tendentious piece of work against the rejection of mixed marriages. Cf. Bal, 'Heroism', p. 47: 'The book of Ruth is an institutionalized *metatext*, which was meant to be read at specific feasts and to comment upon the Torah.'

73. Perez is the last name in the Judah geneaology in Genesis (38.29) and the first one in the genealogy of Ruth (4.18).

74. I.L. Seeligmann, 'Voraussetzungen der Midraschexegese', in *Congress Volume: Copenhagen 1953* (VTSup, 1; Leiden: E.J. Brill, 1953), pp. 150-81; p. 181 characterizes midrash-exegesis in the following way: 'In der Tat wohnt ihr die Spannung eines gewissen Paradoxons inne. Auch nachdem der Midrasch zur richtigen Auslegung eines festen und fertigen Textgebildes geworden ist, bleiben ihm Elemente der Beweglichkeit, des Spiels und der Aktualisierung anhaften; einerseits will er einen abgeschlossenen Text erklären, der eben in dieser Gestalt die höchste Autorität besitzt, andererseits ist er betrebt [!] denselben... offenzuhalten, vor Versteinerung zu behüten und mit immer neuen [!] Leben zu erfüllen—fur [!] jede neue Situation und für jeden neuen Tag!'

Bethlehem become ancestress to the royal dynasty of David. It is quite obvious that in those days people already expected a descendant of this dynasty, who would lead Israel to salvation.[75]

The author of Ruth knows about the problems of her time, caused by prohibiting mixed marriages.[76] Above all, she realizes the problems women have to face. That is why she first of all lets Naomi, the Judahite, go to a foreign country. In Moab the woman of Judah is a foreigner and becomes a childless widow. Mahlon and Chilion, both from Judah, are aliens in Moab and marry native women there.[77] Thus the story of Ruth illustrates through a member of her own people the following principles: all people are aliens everywhere except in their own country.[78] Not until after this example, which is meant to evoke reason, does she deal with the Moabite woman who is alien in Judah. A woman who, like Abraham and Rebekah, leaves her people, her kin, her country, yes even her God, in order to follow YHWH is to be judged in a different way. Her case cannot be treated only with regard to the question of mixed marriages! In standing up for a woman of the Judahite people, the Moabite woman realizes YHWH's kindliness far better than Boaz, the man of rank. Although he has duty of redemption and recognizes the misery of the widows, he does not act, but generously tolerates gleaning, the right of the poor. Thus the author of the book of Ruth shows women in her times (and us nowadays) that, especially in times of crisis, one can rely on strong women, even if they are strangers. They are far better than the so-called 'capable men' of one's own people, who first have to be challenged to perform their duty of solidarity.

In pleading for the priority of women's relations,[79] the author does

75. In Butting's (*Buchstaben*, pp. 22-23, 47-48) canonical approach under a messianic perspective she interprets the book of Ruth as a genealogy of the 'New David'. It is written as a women's story in confrontation with the traditional historiography, which is presented as history of the houses of fathers (p. 31).

76. 'Welche Konflikte der *erzählenden* Zeit lassen die *erzählte* Zeit in dieser Weise erstehen?' Ebach, 'Fremde', p. 283, asks. For detailed reasons of Ruth's opposition against tendencies in Ezra–Nehemiah, see pp. 284-86 (relevant literature in n. 33), as well as LaCocque, *Feminine*, pp. 84-86.

77. Bos, 'Shadow', p. 37, thus sees in Ruth (as well as in Gen. 38 and Judg. 4–5) a 'counter-theme especially to the betrothal alliance', which contravenes the classical 'type-scene' (meeting at the well) in a patriarchal-critical way.

78. See Ebach, 'Fremde', p. 288.

79. J.C. Exum, *Plotted, Shot, and Painted: Cultural Representations of Biblical Women* (JSOTSup, 215; Gender, Culture, Theory, 3; Sheffield: Sheffield Academic Press, 1996), analyzes (in the chapter 'Is this Naomi?', pp. 127-74) the *Wirkungsgeschichte* of the book of Ruth and, impressively, points at the marginalization of

something that is in contrast to the texts of Genesis: In Genesis, whenever women are presented in pairs, conflicts arise. This is the case with Sarah and Hagar and Rachel and Leah. Naomi and Ruth[80] work for and not against each other. The narration of Ruth paradigmatically shows that such a strategy of life is far more beneficial to women than the rivalry over men produced by patriarchy!

5. *The Early 'History of Israel' Continues as Women's History: From Judah to David*

The Torah-exegete who wrote Ruth continues the genealogy of Perez, son of Tamar and Judah, up to David, thus continuing the Genesis story. There she deliberately refrains from her own view of Israel's genealogy being seen as women's history (as she has shown in 4.11-17). This genealogy (4.18-22) has been written, in accordance with Genesis, as an agnatic genealogy in the form of the *tôlᵉdôt*. Nowhere does Genesis refer to *tôlᵉdôt* as far as Jacob's sons are concerned. The '*tôlᵉdôt* of Perez' declare the line of Judah the main line after Jacob–Israel, a line directly leading to the House of David.[81] The author of Ruth uses the androcentric literary genre of the *tôlᵉdôt* in order to anchor her 'feminist' exegesis in tradition. She had already done so in presenting the scene at the city gate from a male viewpoint. So, now she chooses to change her viewpoint in order to increase the credibility of her story in an evidently patriarchal society.

The book of Ruth is often described as a delightful idyll, a trivial romance: two widowed women succeed in getting a man and a child! The genealogy at the end, however, refuses such an interpretation. The two (שְׁתֵּיהֶם, 4.11) women, Leah and Rachel, built up the House of Israel. The two (שְׁתֵּיהֶם, 1.19) women, Naomi and Ruth, built up the House of David. What is narrated as a seemingly *private* story of life is to be read *politically*. Referring to the '*Erzeltern*-narratives', the book of

the (lesbian?) primary relationship between the two women in favour of the heterosexual relationship between Ruth and Boaz: 'The book of Ruth…invites readers to collapse the gender distinctions with which they themselves operate' (p. 174).

80. Cf. also van Dijk-Hemmes, 'Ruth', p. 136.

81. It remains to be seen whether this means a hidden polemic against Num. 3.1-4, the *tôlᵉdôt* of Moses and Aaron. Num. 3.1-4, however, does not continue the line of Moses, but only that of Aaron, thus introducing him as the legitimate descendant of the *Erzeltern*. As the *tôlᵉdôt* of Perez continue the genealogies of Genesis more directly than Aaron's *tôlᵉdôt*, it might be presumed that Ruth 4.18-22 takes a critical view on overvaluing the priestly descendants after the exile. This would explain why the book of Ruth does not say anything about cult and temple.

Ruth composes the *people's* history as *women's* history! The story of Ruth began with Elimelech, whose name means 'my God is king'. He and his sons died. However, the dead man's name is being strikingly carried on through his wife and his daughter-in-law because the God of Israel lets the royal dynasty arise by means of the two women.

In admitting the book of Ruth to the canon, people agreed with the exegete who explains her concern in referring to the tradition. She pursued the right strategy in order to explain sensibly her concern, which is definitely for women, and to make it appear clear and reasonable to men too. In Jewish tradition the scroll of Ruth is read at Shavu'ot. This custom constitutes splendid homage to the exegete who wrote the story of Ruth. The gift of the Torah is being celebrated by means of a story that interprets it in a creative and vigorous way!

RUTH, THE MODEL EMIGRÉE:
MOURNING AND THE SYMBOLIC POLITICS OF IMMIGRATION*

Bonnie Honig

While the Oxford political philosopher David Miller and other contemporary neo-Rousseauvians respond to late modernity's heightened migrations and the politics of multiculturalism by arguing that a sense of kinship and shared purpose is a necessary feature of democracy (social democracy, in particular), Jacques Derrida, in his recent *Politics of Friendship*, asks us, on the contrary, to see how a democratic politics requires an interruption of the symbolics of genetic relation: 'The foundation of citizenship in a nation' occurs in

> the link between this isonomic and the isogonic tie, the natural bond between nomos and physis, if you like, the bond between the political and autochtonous consanguinity ... It is the place of fraternization as the symbolic bond alleging the repetition of a genetic tie.[1]

Instead of working so hard to maintain the genetic fiction, democratic actors would do better to work to decenter democracy's traditional privileging of the near over the distant, the neighbor over the foreigner, the family over the stranger in order to open up the reach of democracy and multiply solidarities, affinities, identifications with others, both here in the temporal-space of the nation-state—and elsewhere.

The biblical *Book of Ruth* provides an excellent opportunity to think through issues of nearness and distance, friendship and strangeness, national identity, kinship and foreignness. Ruth traverses all of these boundaries but her story, for the most part, has been used to recon-

* This essay is a moderately revised version of an essay published in *Political Theory* 25.1 (1997), pp. 112-36. Reprinted by permission of Sage Publications, Inc. My thanks to Sage Publications for permission to republish the essay and to Athalya Brenner for providing me with some helpful suggestions for revision and with the opportunity to republish the essay in revised form.

1. David Miller, *On Nationality* (Oxford: Oxford University Press, 1996); Jacques Derrida, *Politics of Friendship* (trans. George Collins; London: Verso, 1997).

solidate the very divisions it might have called into question. Again and again Ruth, the Moabite, has been recuperated by her readers for a kind of nationalist narrative that Ruth's story does not only nor unambivalently support.

'What good is a legend to a people that makes their hero into an alien?' Freud asks in *Moses and Monotheism*.[2] Freud poses the question rhetorically, as if the answer was obviously 'no good at all'. But what if we suppose otherwise? In this essay, I read the book of Ruth in an effort to answer this (not at all rhetorical) question: What does Ruth, the alien, provide for the Israelites and her later readers that an Israelite heroine could not? What kind of symbolic-cultural work does Ruth's foreignness do for the Israelites and (how) might her story be mobilized now on behalf of a politics that is more cosmopolitan than nationalist in its aspirations? I try to answer these questions by way of a reading of the book of Ruth that emerges out of an engagement with two recent readings of that text: one by Cynthia Ozick, the American literary critic and author, the other by Julia Kristeva, the French psychoanalyst and cultural critic.[3] Like Ozick and Kristeva, I see the book of Ruth as a potential source of new ethical and political inspiration. I differ with them, however, regarding the particular political and ethical guidance that Ruth might have to offer late modern readers seeking to deal responsibly with the politics of immigration, nationalism and cosmopolitanism.

Ruth

The book of Ruth begins with a flashback. A few years earlier a man named Elimelech, his wife Naomi and their two sons left Bethlehem to escape famine. They moved to Moab, having heard that Moab was flourishing while Bethlehem suffered. The move to Moab is controversial. Elimelech has abandoned his community in a time of need, and worse yet, he has gone to live in *Moab*, the home of the historical enemies of the Israelites. This terribly forbidden move, and the famine

2. Sigmund Freud, *Moses and Monotheism* (New York: Vintage Books, 1955), p. 12.

3. Cynthia Ozick, 'Ruth', in Judith A. Kates and Gail Twersky Reimer (eds.), *Reading Ruth: Contemporary Women Reclaim a Sacred Story* (New York: Ballantine, 1994), pp. 211-32. Julia Kristeva has a lengthy reading of Ruth in *Strangers to Ourselves* (trans. Leon S. Roudiez; New York: Columbia University Press, 1991). A briefer discussion of Ruth appears in Julia Kristeva, *Nations without Nationalism* (trans. Leon S. Roudiez; New York: Columbia University Press, 1993).

that occasions it, suggests that the Israelites have fallen away from
their fundamental moral principles.

The Moabites are lacking virtue as well, but theirs is no temporary
corruption. They refused water to the Israelites as they wandered in
the desert from Egypt to the Promised Land. And when the Israelites
camped at Beth Peor, some Moabite women tried to seduce the Israelite men into illicit relations and idol worship. For this, the prohibition
in Deuteronomy against intermarrying with Moabites is uncompro-
mising: 'None of the Moabites' descendants, even in the tenth generation, shall ever be admitted into the congregation of the Lord' (Deut.
23.4).

Elimelech dies soon after settling in Moab. His sons marry two
Moabite women, but these men also die within ten years, leaving
behind three childless widows, Naomi and her Moabite daughters-in-
law Ruth and Orpah. Naomi hears the famine in Bethlehem is over,
and she decides to return home. Her daughters-in-law accompany her
initially, but she soon tells them to 'Turn back, each of you to her
mother's house' in Moab (Ruth 1.8). They refuse, Naomi insists, and
finally Orpah, weeping, agrees to return to Moab but Ruth remains.
And when Naomi tells her again to leave ('See, your sister-in-law has
returned to her people and her gods; return after your sister-in-law'
[v. 15]), Ruth responds poignantly:

> Whither thou goest, I will go
> Whither thou lodgest, I will lodge
> Thy people shall be my people
> Thy god shall be my god
> Whither thou diest, I will die, and there I will be buried (vv. 16-17).

Naomi says nothing in response but she stops protesting and Ruth
accompanies her on her journey.

In Bethlehem, Naomi is welcomed back by the women of the community. She announces her losses to them and declares that her name
is changed from Naomi (which means 'pleasant') to Mara (which
means 'bitter' [1.20]). Naomi and Ruth establish a joint household.
Ruth supports them by harvesting the remnants left in the field of a
man named Boaz, who, it turns out, is a relative of Naomi. Having
heard of Ruth's remarkable loyalty to Naomi, Boaz welcomes Ruth to
his field and sends her home with extra grain.

But Naomi and Ruth conspire together to achieve a more certain
protection than that. Ruth seeks out (and perhaps seduces) Boaz one
night on the threshing-room floor and calls on him to extend his protection to her through marriage, while also redeeming a piece of land

that was left to Naomi by Elimelech. Boaz notes that there is another
male relative who has prior right or obligation to redeem the land, but
he promises to do what he can for Ruth. He goes the next morning to
find the next of kin and convenes a meeting of the town elders to
resolve the question of Elimelech's land. The next of kin's interest in
redeeming the land dwindles when he hears that Boaz intends to
marry Ruth. Knowing that if they have a son, the child could claim
the redeemed land as his own inheritance without recompense, the
next of kin offers his option/obligation to Boaz.[4]

Boaz and Ruth marry and have a son who is given to Naomi to
nurse. The women's community celebrates, proclaims the child
Naomi's son and protector in old age, pays Ruth the highest compli-
ment, declaring her to be of more value to Naomi than seven sons,
and names the child Obed. Ruth never speaks again; and she is, of
course, absent from the book of Ruth's closing patrilineal genealogy
which ends with David, later to be the King of Israel. Ruth's precarious position in the Israelite order is stabilized by a marriage and birth
that provide the founding energy for a new monarchic regime. In
turn, Ruth's migration seems to be the vehicle of this welcome regime
change. The book of Ruth opens in the days when the judges ruled, a
time of famine, barrenness and corruption; and closes amidst plentiful
harvest and a newly born son with a genealogy anticipating the coming monarchy.

But this regime founding leaves us nonetheless uncertain about
Ruth's status as an immigrant. How should we read Ruth's closing
silence? Has she been successfully assimilated, or has she been left
stranded? More generally, what connections between immigration
and founding are presupposed and consolidated by this great short
story? What is a Moabite woman, a forbidden foreigner, doing at the
start of the line of David?

Immigration and Founding

According to two recent readers of the book of Ruth, Cynthia Ozick
and Julia Kristeva, Ruth is a model immigrant. Ozick reads the book
of Ruth as a tale of reinvigoration by way of conversion or assimilation. (This is in line with the dominant, traditional reading of the

---

4.   There is some debate about the details of this scene: is the next of kin being
asked to redeem the land through purchase or to redeem Ruth through marriage?
For a summary of the debate and the single best reading of the scene, see Danna
Nolan Fewell and David M. Gunn, *Compromising Redemption: Relating Characters in
the Book of Ruth* (Louisville, KY: Westminster/John Knox Press, 1990).

story.) Ruth's conversion to Judaic monotheism from Moabite idolatry testifies to the worthiness of the Jewish God. Ruth's devotion to Naomi exemplifies Ruth's virtue, which is an example for everyone and a ground for the rule of David. Ruth, the model immigrant and convert, supplements the Israelite order and saves it from its wayward rule by judges by founding a new sovereign monarchy.

For Kristeva, by contrast, Ruth unsettles the order she joins. Israelite sovereignty is secured by Ruth, but it is also riven by her, by the moment of otherness she personifies as a Moabite. While Ozick's Ruth completes the Israelite order, Kristeva's Ruth makes it impossible for the order ever to attain completeness. And this, Kristeva argues, is Ruth's great service to the Israelites: she disabuses them of their fantasies of identity and makes them more open to difference and otherness. But Kristeva's Ruth does not only disrupt the order she joins. She also adopts its customs and rituals and tries to get along. From Kristeva's perspective, that makes Ruth a valuable model for those contemporary Muslim immigrants who tend to resist absorption into their receiving regimes.[5]

Ozick's and Kristeva's redeployments of the book of Ruth each combines two of the dominant and enduring responses we have to immigrants. Either immigrants are valued for what 'they' bring to 'us' (diversity, energy, talents, industry, innovative cuisines and new recipes, plus a renewed appreciation of our own regime whose virtues are so great that they draw immigrants to join us) or they are feared for what 'they' will do to 'us' (consume our welfare benefits, dilute our common heritage, fragment our politics, undermine our democratic culture). Both responses judge the immigrant in terms of what she will do for (or to) us as a nation.

The first (welcoming) response models immigration as an occasion for citizens (who are perhaps jaded) to re-experience the fabulous wonder of founding, the moment in which the truth or power of their

---

5.   Some doubt that the book of Ruth can be a resource for an account of immigration politics, because the text tells the story of a single migrant, while the contemporary issue is concerned with hordes of people. My own view is that the text's success at dramatizing enduring issues of immigration politics is due partly to its use of the device of personification. Moreover, the story of Ruth has established connections to immigration politics that precede my analysis. Marjorie Garber (personal communication) recalls playing Ruth in the late 1940s in the US in a series of fund-raisers sponsored by Hadassah to help Jewish refugees make their way to Palestine after the war. Interestingly, given Kristeva's use of the headscarf to mark the recalcitrance of Muslim immigrants, Garber, as Ruth, wore a headscarf to mark her character's European (refugee) identity.

regime was revealed or enacted for all the world to see. Notably, Moab is (as President Clinton put it in a speech in the Middle East in the fall of 1994) 'the land where Moses died and Ruth was born'. Ruth is a vehicle through which the Law comes alive again generations after the death of the lawgiver, Moses. She repeats the foreign-founder script first acted out for the Israelites by Moses.[6] Ruth's immigration and conversion re-perform the social contract of Sinai and allow the Israelites to re-experience their own initial conversion, faith, or wonder before the Law. Ruth's choice of the Israelites re-marks them as the Chosen People, a people worthy of being chosen. Here, the immigrant's choice of 'us' makes us feel good about who we are. (In the American context, the pleasure and reinvigoration of having been chosen is illustrated and produced, for example, by the *New York Times*'s periodic publication of a photograph of new citizens taking the oath.[7] That pleasure is further protected by the failure of the United States to keep any continuous official statistics on remigration or emigration.[8])

The second (wary) response to immigrants also suggests a re-experience of the founding. Highlighted here, though, is the impulse to secure a regime's identity by including some people, values and ways of life and excluding others.[9] Here, the immigrant's choice of us endangers our sense of who we are. We might see the book of Ruth as an effort to reinvigorate Israelite identity without also endangering it by combining the story of Ruth's immigration with the story of Orpah's decision not to emigrate. The contrast between Ruth and Orpah highlights the extraordinariness of Ruth's border crossing, as Ozick points out.[10] But the contrast also has another effect: it suggests that Ruth's migration to Bethlehem does not mean that Israel is now a

6. For a discussion of the foreign-founder script in the history of Western culture, see Chapters 1 and 2 of my *Democracy and Foreignness* (Princeton, NJ: Princeton University Press, forthcoming 1999/2000).

7. A brief discussion of the symbolic functions of the iconic new citizen photograph can be found in Honig, 'Immigrant America? How Foreignness "Solves" Democracy's Problems', in *Social Text* 56.16.3 (Fall 1998), pp. 1-27. A more detailed discussion can be found in Chapter 4 of *Democracy and Foreignness*.

8. Estimates are that 195,000 US residents emigrate annually. See Priscilla Labovitz, 'Immigration—Just the Facts', *New York Times*, 25 March 1996.

9. Toni Morrison, 'On the Backs of Blacks', in Nicolaus Mills (ed.), *Arguing Immigration* (New York: Simon & Schuster, 1994), pp. 97-100, calls particularly sharp attention to the exclusionary dimension of the refounding effect of American immigration in relation to American Blacks.

10. Ozick, 'Ruth', p. 221.

borderless community open to all foreigners, including even idolatrous Moabites. Israel is open only to the Moabite who is exceptionally virtuous, to Ruth but not Orpah.

Together, then, Ruth and Orpah personify the coupling of wonder *and* fear, opportunity *and* threat, the sense of supplementation *and* fragmentation that immigrants often excite in the orders that absorb or exclude them. (Is Orpah not threatening? Traditional interpreters give expression to their fears when they claim that Goliath is her descendant.) Personified by the two distinct characters of Ruth and Orpah, these impulses may seem to be attached to different objects, the good immigrant versus the bad, for example. But what if we read Orpah as part of Ruth, a personification of the part of Ruth that cannot help but remain a Moabite even in Bethlehem?[11] The story might then illustrate the deep and abiding ambivalence that (even democratic) regimes tend to have about the foreigners living in their midst.

After all, it is Ruth's *foreignness* that enables her to choose the Israelites in a meaningful way. Indeed, the more radical her foreignness, the more meaningful the sense of chosenness that results from her choosing.[12] The more deep the enmity between Moab and Israel, the

11.   Jack M. Sasson, *Ruth: A New Translation with a Philological Commentary and Formalist-Folklorist Interpretation* (Sheffield: JSOT Press, 1989), pp. 16-17, notes this device of personification elsewhere in the book of Ruth: 'A didactic device frequently resorted to by Biblical writers is to limit the spectrum of choice to two alternatives, only one of which will prove to be correct. An obvious method of putting such a concept in effect is the creation of two brothers, only one of whom will ultimately fare well. Mahlon marries Ruth—he will live on' (through the posterity of Obed). Other biblical examples noted by Sasson are Cain and Abel, Jacob and Esau, Ishmael and Isaac—all male. Why does Sasson not include Ruth and Orpah in his list? Perhaps because of his Proppian assumption that Orpah is a merely marginal character, not central to the tale and not worthy, therefore, of further interpretive attention.

12.   Another reason for the supplementary powers of foreign choosing in the case of the Israelites is suggested but never really investigated by Freud, when he argues that the Israelites covenanted under Moses with an 'alien' god, YHWH, whose alienness was then hidden by YHWH's retrodictive claim that 'he had been the God of those patriarchs', Abraham, Isaac and Jacob (p. 53). Freud finds 'astonishing' the idea of a 'god suddenly "choosing" a people , making it "his" people and himself its own god. I believe it is the only case in the history of human religions. In other cases the people and their gods belong inseparably together; they are one from the beginning' (pp. 54-55). (Equally astonishing is that fact that Freud never asks whether these *other* peoples' original unitariness is *any truer than that of the Israelites.* He only questions the latter's.) 'Sometimes, it is true, we hear of a people adopting another god, but never of a god choosing a new people.' Freud interprets this unheard of divine choosing as a way of remembering the repressed

more profound the friendship that is declared in its midst. The more radically particular the convert, the more obviously universal the divinity that compels her to join up. The Israelites' own insistence that *their* god is (uniquely) universal is what puts them in need of periodic new testimony to his charms. Even as they eschew converts, they rely on them in this deep way. The most powerful testimony to Judaic monotheism's attractions is the testimony provided by the *most* unlikely person, the one coming from the most radically particular and hostile culture. It is because Ruth is a Moabite that her conversion, if a conversion it was, is fabulous. Indeed, were it somehow possible to cleanse Ruth of her foreign Moabite identity, the price of such a cleansing would be the very gift she has to offer.

And yet, that same foreignness makes Ruth deeply threatening to the order she might otherwise simply reinvigorate. There is no way around it: a *Moabite* has come to live in Bethlehem!

Ozick's Ruth: Convert or Migrant?

Traditional interpreters of Ruth 'solve' the problem of Ruth's founding foreignness by way of Orpah, the sister or sister-in-law who chooses to stay in Moab rather than migrate to Bethlehem. Cynthia Ozick's reading of Ruth provides a perfect illustration of this traditional 'solution'.

Ozick's reading of the book of Ruth is indebted to the rabbinical interpretations but departs from them significantly, 'I mean for the rest of my sojourn in the text to go on more or less without [the rabbis]', she says.[13] Where earlier readers interpreted Orpah in terms of her unfavorable comparison with Ruth, Ozick pauses to look to Orpah in her own right. 'Let us check the tale, fashion of a hiatus, and allow normality to flow in: let young stricken Orpah not be overlooked.'[14] Orpah is noteworthy not just for her failure, by contrast with Ruth, to emigrate to Bethlehem for the sake of Naomi and monotheism. Orpah stands out for her own admirable action: she married

---

choice made by the Egyptian, Moses, who 'had stooped to the Jews, [and] had made them his people' (p. 55). Whatever its real source (whether Jehovah, the foreign god, or Moses, the foreign lawgiver), Ruth replays the script, in which the (frightening) foreigner chooses the Israelites as her people and thereby reperforms the choice that made them 'chosen' (Sigmund Freud, *The Standard Edition of the Complete Psychological Works of Sigmund Freud*. XVIII. *Beyond the Pleasure Principle* [ed. James Strachey; London: Hogarth Press, 1953–74]).

13. Ozick, 'Ruth', pp. 219-20.
14. Ozick, 'Ruth', p. 221.

an Israelite in Moab (not a popular thing to have done, certainly) and came to love Naomi. Orpah may not have been up to the tests of monotheism and emigration, but she was an 'open-hearted) woman',[15] beyond the confines of 'narrow-minded', conventional prejudice.[16]

Ozick's Orpah was special, but ultimately, in the crucible of the decision to emigrate or not, the true principle of her character is revealed. She represents 'normality', not 'singularity'.[17] Her wants are mundane; her imagination does not soar. In returning to her mother's house she returns also to her idols. Orpah 'is never, never to be blamed for' her choice, Ozick says, but she suggests nonetheless that history has, indeed, judged Orpah ('Her mark is erased from history; there is no *Book of Orpah*'[18]). Ozick resists the judgment of history by pausing to reflect on Orpah. But Ozick also consolidates history's judgment by depicting Moab's (and Orpah's) disappearance from the world stage as deserved rather than contingent and by figuring Orpah's decision as ordinary and immature by contrast with Ruth's decision which is 'visionary'.[19] 'Ruth leaves Moab because she intends to leave childish ideas behind.'[20]

The contrast between Ruth and Orpah, though softened by Ozick's appreciative hiatus, instantiates Ozick's distinction between the normal and the singular. But it also does something else. Ozick's contrast between Ruth and Orpah effectively works to undo the undecidability of the immigrant who both supports and threatens to undermine the order that both depends upon and is threatened by her. Ozick positions Ruth, the immigrant, to reinvigorate the Israelite order without at the same time threatening to corrupt it. The threat of corruption, along with the specter of unconvertible foreignness, is projected onto Orpah, whose failure to emigrate symbolizes a failure to convert (and vice versa). If by staying home Orpah stayed with her gods then, by leaving home, Ruth left her gods behind. The contrast leaves no doubt about Ruth's conversion. There is no danger in her presence in Bethlehem. She is surely one of 'us'.

The unthreatening character of Ruth's reinvigorative immigration is further consolidated by another moment in Ozick's essay. In a lovely

15. Ozick, 'Ruth', p. 224.
16. Ozick, 'Ruth', p. 222.
17. Ozick, 'Ruth', p. 220.
18. Ozick, 'Ruth', p. 221.
19. Ozick, 'Ruth', p. 224.
20. Ozick, 'Ruth', p. 227.

insight into Naomi, Ozick sees her instruction to Ruth to follow Orpah and return to 'her people and to her gods' as evidence that Naomi 'is a kind of pluralist', *avant la lettre*.[21] Naomi is not a zealot, Ozick says. Orpah has her gods, Naomi has hers, and Naomi knows and accepts that. But Naomi's acceptance of Moabite idolatry is tied to the fact that Moabite idol worship occurs in Moab. Her pluralism is territorial. When Naomi says that Orpah has returned to her people and to her gods, Naomi implies (and Ruth surely picks up on this) that it is not possible to go to *her* people in Bethlehem with Moabite gods. In Naomi's pluralism, people and their gods are tied together and positioned in their proper territorial places. Ozick is right that this is a valuable pluralism by contrast with the forms of imperialism and zealotry that tolerate difference nowhere on earth. Its limits are more evident, however, by contrast with forms of pluralism that demand a more difficult toleration, that of differences that live among us, in our neighborhoods, right next door, in our own homes.

Ozick's positioning of Ruth and Orpah as personifications of singularity and normality combined with her territorialization of cultural difference establish a safe and secure distance between Ruth and Orpah. This distance (intentionally or not) works to enable Ruth to serve as a vehicle of the reinvigoration Ozick seeks without also jeopardizing the identity of the Israelites. Ozick's Ruth is able to supplement the Israelite order without at the same time diluting or corrupting it because the undecidable figure of the (Moabite) immigrant, both necessary for renewal and dangerous to the community, has been split into two: Orpah the practical, material Moabite who stayed at home with her idols, in her 'mother's house',[22] figures the Other whose absence keeps the community's boundaries and identity secure; while Ruth, loyal, devoted to Naomi, possessed of the mature, abstract imagination needed to be faithful to the one invisible God and refurbishes the order's boundaries through her conversion to it.

---

21. Ozick, 'Ruth', p. 223.

22. In psychoanalytic terms, Orpah's (over)attachment to her mother(land)—represented by the phrase 'her mother's house' (an unusual locution for the Bible)—prevents her, as it did Antigone (who clung to Polynices, the displaced site of her longing for her mother Jocasta), from entering the (paternal or monotheistic) Law, the realm of the Symbolic (as Luce Irigaray argues in *Speculum of the Other Woman* [Ithaca, NY: Cornell University Press, 1985]). Irigaray, moved by a sensibility more tragic than Ozick's, finds a subterranean location for Antigone, who eternally unsettles the dominant order. Ozick pauses to reflect on Orpah, but she does not look to Orpah as a source of eternal dissonance or (in Irigaray's appropriation of Hegel's term) irony.

This splitting protects the Israelite order from Moabite corruption while allowing it to profit nonetheless from the supplement of Ruth's migration. In short, Ozick does not see the undecidability of the (im)migrant and the lingering foreignness of Ruth, so intent is she on mobilizing Ruth's reinvigorating virtue and conversion for a national project.

But Ruth's incorporation into the Israelite order is less complete and more ambivalent than Ozick suggests. Where Ozick sees virtue, conversion and assimilation, the text of the book of Ruth suggests complication, recalcitrant particularism and prejudice. The following four examples illustrate how this radically undecidable foreign founder resists Ozick's decisive narration.

First, the book of Ruth repeatedly refers to Ruth as Ruth the Moabitess,[23] suggesting that she in some sense *stays* a Moabite, forbidden, surely noticed and perhaps despised by her adopted culture even while also celebrated by it.

Secondly, the book of Ruth makes a point of the fact that Naomi takes Obed from Ruth to nurse. Why?[24] The taking is reminiscent of the story reported by Herodotus of the 'Pelasgian inhabitants of Lemnos, who carried off Athenian women from Brauron and had children by them. When their mothers brought them up in the Athenian way, the fathers became afraid and killed both mothers and their children.'[25] The Israelites' appreciation of Ruth's re-enchantment of their way of life finds expression in the women's community's celebration of her. But when Naomi takes Obed from Ruth, that signals the community's continuing fear of Ruth's foreignness. Ruth the Moabite cannot be trusted to raise her son properly, in the Israelite way.

Thirdly, another pivotal scene, this one misread rather than ignored by Ozick: What happened that night on the threshing-room floor? Most commentators, including many of the rabbis, treat the scene as a seduction. Ozick, however, says that the scene depicts 'a fatherly tenderness, not an erotic one, though such a scene might, in some other

---

23. 1.22; 2.2, 6, 21; 4.5, 9.

24. One commentator argues that this is because childbirth was never Ruth's desire but rather Naomi's all along (Gail Twersky Reimer, 'Her Mother's House', in Judith A. Kates and Gail Twersky Reimer [eds.], *Reading Ruth: Contemporary Women Reclaim a Sacred Story* [New York: Ballantine, 1994]), pp. 97-106 (105). Reimer's reading is a good one. My own explanation has more to do with Ruth's status as an immigrant or a foreigner.

25. Gail Horst-Warhaft, *Dangerous Voices: Women's Lament in Greek Literature* (London: Routledge, 1992), p. 211 n. 54, citing Herodotus, *Histories* 6.6.138.

tale, burst with the erotic'.[26] Indeed. Another commentator, Jack Sasson, does better. Focusing on Boaz's initial fright upon awakening, Sasson speculates that Boaz mistook Ruth for a 'Lillith'. A Lillith is a demonic woman/spirit thought to be responsible for nocturnal emissions and male impotence.

> [U]pon awakening, Boaz discerns the figure of a woman. Fearing that it might be that of a Lillith, he shudders in fear. The storyteller's joke is that Ruth turns out to be equally as aggressive in her demands to be accepted as a mate. In this case, we shall be shortly reassured (if we do not know it already) that matters will turn out well for all concerned.[27]

The 'joke' of the scene depends upon Boaz's misidentification of Ruth as a Lillith. But the joke of the scene is not on Boaz. It is on this commentator. Because of course Ruth is a Lillith. What Sasson does not note is that Boaz's 'error' is overdetermined not simply by Ruth's sex/gender but also by her Moabite identity. Moabite women were particularly feared by the Israelites as temptresses and seductresses. This scene is much more (or less) than a joke, then. In it, Boaz is allowed to experience his worst fears about Ruth: that, her conversion/immigration notwithstanding, she is truly a Moabite after all, a bearer of desire that will not respect the proper boundaries of male, Israelite subjectivity.

The key to the scene is Boaz's question (Ruth 3.9) upon awakening: *mî'att*— 'Who are you?', as in: 'Who goes there?' It is a border guard's question. Boaz may ask it because he really does not know who this figure is. It is dark. But we know he can see *some*thing, because he says *mî'att*, which addresses the question to a female. He would otherwise have asked *mî'atta* or *mî'zeh*, using the universal masculine.

Still, Boaz may ask because he really does not know. Or… he may ask because in this night-time encounter it occurs to him for the first time as a really pressing concern that he really does not know *who Ruth is!* Is she a new Moses, risen from the dead in Moab, come to save and inspire and regenerate the Israelites? Or is she a Moabite? Is she friend or enemy? Founder or foreigner? Who *is* she? The answer comes: 'I am Ruth, your handmaid.' Not just 'I am Ruth' but also

---

26.   Ozick, 'Ruth', pp. 229-30. And yet the Hebrew term used here for 'feet' is a pun for genitals. Ozick's claim echoes Hegel's that the brother–sister relation, of which he takes Polynices and Antigone to be examplars, is unerotic. As Jacques Derrida points out, the claim is astonishing given the incestuous origins of this pair: 'Antigone's parents are not some parents among others' (*Glas* [Lincoln, NE: University of Nebraska Press, 1986], p. 165).

27.   Sasson, *Ruth*, p. 78.

'your handmaid' (v. 9). She tries to reassure. Nothing to fear here, she seems to say. But what does she know? She can hardly reassure in this matter. Besides, if the rabbis are right, Boaz will soon die, on the night of his wedding to Ruth. It seems there was something to fear after all.

Finally, let us turn to the most famous scene of this short story, the scene in which Ruth declares herself to Naomi. *What* is Ruth saying when she says: 'Whither thou goest, I will go, Whither thou lodgest, I will lodge, Thy people shall be my people, Thy god shall be my god, Whither thou diest, I will die, and there I will be buried' (1.16-17)?

Some commentators, such as Julia Kristeva, treat this speech as a declaration of woman-to-woman love and friendship. Ruth will stick with Naomi, no matter what, 'til death does them part'. (Indeed, in our own time, this speech serves as a wedding or commitment vow for many lesbian couples.) For Ozick, however, Ruth is saying not only that she loves Naomi *but also that she* feels the pull of the one true god. Why would Ruth say, 'Thy god shall be my god' if she was not moved by faith? Why would she even move to Bethlehem? 'Everything socially rational is on the side of Ruth's remaining in her own country.'[28]

Ozick's reading is not implausible, but there is nothing *in the text* to rule out other rival readings: the social rationalities of the situation are unclear, after all. It cannot have been easy to return to Moab as the childless widow of an Israelite.[29] Desperate to get out of there, Ruth may have spoken to Naomi neither out of love, nor faith, but rather out of immigrant practicality: Please take me with you, she pleads, knowing that Naomi does not want to. Naomi has just said to her, 'See, your sister-in-law has gone back to *her people* and to *her gods; return, too, as your sister-in-law has done*' (v. 15), and Ruth may detect in this instruction a concern that she, Ruth, a Moabite, with her own people and her own gods, will be unacceptable and unassimilable in

---

28. Ozick, 'Ruth', p. 225.

29. *Contra* Ozick, Orpah's course was courageous too. The difficulties of such a return are occluded by Ozick, who comments on the unusualness of Orpah's exogamy but then assumes that Orpah's life in Moab will be unproblematic: 'soon she will marry a Moabite husband and have a Moabite child' (p. 224). Fewell and Gunn have a better grasp of the situation: 'What are Ruth's opportunities in Moab? Who would want to marry a barren widow, much less one that had been living with a foreigner? And would she be known as the "Israelite-lover," the one too good for her own people?... In the end, we might ask, what takes more courage, the staying or the leaving?' (*Ruth*, pp. 97-98; cf. Rosa Felsenburg Kaplan, 'The Noah Syndrome', in Susanna Heschel [ed.], *On Being a Jewish Feminist* [New York: Schocken Books, 1983], pp. 167-70 [167]).

Bethlehem. Do not worry, Ruth responds. I may not know all the customs but I will go where you go, live where you live, *your people shall be my people* and *your god shall be my god*.[30] As far as the text is concerned, Ruth may simply be reassuring Naomi—as so many

30. These three readings of Ruth's speech suggest that that it traffics in all three of the kinds of friendship distinguished by Aristotle in the *Nicomachean Ethics*: virtue (Ozick's version in which Ruth's declaration is a conversion), pleasure (Kristeva's version in which Ruth's speech declares a deep love for Naomi) and use (my own reading, in which Ruth's speech is an expression of immigrant practicality). Jacques Derrida points out that Aristotle knows that the borders among these kinds of friendship are porous and cannot be fully policed: 'Aristotle never gives up analysing the ruses that enable one friendship to be smuggled into another, the law of the useful into that of pleasure, one or the other into virtue's mask' (Derrida, *Politics of Friendship*, p. 105). Notwithstanding Aristotle's claim that only friendship as usefulness is *political* friendship, Derrida considers whether what marks friendship as a political relation are the perpetual confusions among its three registers: 'Each time a grievance consequently arises, not between enemies but between friends who, as it were, have been misled, and have misled each other because they have first mistaken friendships, confusing in one case friendship based on virtue with friendship based on usefulness, in another, legal and ethical friendship, etc.' (p. 206).

Reading Ruth under the sign of virtue and pleasure respectively, both Ozick and Kristeva seek to position her relation to Naomi on a single register of friendship. In so doing, both effectively rid Ruth of her troubling foreignness. Ruth is only a friend; she is not an enemy at the same time. Ozick maps Ruth's relation to Naomi as one of strictly virtue friendship for the sake of a pure Israelite monotheism, which is reliable and universal, in Ozick's view, only to the extent that it is untainted by eros (hence her rejction of any erotic quality to the nightime meeting with Boaz) or instrumental calculations of usefulness. Kristeva privileges the woman-to-woman eros reading for the sake of a cosmopolitanism that needs the animation of an erotic motivation but seeks to avoid an overly universalizing virtue on the one hand and an inadequately passionate—merely instrumental—regard for Others, on the other hand. In both readings, Ruth's Moabitic identity is transcended, whether by the pull of virtue or by love. Without the continuing taint of her foreignness, however, Ruth's capacity to (re)found the people or, as in Kristeva's case, Ruth's capacity to model any meaningful kind of cosmopolitanism, is severely diminished.

Reading Ruth's speech to Naomi—as I do—as an expression of friendship as usefulness may serve as an antidote to these other readings insofar as it resists the impulse to rid Ruth of her foreignness and seeks not to overstate her membership and acceptance in the Israelite community. But this reading may also be too univocal. For it may be that the undecidability of Ruth's speech—a speech precariously perched on all three registers of friendship (virtue, pleasure and use)—is what best accounts for how it is that Ruth is always both friend and enemy at the same time. For a more detailed discussion of these issues, see the chapter-length version of this essay in *Democracy and Foreignness*.

immigrants have reassured their hosts and sponsors before and since—that she will be no trouble.

These complications are absent from Ozick's reading because she sees the undecidable figure of the immigrant as two distinct figures: the one who supplements the order (Ruth) and the one who might dilute or corrupt it (Orpah). Ozick sees things this way because she counts on Ruth to perform a function not unlike that of the legislator in Rousseau's *On the Social Contract*, whose combination of foreignness (he comes from elsewhere) and exemplary virtue enables him to restore a wayward order to its forgotten first principles. Rousseau solves the problem of the stranger's dangerous undecidability by having him leave as soon as his restorative work is done. (There is no provision for the office of the legislator in the regime's constitution.[31]) Ozick tries to solve the problem as many multicultural Western democracies have since: by having the helpful (part of the) foreigner/stranger (Ruth) assimilate and by ensuring that the dangerous (part of the) foreigner (Orpah) leave or stay behind.

Kristeva's Ruth: The Ideal Immigrant

Julia Kristeva tries to recapture the undecidability of the immigrant in her own reading of *Ruth* as a potentially alternative model of a founding myth.[32] She points out that Ruth, 'the outsider, the foreigner, the excluded', founds a monarchic line that is riven by difference from the beginning. The rift is generative: 'If David is also Ruth, if the sovereign is also a Moabite, peace of mind will never be his lot, but a constant quest for welcoming and going beyond the other in himself'.[33]

There is, however, no trace of this idealized ('welcoming') relation to the other in David's lament (cited by Kristeva) that 'the people often speak to him wrathfully, saying "Is he not of unworthy lineage? Is he not a descendant of Ruth, the Moabite?"', nor in David's wish (also cited by Kristeva) to be rid of his Moabite ancestry so that the

31. Jean-Jacques Rousseau, 'On the Social Contract', in *idem*, *The Basic Political Writings* (trans. Donald A. Cress; Indianapolis, IN: Hackett), Bk II, Ch. 7.

32. Noting Ruth's love for Naomi, Kristeva calls attention to the woman to woman passion at the base of the Davidic line, a passion that seems to fly in the face of structuralist assumptions about the order-constituting function of the male homo-social exchange of women. One might well add to this the observation that the order constituting exchange in this text is that of a male—Obed—who is passed from one woman, Ruth, to another, Naomi. On the other hand, one could just as well say that Ruth is passed from Mahlon to Boaz by way of Naomi.

33. Kristeva, *Strangers*, pp. 75-76.

people might properly revere him.[34] David was more zealous than Kristeva suggests in dealing with Others. He certainly outdid Saul in his willingness to destroy his enemies. Later rabbinic interpreters imagine David complaining about being identified with Ruth because he thinks (certainly the later interpreters think) the foundation of his regime will be more stable and more secure without her. At the same time, however, David needs Ruth, not to 'worry' his sovereignty (as Kristeva puts it[35]), but to supplement his own well-known deficiencies with the story of her exceptional virtue and also to support his efforts to expand Israel's sphere of influence to Moab.

Kristeva argues that Ruth's gift to the regime *is* her foreignness and its worrying of Israelite sovereignty. But this misses the fact that for the Israelites, as for Ozick, Ruth's virtue is in spite of her foreignness or apart from it. Her gift to the regime is her exemplary character and faith, manifested in her willingness to leave Moab for Naomi and to convert to monotheism. Ruth's foreignness is what makes her choice of the Israelites so powerful, but her foreignness, per se, is no gift.

Kristeva is right, however, to see some promise in the Judaic embrace of Ruth and in the various biblical requirements charging Israel with hospitality to strangers or foreigners.[36] But she reads Ruth without Orpah (who is barely mentioned), and so Kristeva's Ruth easily becomes (as in Ozick's reading) a figure of virtue for her willingness to convert to Israelite monotheism while leaving all really disruptive differences behind in Moab. Without Orpah and all she represents (e.g. the recalcitrance of difference, the home-yearning of immigrants, the forbiddenness of Moabites), Kristeva loses hold of the undecidability of foreignness.

Orpah's absence from Kristeva's retelling of the story is significant. Kristeva seems to count on the ethics-generating power of stories about strangers to move us out of our insistence on national or ethnic self-identity, but in the end her own acceptance of strangeness turns out to depend upon the stranger's willingness to affirm the existence and the worth of the order she supplements and disturbs. Ruth is the model immigrant, for Kristeva no less than for Ozick, because of Ruth's willingness to swear fidelity to Naomi, her people and her god. Indeed, Kristeva's cosmopolitanism depends upon similar pledges of allegiance from French citizens and immigrants alike.[37]

34. Kristeva, *Strangers*, p. 74.
35. Kristeva, *Strangers*, p. 75.
36. Kristeva, *Strangers*, pp. 65-69.
37. Kristeva, *Nations*, p. 63.

Kristeva's Orpahs: Cosmopolitanism without Foreignness

In *Nations without Nationalism* Kristeva returns to Ruth, the border-crossing convert, to figure a cosmopolitanism that Kristeva directs at French nationalists and at recent immigrants to France, such as the Maghrebi denizens and citizens who 'wear the Muslim scarf to school'.[38] These immigrants resemble Ruth in their willingness to emigrate from their original homes, but they also resemble Orpah insofar as they remain attached to the particular culture of their home countries.[39] Is there nothing French to which immigrants might feel allegiance?[40]

The enduring attachment of many Algerian immigrants to their culture and homeland, and their option since 1963 of citizenship in an independent Algeria, lead many of them either to reject French citizenship or to relate to it in purely instrumental terms. In response, those on the French Right have in the last ten years been calling for tighter controls on immigration and demanding that citizenship be awarded only to those who relate to France affectively. Those on the French Left resist efforts to control immigration and reject attempts to inscribe citizenship as an affective practice.[41]

Charging that the first response is too 'nationalist' and the second too 'world-oriented' (the Left is too ready to 'sell off French national values'),[42] Kristeva carves out a middle ground between them and offers up a cosmopolitanism that is distinctively French, in which the nation is still an important but not all-encompassing site of identity, centered not on *Volk* but on compact.[43] Kristeva resignifies the nation from a final site of affiliation to, in psychoanalytic terms, a *transitional object*. (The object is a device, such as a favorite blanket or stuffed animal, that empowers the child to separate from the mother[land] and eventually, in theory anyway, move on to an independent—blanketless/post-nationalist—existence.) Brilliantly cutting across the French Right–Left divide, Kristeva's cosmopolitanism is rooted and

38. Kristeva, *Nations*, p. 36.
39. Kristeva, *Strangers*, p. 194.
40. Kristeva, *Nations*, p. 60.
41. Rogers Brubaker, *Citizenship and Nationhood in France and Germany* (Cambridge, MA: Harvard University Press, 1992), pp. 138-64, and James Hollifield, *Immigrants, Markets and States: The Political Economy of Postwar Europe* (Cambridge, MA: Harvard University Press, 1992), chs. 6–7.
42. Kristeva, *Nations*, p. 37.
43. Kristeva, *Nations*, p. 40.

affective, but attached finally to a transnational not a national object.

Kristeva's cosmopolitanism secures and is secured by affective relations to a series of 'sets'—specifically: self, family, homeland, Europe, and mankind—in which each set operates as a transitional object for the next.[44] By locating the sets in a progressive, sequential, trajectory of transition, Kristeva avoids the issue of possible conflicts among them. She also avoids the question of a specifically French affiliation by using the abstract term 'homeland' for *that* set. But her call for an identification with *Europe* positions French and Maghrebi subjects asymmetrically in relation to her cosmopolitanism.[45] And because her cosmopolitanism (as she says repeatedly) 'make[s] its way through France',[46] specifically by way of Montesquieu, it works to shore up a uniquely French identity, even while claiming to overcome or transcend it. '[T]here is no way for an identity to go beyond itself without first asserting itself in satisfactory fashion', she says.[47] (But this generous recognition of the need to affirm identity before overcoming it is is not extended to France's immigrant communities.)

There is surely no way out of this paradox, in which cosmopolitanism must be striven for through the particular, albeit heterogeneous, (national) cultures that shape us. But Kristeva does not explore the paradox and she tends to leave the heterogeneity of France behind in her embrace of one particular strand of French Enlightenment thought. She is right to say we must 'pursue a critique of the national tradition without selling off its assets', but her account of French cosmopolitanism ultimately protects (what she sees as) the nation's assets from critique and from critical engagement with others:

> Let us ask, for instance, where else one might find a theory and a policy more concerned with respect for the *other*, more watchful of citizens' rights (women and foreigners included, *in spite of blunders and crimes*), more concerned with individual strangeness, in the midst of national mobility?[48]

The limits of Kristeva's cosmopolitanism emerge again when, echoing Ozick's preference for Ruth over Orpah, Kristeva suggests that the '"abstract" advantages of a French universalism may prove to be superior to the "concrete" benefits of a Muslim scarf', implying that

44. Kristeva, *Nations*, p. 41.

45. See Norma Moruzzi, 'A Problem with Headscarves: Contemporary Complexities of Political and Social Identity', *Political Theory* 22 (1994), pp. 653-72 (665).

46. Kristeva, *Nations*, p. 38.

47. Kristeva, *Nations*, p. 59.

48. Kristeva, *Nations*, pp. 46-47; my emphasis.

the scarf, unlike the nation, is essentially a fetish and is therefore unable, as such, to serve as a healthy transitional object.[49] She seems to have those who wear the scarf in mind when she says there 'are mothers (as well as "motherlands" and "fatherlands") who prevent the creation of a transitional object; there are children who are unable to use it',[50] Kristeva sees these veiled women much as Ozick sees Orpah: tethered to their idols, their mothers and motherlands, capable of some bold mobility but ultimately incapable of proper and mature transition, they mark (what Kristeva calls) the 'melancholy' of nationalism.[51]

Kristeva quite rightly sees a generative possibility in a differently conceived French *nation*.[52] Why not accord the same possibility to the Muslim scarf? In *Women and Gender in Islam*, Leila Ahmed highlights the transitional properties of veiling in a particular context, arguing that for Muslim women in contemporary Egypt the veil, worn increasingly by professional and university women, operates as a kind of transitional object, enabling upwardly mobile women to move from the familiar settings of their rural homes 'to emerge socially into a sexually integrated world' that is 'still an alien, uncomfortable social reality for both women and men'.[53] Ironically, if Ahmed is right and veiling *can* function as a healthy transitional object, then Kristeva's figuring of the veil as a concreteness that may have to give way to the welcome abstraction of cosmopolitanism puts her in the very position of those mothers whom she criticizes, those 'mothers (as well as "motherlands" and "fatherlands") who prevent the creation of a transitional object'.[54]

49. Kristeva, *Nations*, p. 47. Kristeva does note the tenuousness of the distinction between fetish and transitional object when she concedes that the transitional object is 'any child's indispensable fetish' (Kristeva, *Nations*, p. 41).

50. Kristeva, *Nations*, pp. 41-42.

51. Kristeva, *Nations*, p. 43.

52. Kristeva, *Nations*, p. 47.

53. Leila Ahmed, *Women and Gender in Islam* (New Haven: Yale University Press, 1992), pp. 223-24.

54. Ahmed studies veiling in Egypt, not France, but her argument was recently echoed by France's Federation of Councils of Parents of Pupils in Public Schools (FCPE), which opposed the expulsions of over 70 girls who wore headscarves to their schools in Lille and the Paris region: 'These expulsions carry with them the immense inconvenience of confining these young girls to within their family circle and of limiting any possibility of emancipation' (*Migration News Sheet*, November 1994, p. 2). Kristeva never questions why she (like so many others) expresses her concerns about Muslim particularism through Muslim *women*. This is not a new

The pleasing irony of this insight should not, however, blind us to the fact that the problem with Kristeva is not simply her failure to explore the transitional properties of veiling, while managing nonetheless to see the transitional possibilities of the nation. Were that the case, she could simply change her position on veiling and the problem would be solved.[55] Instead, the problem with Kristeva is her failure to engage Others in her deliberations about the project goals and instruments of a cosmopolitanism she values too much to risk by including it in the conversation as a question rather than as the answer. Kristeva ends up in this awkward position because she neglects what Judith Butler calls the 'difficult labor of translation', an ongoing project of political work that always also involves a critical self-interrogation and courts the risk of transformation.[56] Without a commitment to such a labor, Kristeva's cosmopolitanism already knows what it is—and what it isn't, and so it *risks* becoming another form of domination, particularly when it confronts an Other that resists assimilation to it, an Other that is unwilling to reperform for 'us' the wonder of our conversion to world (or French) citizenship.

When Kristeva does invite an exchange with 'foreigners, [which] we all are (within ourselves and in relation to others)', she imagines it will 'amplify and enrich the French idea of the nation'.[57] But this imagined exchange, in which Others join to complete the French idea, calls attention to the need for a different cosmopolitanism in which cosmopolitans risk their cosmopolitan (and nationalist) principles by engaging Others in their particularities, while *at the same time* defending and discovering located universalisms, such as human rights and the equal dignity of persons. There is not enough evidence of such a risk in the questions put to immigrants by Kristeva: 'What does each immigrant community contribute to the lay concept of *national spirit*

question. It was posed by Fanon in 'The Unveiling of Algeria', in *A Dying Colonialism* (trans. Haakon Chevalier; New York: Grove Press, 1965). Winifred Woodhull hazards an answer to it, albeit not with Kristeva in mind. Echoing Fanon, she says, 'In the eyes of many French people, girls of Maghrebian descent are generally diligent students and compliant people—in short, the most assimilable element of the immigrant population; if they begin to defend their right to "difference," the whole project of integration seems to be jeopardized' (*Transfigurations of the Maghreb: Feminism, Decolonization, and Literatures* [Minneapolis: University of Minnesota Press, 1993], p. 48).

55. Thanks to Pratap Mehta on this point.

56. Judith Butler, 'Kantians in Every Culture?', *Boston Review*, October–November 1994, p. 18.

57. Kristeva, *Nations*, p. 47.

as esprit general reached by the French Enlightenment? Do these communities recognize that *esprit general* or not?'[58]

Mourning, Membership, Agency and Loss: *Ruth's Lessons for Politics*

I return to Ruth by way of a psychoanalytic account of transitional objects. Transitional objects play a central role both in Kristeva's account of immigration and in Ozick's reading of Ruth, in which Naomi is in effect the transitional object that enables Ruth to make the (progressive) move from Moab to Israel.[59]

Modeling issues of separation and autonomy in terms of the child's developing independence from the mother, the object relations school of psychoanalysis emphasizes the role of transitional objects in the process of individuation.[60] Drawing on the work of D.W. Winnicott, who emphasizes the loss that attends and occasions individuation and separation, Eric Santner argues that transitional objects enable successful separation only if certain necessary conditions are met. First, the separation must not be traumatic; it must be temporary. Secondly, there must be a healthy environment conducive to transitional object play. And thirdly, that play must have an intersubjective dimension; that is to say, it must be witnessed periodically by the figure whose (temporary) absences are being borne. If these conditions are met, the space of object play can serve as a site of healthy mourning for the loss entailed by transition. At play with the transitional object, the subject acts out her bereavement and is thereby

---

58. Kristeva, *Nations*, p. 60; emphasis original.

59. Ozick, 'Ruth', pp. 227-28. That the cultural-symbolic connections among nationalism, immigration, psychoanalysis and transitional objects are well established was evidenced by the *New York Times Book Review*'s use of a flag-stuffed baby bottle to illustrate its review of Michael Lind's *The Next American Nation* (summer 1995).

60. I borrow from one version of this account but I distance myself from psychoanalysis's reliance on the model of an original maternal relation. Separation and transition are issues not just for children or immigrants but for all of us throughout our lifetimes. I also seek to avoid the progressive trajectory of developmental accounts. That trajectory infantilizes the immigrants whose transitions are part of what is at issue here, and it works to affirm Western receiving regimes' perceptions of sending regimes as a 'past that the West has already lived out' and can be left behind without loss (Shiv Visvanathan, 'From the Annals of the Laboratory State', *Alternatives: A Journal of World Policy* 12 [1987], pp. 37-59 [41]). Kristeva's and Ozick's progressive accounts tend to feed these prejudices too.

empowered for separation and individuation (as in the 'fort-da' game—a kind of peek-a-boo—described by Freud). There is empowerment here, not just mourning: the play provides the subject not simply with a substitute (for the loss being mourned) but with a lesson in what Peter Sacks calls 'the very means and *practice* of substitution'. At best the subject learns *agency* in the face of loss (perhaps even as a result of it, if the conditions are right for such a learning).[61]

If these conditions are not met, neither mourning nor empowerment will ensue. Instead, the subject will first make a fetish of the object, engaging it in a furious and hyperbolic play that signals her denial of her loss. Second, the object will ultimately lose all meaning for the subject and she will abandon the object entirely, leaving it stranded. The evacuation of the object's meaning can result in 'signification trauma', which leaves the subject stranded, silent and speechless, outside the world of language, play and mourning. Emphasizing all three dimensions of transitional object play—mourning, empowerment and intersubjectivity—Santner summarizes Winnicott's view with the aphorism: 'Mourning without solidarity [i.e. transitional object play in the absence of intersubjective witnessing] is the beginning of madness.'[62]

How might this account apply to *Ruth*? By pointing out that successful transitions are determined not by the nature of the transitional object itself but by the context in which it operates, Santner calls attention to the role of institutions, culture, community and politics in projects of transition and translation, something to which Kristeva does not adequately attend in her critique of immigrant particularism. And Santner's focus on mourning, empowerment and intersubjectivity calls attention to the fact that none of these three components of successful transition is available in Ruth's case. Ruth's separation from Orpah (who, on my account, personifies Moab) is traumatic. There is no healthy space for transitional object play, no intersubjective witnessing and no possibility of proper mourning because Ruth is not given cultural, juridical or psychological permission to mourn Orpah–Moab. Nor are we. Ruth made the right choice. Ozick and Kristeva agree on that. What could there be to mourn?

61. Eric Santner, *Stranded Objects: Mourning, Memory and Film in Postwar Germany* (Ithaca, NY: Cornell University Press, 1990), pp. 19-26, and Peter Sacks, *The English Elegy: Studies in Genre from Spenser to Yeats* (Baltimore: The Johns Hopkins University Press, 1985), p. 8. Santner is working with D.W. Winnicott, *Playing and Reality* (London: Tavistock, 1971) and Freud, *Beyond the Pleasure Principle*.

62. Santner, *Stranded Objects*, pp. 26-27.

Ozick and Kristeva both seem to assume that their affirmation of the rightness of Ruth's choice (and their marginalization of Orpah) secures Ruth's transition from Moab. But, if Santner and Winnicott are correct, the opposite is true: Naomi's power as a transitional object for Ruth *depends upon* the proper mourning of Orpah and upon a kind of continued (perhaps hyphenated?) relation with her. It depends upon recognizing that Orpah (Moab) is part of Ruth. In Ozick's and Kristeva's terms, we might say that Ruth's insight into a universality is touched by a particularity with which it may be in tension but by which Ruth and her insight are nonetheless also nourished.

Indeed, *contra* Ozick and Kristeva, the book of Ruth can be read as a tale of incomplete mourning, a fable of failed transition. Through the lens provided by Santner, Ruth's famous loyalty to Naomi no longer signals simply the selfless devotion of a virtuous or passionate woman, nor is it only a mark of Ruth's immigrant practicality (a possibility I myself raised earlier, along with Fewell and Gunn). What if this clinging is a symptom of Ruth's denial of her loss of Orpah–Moab, a sign of Santner's first stage in which the subject's denial of her loss leads to a frenzied attachment in which the transitional object is fetishized?

And Ruth's closing silence can no longer be taken to signal merely successful and complete absorption. Instead, that silence may be a mark of Santner's second stage, in which the subject suffers from a 'signification trauma'. In Ruth's case, the trauma is produced by the separation from Orpah–Moab and the loss of any meaningful relationship to Naomi, Ruth's adopted (transitional) mother. That second loss is finally symbolized by Naomi's adoption of Obed in place of Ruth but it is foreshadowed by, among other things, Naomi's failure to introduce or even mention Ruth to the women who welcome Naomi back to Bethlehem.

These two moments in Ruth's story mark two familiar moments of immigration dynamics as they are modeled in contemporary multicultural democracies. One, a furious and hyperbolic assimilationism in which all connections to the motherland are disavowed. And two, a refusal of transition and a retreat into a separatist or nationalist enclave that leaves the immigrant stranded in relation to the receiving country *and* in relation to the lost homeland. The two moments are figured developmentally by Santner and Winnicott, but they actually make simultaneous claims upon immigrants and receiving regimes.

This binary of absorption versus enclavism is animated by efforts to recuperate foreignness for national(ist) projects. It is the (not very well) hidden nationalism of Kristeva's cosmopolitanism that leads her to see newcomers to France in terms of this stern binary. She does not explicitly invoke the sense of kinship that David Miller thinks is a necessary condition of social democracy, but neither does she see foreignness as itself an occasion of democratic re-fashioning. The history of interpretative engagements with Ruth illustrates the consequences of this approach. Democracy is unexpanded and untested by the insistence that others become 'us' or go back whence they came. That often punitive insistence itself plays a (never acknowledged) role in producing the very tendencies it excoriates—withdrawalism, recalcitrant particularism, separatism.

Retold, the book of Ruth is not only a fable of founding and immigration; it is also—appropriately—a parable of mourning and membership. It suggests that there are institutional and cultural conditions for the proper work of mourning and it teaches the importance to a meaningful and empowered agency of intersubjective spaces, actions in concert, multiple solidarities, civic powers and (always contested) connections to the past. Because such spaces, actions, powers and connections are available to Naomi in Bethlehem (Boaz is her relative, the women of Bethlehem are her friends, and her connection to Moab is preserved by Ruth), Naomi is restored to plenitude and agency. Ruth's fate is different because Bethlehem positions her and Naomi asymmetrically in relation to their losses. Naomi's dead sons and husband can be mourned in Bethlehem, but Ruth's loss of Orpah–Moab cannot even be articulated as such. The women's community provides Naomi with support and sympathy. They witness her ritually mournful name change to Mara (though they never call her by that name), and she is empowered for agency (symbolized by maternity).

'The homeopathic constitution and (reconstitution) of the self takes place not in a vacuum', Santner says, 'but always in a particular social context'.[63] Ruth's resources and context are limited because her losses are not seen as such and her transnational connections to Orpah–Moab (a potentially alternative site of support and power) are severed. Like Antigone's mourning of Polynices, Ruth's mourning of Orpah is forbidden for the sake of a regime's stability and identity. Thus, Ruth's mourning—like Antigone's—is endless, melancholic. Her losses get in the way of the closure this community seeks to attain through her *and* in spite of her. Indeed, the fact that Naomi's restoration to the community is finally marked by her occupation of Ruth's position as mother to Obed suggests that the reinvigoration of

63. Santner, *Stranded Objects*, p. 24.

this community and the stabilization of David's monarchy depend not only upon the supplement of Ruth's inspiring example but also, and at the same time, upon her marginalization. The Israelites need Ruth's foreignness to shore up their identity as a Chosen People; but that identity is also deeply threatened by her foreignness (which must then be hidden or managed under the umbrella of her supposed conversion and assimilation) and there is no way out of this dynamic as long as a unitary, kinship-style (national) identity rather than a challenged and contested democracy is the goal.

It might be possible, however, to take the affective energies of kinship and redeploy them on behalf of a politics that is more cosmopolitan than nationalist in its aspirations. Ruth's severed sororal relation to Orpah calls to mind another sororal relation, that of sister-cities, those affective sites of transnational connection that bypass state apparatuses to pursue shared goals and establish relations of long standing. Sister-cities are usually founded by local civic energies and initiatives. They are not limited 'to carrying out a single project' and this makes them an important complement to more temporary, issue-oriented forms of local and international solidarity that are coalitional.[64] Most important, sister-cities interrupt projects of (re-) nationalization by generating practices of affective citizenship that exceed state boundaries and sometimes even violate state foreign policy.[65] They are one site of enacted cosmopolitanism. They are sites of leverage in national(ist) politics and they also serve as settings in which mourning, empowerment, solidarity and agency can develop for foreigners, residents and citizens alike. Sister-cities commemorate Ruth and Orpah by enacting a forbidden sorority rather than inheriting the permitted kind. In so doing, they contest the tendency to model state citizenship in terms of kin relations, while also dispersing the sites of democratic politics beyond and within the states that would like to be democracy's privileged and exclusive centers.

64. Wilbur Zelinsky, 'The Twinning of the World: Sister Cities in Geographical and Historical Perspective', *Annals of the Association of American Geographers* 81.1 (1991), pp. 1-31 (1).

65. Liz Chilsen and Sheldon Rampton, *Friends in Deed: The Story of U.S.–Nicaraguan Sister Cities* (Madison: Wisconsin Co-ordinating Council on Nicaragua, 1988).

FACING THE OTHER:
RUTH-THE-CAT IN MEDIEVAL JEWISH ILLUMINATIONS

Carole R. Fontaine

Medieval Hebrew Manuscripts: Unexpected Treasures

For students of mainstream art history, it is almost a commonplace to say that Jewish manuscripts do not receive much attention when one is studying the making of the medieval book. Presumably the second commandment of the Decalogue, forbidding all representations, is responsible for this dearth of codices with iconographic materials. Judaism, taking its cue from this ancient injunction, speculates, exegetes and comments, the experts (Jewish and Christian alike) tell us;[1] it does not paint or sculpt its faith in the ways that Christian communities do. Further, the assumption that Jews were excluded from monastic or secular Christian ateliers led art historians to relegate studies of Hebrew manuscripts to the realm of codicology or calligraphy, since of course whatever manuscripts we may have could not possibly contain figurative paintings, or, if they did, they must have been executed by Christian artisans.[2]

Actually, the case is rather different than the textbooks would lead us to conclude: Sephardic and Ashkenazi illuminated manuscripts of the Hebrew Bible, prayer and ritual texts *do* exist in fact, and are becoming a fertile field of study in their own right/write/rite.[3] These

---

1.   Joseph Gutmann, *Hebrew Manuscript Painting* (New York: George Braziller, 1978), pp. 8-9.

2.   I choose the term 'artisan' here because scribes, painters and illuminators (those who apply metallic leaf to the compositions) are usually not the same person. Typically, only scribes' names appear on the manuscripts of this period.

3.   Malachi Beit-Arié, *The Makings of the Medieval Hebrew Book: Studies in Paleography and Codicology* (Jerusalem: Magnes Press; Hebrew University, 1993); Thérèse Metzger and Mendel Metzger, *Jewish Life in the Middle Ages: Illuminated Hebrew Manuscripts of the Thirteenth to the Sixteenth Centuries* (New York: Alpine Fine Arts Collection, 1982); Bezalel Narkiss, *The Golden Haggadah* (Rohnert Park, CA: Pomegranate Art Books, 1997); Bezalel Narkiss, *Illuminated Hebrew Manuscripts*

brilliantly glowing treasures provide not only an important link for
the study of religious manuscripts, but also provide us with contemporary iconographic information[4] on Jewish rituals, customs and
world view from the medieval and early modern period, an 'ideo-
graphic summarizing of elements of medieval Jewry's spiritual experience'.[5]

These works also bear written witness to the ongoing struggle of
Jewish communities in Northern and Southern Europe to preserve
their own traditions in the face of a hostile Christian church and secular bodies who, quite without a second thought, naturally endorsed
the anti-Judaism of the dominant religious hegemony. Scribal colo-
phons in our texts are often followed with various notes by Christian
censors who had been authorized by the Church to expurgate or burn
any Jewish books found 'blasphemous' to the Christian faith or
sensibilities. Long before the Nazi persecutions of this century made
burning Jewish books a fashionable public activity, the Church had
instituted much the same practice. We might note, however, that
Christian scribes and booksellers knew wasteful practices when they
saw them: though most books were destroyed during these official
cleansings of 'Jewish lies',[6] many technicians rescued the parchment
leaves from the flames when they could, and recycled this highly
prized writing surface[7] for other uses. It is the case that one may find
secular documents in town halls and archives still wrapped in pages

(New York: Alpine Fine Arts Collection, 1983); Binyamin Richler, *Hebrew Manu-
scripts: A Treasured Legacy* (Cleveland: Ofeq Institute, 1990); Gabrielle Sed-Rajna,
The Hebrew Bible in Medieval Illuminated Manuscripts (trans. Josephine Bacon; New
York: Rizzoli, 1987).

    4.   That is, these manuscripts illustrate biblical scenes using characters, dress,
and backgrounds drawn from the world of the scribes and illuminators who created them, rather than trying to archaize the depictions presented in these liturgical texts.

    5.   Gutmann, *Painting*, p. 15.

    6.   Joshua Tractenberg, *The Devil and the Jews* (Philadelphia: Jewish Publication
Society of America, 2nd edn, 1983), pp. 68, 179.

    7.   In fact, the parchment prepared by medieval Jews is of significantly higher
quality than that used by Christians. By a technique now lost to us, Jewish artisans
were able to prepare both hair and flesh sides in such a way that either side had a
fine velvety texture suitable for miniature painting and illumination. Normally,
only the flesh side of the parchment was finely grained enough for art purposes,
causing the quires of the codex to be folded in such a way that flesh side faced
flesh side, while facing pairs of hair side were used only for script. This factor
meant that Jewish ateliers used their materials in a more cost-effective and artis-
tically liberating way.

from a Hebrew codex, with the Hebrew script plain to see.[8] What we might find in all these fragments, could they be collected, catalogued and made available for scholarly purposes remains a tantalizing question.

While art historians debate the existence of Hebrew manuscript models with illustration cycles to be copied by subsequent scribes, a line of inquiry opened by considerations of the Synagogue paintings of late antiquity from Dura-Europos,[9] it is generally thought that Hebrew illuminations do not reflect a particular 'Jewish style' of art. Rather, Christian and Islamic trends and various regional variants all find their way into Hebrew manuscripts, reflecting the realities of a Jewish diaspora spread throughout the known world and living in the midst of the currents of the artistic worlds that surrounded them.[10] It is the case, however, that one will find significant differences between Sephardic and Ashkenazi traditions of illustration, script and organization, as well as regional manuscript preferences, such as the 'carpet page' micrography of Yemenite codices, which were influenced by Islamic aniconic tendencies.[11] The earliest illustrated Hebrew manuscripts, as far as current evidence permits us to say, seem to begin in the Near East around the ninth–tenth centuries, with the most lavishly painted and illuminated examples coming from late medieval Spain and Renaissance Italy.[12] Out of all of these variants, this essay will address only the twelfth–fourteenth Ashkenazi traditions of Romanesque liturgical compilations from south Germany, since it is here that we find a scene depicting Ruth gleaning in the fields with Boaz's young men (Ruth 2.15-16).

8.　Richler, *Legacy*, p. 86.

9.　K. Weitzmann, 'The Question of the Influence of Jewish Pictorial Sources on Old Testament Illustration', in Herbert L. Kessler (ed.), *Studies in Classical and Byzantine Manuscript Illumination* (Chicago: University of Chicago Press, 1971), pp. 76-95; H.L.C. Jaffé, 'The Illustrations', in M. Spitzer (ed.), *The Bird's Head Haggada of the Bezalel National Art Museum in Jerusalem* (2 vols.; Jerusalem: Tarshish Books, 1965–67), I, pp. 31-88 (68).

10.　This is not to deny the distinctive Jewish characteristics of these illuminations, however: subject matter was drawn from Bible or midrash; initial-word panels (rather than illuminated first capital letters; depiction of halakhic traditions, etc. (Narkiss, *Manuscripts*, pp. 14-16). The common source for the graphic traditions in Islamic, Christian and Jewish manuscripts of this early period is folkloric embellishment of scriptural themes.

11.　Gutmann, *Painting*, pp. 13-15.

12.　Richler, *Legacy*, p. 47.

Jewish Manuscript Art in the Romanesque Period

Influenced by the monastic ascetic preferences in the presentation of theological subject matter as well as the aniconic struggles of Byzantium and rooted restrictions against human representation in Muslim manuscripts, scholars speculate that Jewish asceticism developed in twelfth-century Germany and northern Italy as the group's response to these dominant trends. Judah the Pious (twelfth century) and his circle in south Germany produced mystical literature which records mention of depiction of bird- and dog-headed humans, a consistent feature of S. German illuminations up until the fourteenth century.[13] By the end of the thirteenth century disapproval of even this deformed method of portraying humans was being expressed, but not for reasons having to do with the transgression of the second commandment. R. Meir of Rothenburg writes in a *responsum:*

> I have been asked about those who paint prayer-books (Maḥzorim) with figures of animals and birds, whether it is right to do so or not. And I have answered that it is certainly not good to do so, since when they look at those figures they divert their hearts from the Almighty; but these do not fall under the prohibition [of the second commandment] Thou shalt not make… (*Tosafot* to *Yoma* 54b).[14]

Scribes and illuminators from this region used a variety of methods to circumvent any prohibition against figural representations. Typically, the so-called 'zoocephalic' approach prevailed, with beaked birds' heads being used in place of human faces (see Fig. 1).[15] This motif had been common in representations of the Gospel Evangelists (eagle, lion, calf/ox, man; see Fig. 2), and depiction of fabulous and domestic animals was familiar from Roman Catholic breviaries used by the clergy.[16] This convention, however, did not exhaust the ingenuity of pious illustrators: they also show humans with turned heads, from the back with faces not shown,[17] faces covered with helmets,

13. Gutmann, *Painting*, p. 25.

14. Jaffé, 'Illustrations', p. 70; Narkiss, *Manuscripts*, p. 15.

15. B. Narkiss, 'On Zoocephalic Phenomenon in Mediaeval Ashkenazi Manuscripts', in *Norms and Variations in Art: Essays in Honor of Moshe Barasch* (Jerusalem: Magnes Press; Hebrew University, 1983), pp. 49-62.

16. Bernard Meehan, *The Book of Kells: An Illustrated Introduction to the Manuscript in Trinity College Dublin* (London: Thames & Hudson, 1994), pp. 36-43; see especially folio 129v of *The Book of Kells*; Elizabeth B. Wilson, *Bibles and Bestiaries: A Guide to Illuminated Manuscripts* (New York: Farrar, Strauss & Giroux, 1994).

17. So, too, the figure of Abraham in the sacrifice of Isaac from the Dura-Europos Synagogue.

Fig. 1 Bird-headed woman (in a bird-headed hat) at Passover (after Spitzer [ed.], *Bird's Head Haggada*, II). All drawings by the author unless otherwise noted

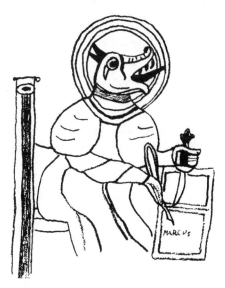

Fig. 2 The Leofric Gospels, St Mark, Eleventh century (after Jonathan J.G. Alexander, *Medieval Illuminators and their Methods of Work* [New Haven: Yale University Press, 1992], Illus. 123, p. 77)

draperies or hats, or disfigured by bulbous facial features. While the will-to-distort human faces may have emerged from Persian and Muslim circles, in southern Germany the artisans creating manu-scripts seem to have adopted it as a form of self-censorship. Others have speculated that this motif is derived from texts from the classical and medieval stage with its use of masks (see Fig. 3), but no conclu-sive evidence of direct dependence can be cited.[18] The zoocephalic convention is used broadly to portray eschatological scenes (the Righ-teous feasting in Paradise), scenes from the Bible, and especially to draw angelic, divine or celestial entities.[19] A whole school of manu-scripts display this trait, along with other more general Romanesque features,[20] and are attributed to a Jewish scriptorium in Rhineland, although, again, there is no direct evidence of the existence of such an atelier. The manuscripts belonging to this group are *The Worms*

Fig. 3 Scene from Terence's *Andria* (Alexander, *Illuminators*, Illus. 178, p. 107)

18. Gutmann, *Painting*, p. 25.
19. Narkiss, *Manuscripts*, pp. 29-31.
20. Architectural motifs drawn from the contemporary styles, gently folded draperies, strong blue, red and sepia colors, and most especially, the use of distinct outlines around figures, drawn from world of stained-glass portraiture in churches (Michelle P. Brown, *Understanding Illuminated Manuscripts: A Guide to Technical Terms* [Malibu, CA: J. Paul Getty Museum, 1994], pp. 110-11).

Maḥzor,[21] *The Ambrosian Bible*,[22] *The Bird's Head Haggadah*,[23] *Laud Maḥzor*,[24] *The Leipzig Maḥzor*[25] and *The Tripartite Maḥzor*,[26] the second volume of which will be considered here.

Maḥzorim

Maḥzor means 'cycle' in Hebrew. This communal prayer book was a collection of liturgical poems (*piyyutim*, sung by a *ḥazzān* or cantor) for the seven special Sabbaths and all the holiday festivals appearing through the year, and may be considered similar to Christian breviaries (even called *Breviarium Judaicum* in one inscription). The maḥzorim of southern Germany were executed during a hundred-year period from about 1250 to 1350 CE. Oversized for synagogue use, the dimensions are probably derived from the huge lectern-style bibles and breviaries used in Christian churches of the era. The maḥzor typically contained illuminated 'initial word' panels (rather than the 'historiated initials' of Latin manuscripts), marginal illustrations, and developed a specialized iconography based on midrashic traditions. This often included scenes of the 'special food' of Paradise (the meat of Leviathan and Behemoth), signs of the Zodiac, ornate illustrations from the book of Esther and the sacrifice of Isaac.[27]

While the earlier versions of this manuscript type relied mostly on bird's beaks[28] to deform the faces of *all* of the human figures, by the

21. Ms. Heb. 4°781/1, Jerusalem National and University Library.

22. Ms. B. 32, INF., Ambrosian Library, Milan, Italy.

23. Ms. 180/57, Israel Museum, Jerusalem.

24. Ms. Laud Or. 321, Bodleian Library, Oxford.

25. Ms. V. 1102/I-II, Karl Marx-Universitätsbibliothek, Leipzig.

26. Vol. I, Ms. A 384, Library of the Hungarian Academy of Sciences, Budapest; Vol. II, Ms. Add. 22413, British Museum, London; Vol. III, Ms. Mich. 619, Bodleian Library, Oxford.

27. Sed-Rajna, *Hebrew Bible*, p. 161; Gutmann, *Painting*, pp. 23-24; Narkiss, *Manuscripts*, p. 32.

28. I suspect that the choice of birds' heads for human faces is related not only to the portraits of Evangelists, but to depictions of the Holy Spirit—the source of inspiration for Christians—in the form of a bird. Whether this convention, in turn, recalls the bird-headed goddesses of Old Europe requires more study. On traditions of Jewish figurative art from biblical times, see Sylvia Schroer, ' "Under the Shadow of your Wings": The Metaphor of God's Wings in the Psalms, Exodus 19.4, Deuteronomy 32.11 and Malachi 3.20, as Seen through the Perspectives of Feminism and the History of Religion', in Athalya Brenner and Carole R. Fontaine (eds.), *Wisdom and Psalms: A Feminist Companion to the Bible (Second Series)* (The Feminist Companion to the Bible, 2; Sheffield: Sheffield Academic Press, 1998), pp. 264-82.

time of our text, *The Tripartite Maḥzor*, the artists executing the work were no longer clear about the reasons for this convention and use it differently.[29] In our manuscript the men usually have ordinary human heads, but the women all have animal heads (cf. vol. II, fol. 3, 'Revelation at Sinai' panel, read for Shavuot, the Feast of Weeks).

Although the book of Esther received ornate illustrations in Hebrew manuscripts of the Middle Ages, Ruth rarely receives such treatment (though *The Worms Maḥzor* features a pen drawing, probably from the fifteenth century).[30] One wonders whether the ethnic identity of the heroines of these stories of 'successful' intermarriages is at work in the artists' decisions on illustration and the community's reception of the work. Esther is a *Jewish* queen, whose nationality is at first hidden and later revealed as she saves her people from persecution: here sexuality is salvific and the marriage provides a model of survival hallowed by long antiquity.

Ruth is another matter entirely: a hated Moabite, originally barren and suspiciously widowed, she has only low status as she follows her mother-in-law Naomi back to Israel. Though Esther uses trickery in assuming her high position, for she hides her ethnicity from the king and his servants, Ruth's escapade on the threshing floor with Boaz is trickery of another order, for here she hides not her *ethnicity* but the presence of one of her *gender*.[31] The story is quick to bless her, and characterizes her attentions to Boaz as a form of *ḥesed* (3.10). Though she is declared to be a 'valiant woman' (lit. 'woman of worth', as in Prov. 31.10),[32] nevertheless Boaz is all haste to 'cover up' her presence at a festival where men's hearts were merry, and get her home to Naomi undetected. *Why* all the rush?

Ruth-the-Cat in the Tripartite Maḥzor

Ruth and Boaz's game of sexual 'cat-and-mouse' may be at the heart of the iconographic treatment in the *Tripartite Maḥzor*, vol. II, folio 71r (see Fig. 4). This multivolumed *maḥzor*, now separated, is slightly

---

29. Narkiss, *Manuscripts*, p. 32.
30. Gutmann, *Painting*, p. 95.
31. Note Boaz's surprise in 3.8: 'behold, a woman lay at his feet!'
32. And he said, 'May you be blessed by the LORD, my daughter; you have made this last kindness greater than the first, in that you have not gone after young men, whether poor or rich. And now, my daughter, do not fear, I will do for you all that you ask, for all my fellow townsmen know that you are a woman of worth' (3.10-11, RSV).

Fig. 4 Ruth Gleaning, *The Tripartite Maḥzor*, II, folio 71r (Gutmann, *Painting*, Pl. 28, p. 94)

smaller than its earlier siblings of the same genre (*Worms Maḥzor*, *Laud Maḥzor*), a feature that, when taken with the development of the zoo-cephalic heads for women, only leads to the conclusion that we are seeing a specific stage of the development of the genre. Like the *Worms Maḥzor*, it includes among its illustrations signs of the Zodiac, along with the 'labors of the months' portrayed in medallions alongside the Zodiac signs.[33] The manuscript, dated to about 1320, is signed by the scribe *Hayyim*, who worked in southern Germany around 1300. His signature also appears on the *Schocken Bible* and in the *Duke of Sussex Pentateuch*, both of which are nicely tricked out with dragons and other hybrid 'grotesques'.[34] This, of course, does not mean that Hayyim was the illuminator or even that he prepared these particular manuscripts, since master scribes were in the habit of signing all the

33.   While signs of the Zodiac are featured in synagogue mosaics of late antiquity, nevertheless such imagery must be considered originally foreign to Jewish art.

34.   Narkiss, *Manuscripts,* p. 31; cf. Pls. 31 and 32.

work produced in their ateliers, whether by their own hand or not. Still, we *do* have a name, *and* a set of artistic family resemblances among the manuscripts signed by Hayyim.

Ruth appears twice in this initial-word panel. On the right she gleans amid four other figures, one of whom is donkey-headed and another has a bird-like face, amid two naturalistically depicted men. Ruth holds a sickle in one hand, as she sets to work on the grain, and wears a peculiar cone-shaped headdress, which is not entirely unlike the truncated version of the medieval 'Jew's hat' shown on a young man to the left. Ruth appears again on the left, with two human-headed males. This time her long yellow hair falls from her uncovered head, while Boaz (probably[35]) gives her six measures of barley (2.3-15). In both paintings she has an animal head, which Gutmann identifies as a cat.[36]

It is clear from the study of Jewish manuscripts that various animal figures held particular symbolism for the communities producing these texts. Deer and other cervine creatures, for example, usually 'stood for' gentleness, piety, devotion and acceptance of divine will. When featured with hounds and hunters, the 'hunt' of the European nobility, they became a fitting symbol of the Jewish community suffering persecution at the hands of Christians. However, animal and hybrid symbolism was not systematically fixed: unclean animals, such as predators, might be used for their predatory (= evil, dangerous) nature in one scene but be taken for their outstanding salient positive characteristics in another.[37] For those acquainted with classical and Christian bestiaries, such 'proverbial' use of animals was an accustomed sight, and biblical passages were frequently the source for the judgments made on animals illustrated. Isa. 11.6-8 and 65.25, for example, speaks of lions, leopards,[38] bears and wolves that attack

35. But not certainly or unambiguously, since manuscripts by this scribe feature men with natural heads and only women appear with the zoocephalic technique. Elsewhere (Revelation at Sinai panel, vol. II, fol. 3) there is a donkey-headed figure among the animal-headed women, while all the men have human faces.

36. Gutmann, *Painting*, p. 95; Sed-Rajna identifies the Ruth head on the left as a gryphon and the one on the right as a dog's head (*Hebrew Bible*, p. 147). Although we are exploring Ruth's identity primarily as a (pussy-)cat here, it is clear that she is shown as a hybrid creature, as are other women in depictions by this scribe (and/or his apprentices).

37. Metzger, *Jewish Life*, pp. 21-22, 32-34. For example, the eagle symbolized swiftness, the leopard strength, the donkey patient service, etc.

38. Cf. Jer. 5.6.

God's people, setting the tone for interpreting these large predators as personifications of various earthly evils.

Lions were the most widely illustrated of the great and dangerous beasts, but we also see panthers, leopards and cheetahs here and there. By the thirteenth century, in Barcelona, Jews were in charge of the care of lions housed in the menageries of the wealthy, so that the big cats were by no means as exotic as the elephant or unicorn. Clearly, lions embody a significant biblical multivalence. They are associated with the tribe of Judah and justice in Gen. 49.9, and are adornments guarding the steps of Solomon's throne—a venue not unassociated with Ruth's story, after all—in illustrated midrashim occurring in the *mahzorim*. This attests to the lion's ubiquitous and varied presence[39] in the thought world of medieval Jewish illustrators and the communities that used their work.[40]

If the biggest cat of all appeared often, carrying multifaceted meanings, what can be said of its domestic cousin, *Felis Catus*, the only member of *Felidae* family to be called 'happy'?[41] I[42] remind the reader of the traditions of ancient Egyptian iconography and cultural practice concerning the domestic cat for discussion of the meaning of the feline Ruth, since many ideas had attained the status of 'classical' representations by Greco-Roman times. It will be recalled that the cat goddess Bastet, the 'tame' sister of the dread battle lion goddess Sekmet, featured a woman's body and a cat's head. Both goddesses could be understood as guardians of the royal household. Lion hunting was all the rage for royals in Egypt, as it had been Mesopotamia, but the domestic cat found a much more felicitous place in the life of the Egyptian people. A symbol of joy, love, fertility and the 'wild-made-tame' (i.e. acculturation), the house cat[43] is frequently pictured in tomb paintings, found mummified just as a beloved and well-off human would have been and, often, wears jeweled collars and earrings. On leashes, cats were used to hunt small creatures in the

---

39. For a fuller discussion of the lion in proverbial and biblical texts, see my 'More Queenly Proverb Performance: The Queen of Sheba in Targum Esther Sheni', in Michael L. Barré, SS (ed.), *Wisdom, You Are my Sister: Studies in Honor of Roland E. Murphy, O.Carm., on the Occasion of his Eightieth Birthday* (CBQMS, 29; Washington: Catholic Biblical Association, 1997), pp. 216-33.

40. Metzger, *Jewish Life*, pp. 21-22, 32-34.

41. 'Felix' the Cat, a noted cartoon personality.

42. A 'cat' person, as opposed to a 'dog' person.

43. *Miȝw* in Egyptian; cats in wall paintings bear ticked, striped coats, looking much like an early relative of the current 'Abyssinian' breed, known for their affectionate, intelligent and demonstrative natures.

company of their human partners. Mythologically, the cat was attributed with protective duties in warding off snakes and rats, so must
have been considered useful as well as decorative in the home. A
household with many cats could be counted upon to produce many
children, another felicitous feature in a pre-modern age where fertility
was a means of status for women.

Domesticated first by the Egyptians probably around 2500 BCE, the
'Caffre' cat, a species of African wild-cat (*F. Libycus*), was probably the
origin of today's domestic cat. This cat was traded by Phoenicians,
taken to Britain by Romans and imported to Europe by Crusaders in
the late Middle Ages. It was known for its excellent hunting skills,
nocturnal habits and marvelous night vision, prodigious breeding
habits (several breeding seasons a year, producing about four kittens
per litter), grace in leaping, intelligence in learning and friendly but
aloof disposition.

In one of the worst of all its omissions, the Hebrew Bible fails to
mention these sleek ambassadors of wildness in the midst of culture
even once,[44] a glaring blunder that is corrected in the Babylonian
Talmud.[45] It is clear that the cat was considered useful by the rabbis:
cats protect a house from infestation by snakes (*Pes.* 112b); for such
reasons, it is permissible to breed them along with dogs, apes and
porcupines, as they keep a house clean (*B. Qam.* 80a-b). The cat also
appears as subject of proverbial observations, often paired with dogs
or mice.[46] 'Thus the people say, "The weasel and cat (when at peace
with each other) feast on the fat of the luckless"' (*Sanh.* 105a). The
habits of cats also form a subject for study: one's own cat (but *not* a
neighbor's) may be given a drink of water that has been left uncovered[47] (*'Abod. Zar.* 31a; cf. *Šab.* 128a); and fed with foreskins (*Sanh.*
19b, commenting on 1 Sam. 18.25) or duck entrails (*Šab.* 142b; *Beṣ.* 33a).
If a cat has clawed a food animal, it is not unclean unless the claw has
pierced the abdominal cavity (*Ḥul.* 52b). Cats appear in the context
of menstrual blood (see below on female sexuality) and the wood of
an *Asherah* in *Šab.* 75b,[48] linked to the folk idea that an animal who

44. Jeremiah's spot-changing leopard (13.23), even though displaying features
of the ticked-coated African bush-cat, does not count.

45. 'Cat, Domestic', *Microsoft® Encarta® 97 Encyclopedia* (Redmond, WA:
Microsoft Corporation, 1993–96).

46. *Ket.* 41b; *B. Meṣ.* 97a; *Sanh.* 19b; *Ḥul.* 53b; *B. Qam.* 80a.

47. In fact, cats will not drink tainted water, so they are used as a guide to the
potability of water that might have been fouled.

48. Note, too, that the Canaanite goddess Asherah and her West Semitic coun-
terparts are routinely imaged as standing on lions or leopards (Judith M. Hadley,

consumes the blood of a person will cause that person to become ill. On the well-noted aloof quality of personality that keeps most cats from behaving in an undignified doggiesque manner (answering to their names, fawning over their owners, etc.), the rabbis find that it is the *mouse* who is responsible for this behavioral trait: since eating food that has been nibbled by a mouse causes memory loss in humans, how much more memory is lost by the animal who eats the mouse *whole*! (*Hor.* 13b). In a comment on Job 35.11, R. Johanan suggests that, even if there had been no Torah, humanity could have simply observed the world of creation: the cat, for instance, would have taught us modesty.[49]

The Cat in Medieval and Early Modern Times

Unfortunately, the high status enjoyed by the domestic cat in antiquity was replaced by a far more ambivalent set of 'folk ideas' during the medieval period in Europe. Though cats were kept in both northern and southern Europe as a defense against vermin, they were nevertheless often the objects of human violence and torture. Like most persons of that age, Jews probably also believed that 'evil spells' could change a person into a cat, wolf or donkey.[50] Cats had become indissolubly linked with witchcraft and heresy in the popular mind; nursery rhymes that viewed the Jew as a shape-changer who took cat form are recorded, as are numerous occasions of linkage between the Jew as heretic par excellence and the cat, the witches' demonic familiar.[51] These unearthly features of cats are underscored in their characterization in *Hausmärchen*, such as 'Puss in Boots'.

Well into the early modern period, cats continued to suggest occult power, such that maiming one could prevent harm to one's self, family or crops. An added bonus for this apotropaic behavior was the deep-throated scream a cat might produce, whether during mating or

---

'From Goddess to Literary Construct: The Transformation of Asherah into Hokma', in Athalya Brenner and Carole R. Fontaine (eds.), *A Feminist Companion to Reading the Bible: Approaches, Methods and Strategies* (Sheffield: Sheffield Academic Press, 1997), pp. 360-99.

49. '*Erub.* 100b; one wonders what sorts of cats the Babylonian Talmud is referring to for the discussion of the quality of modesty (cleanliness? daintiness?); cats are well-known in folklore for their self-satisfied view of themselves and their place in the world, as the rabbis are well aware.

50. Metzger, *Jewish Life*, p. 31.

51. Tractenberg, *Devil*, pp. 72, 205-206, 208, 218. Note that folk etymologies in German traced the word *Ketzer*, 'heretic', to *Kater*, 'tomcat'.

torture, which was strongly reminiscent of those torn from human throats, making the cat an idea choice for ritual events.[52] The newly Protestant English might burn wicker effigies of the hated Pope, filled with cats, whose screams delighted the watching crowds. In carnivals preceding Lent in France, youths would *faire le chat*, mocking various human targets while making a cat scream as fur was torn out. In Germany, the term *Katzenmusik* referred to much the same events of group torture, but could also refer to the energetic howls produced at night by mating felines.[53]

As if all these associations were not bad enough (for the cat, at least, if not for the folklorist), the cat also accrued symbolic associations with female sexuality, a favorite target of androcentric belief systems then as now. In French vernacular, the terms for cat—*le chat, la chatte, le minet*—became slang for the female genital triangle, much like its English counterpart, the 'pussy-cat'. A fifteenth-century proverb, 'He who takes good care of cats will have a pretty wife', makes this point quite blatantly, as does the statement about an adulterer, 'He has other cats to whip'. A lusty maiden might be said to be 'in love like a cat'; if pregnant, she had 'let the cat go to the cheese', and eating a cat might itself cause a girl to give birth to kittens. Attacks on a woman's pet cat might well be interpreted by her as a grievous sexual insult/ assault.[54]

The Cat in Illuminated Manuscripts

For all these various reasons, it is not surprising that we find the domestic cat, as well as its wild siblings, depicted in illuminated manuscripts. One of the more famous depictions is from the Irish *Book of Kells*, where a cat is pictured chasing a mouse who has just stolen a communion wafer (see Fig. 5).[55] Vermin were particularly bothersome to illuminators and scribes, it would seem: in a famous self-portrait in a manuscript of *Civitas Dei*, the scribe Hildebertus swears at a mouse who has just stolen part of his meal and knocked a roast chicken to the floor (*Pessime mus, sepius me provocas ad iram, ut te deus*

---

52. Some speculate that the cat is a chosen target also because the average adult cat is approximately the size of a human infant.

53. Robert Darnton, *The Great Cat Massacre and Other Episodes in French Cultural History* (New York: Basic Books, 1984), pp. 82-91.

54. Darnton, *Cat Massacre*, pp. 94-95.

55. Folios 48r and 34r (Meehan, *Kells*, p. 45); see Fig. 5.

Fig. 5 The Kells Cat (after Meehan, *Kells*, p. 45)

perdat!, 'Accursed mouse, you anger me so often—God take you!').[56] Though no domestic cats are portrayed—too bad for Hildebertus's ruined dinner—a mighty lion is carved into the stand which holds the manuscript on which the monk is currently at work.

Cats and mice appear as a 'proverbial word-pair' translated into image in both Ashkenazi and Sephardic manuscripts as well (Figs. 6 and 7). Cats are pictured eating mice, or by themselves, but with no noticeable negative connotations. In fact, cats may have played an enhanced role in the domestic organization of the households of Jewish moneylenders. Cats were a necessity for the protection of pledged items, such as books or clothing, from vermin, and so moneylenders were required to keep them.[57] Though not so metaphorically well-connected as the lion, the cat nevertheless makes its share of appearances in the Jewish household. Perhaps the fear and loathing in which the cat was usually held by Christians triggered a kind of 'fellow-feeling' of kinship in the community that suffered from similar slights.

The Kittycat on the Threshing Floor

Returning to our portrait of Ruth as a feline—or at least, an animal-headed hybrid—we readily see that the charming illustration in *The Tripartite Maḥzor* draws not only on the iconographic traditions of south Germany, but on the rich vein of Talmudic lore on cats, as well as metaphorical associations from the world of European folk ideas. *Why* is Ruth a cat? And why should she *not* be, given the context of her story? She is, like the domestic cat, a fertile and useful addition to

56. Ms. A. XXI/1, folio 153v, Metropolitan Library, Prague (Alexander, *Illuminators*, p. 15).

57. Metzger, *Jewish Life*, pp. 21, 201, esp. p. 292 n. 43.

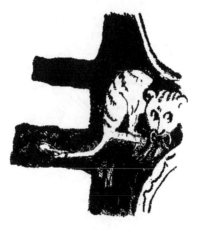

Fig. 6 Hebrew Cat, British Museum Ms. Add. 11639, folio 433v (after Metzger, *Jewish Life*, Illus. 287, p. 202)

Fig. 7 Hebrew Cat with Mouse (Metzger, *Jewish Life*, Illus. 288, p. 202)

the household of the future King David, the Lion of Judah. She is valuable in the fields, and well beyond; she is willing to eat scraps thrown to her from the master's table. Her 'night vision' guides her hunt on the threshing floor of the 'House of Bread',[58] where cats have the advantage over mice who try to nibble away at the community's harvest. Her purring presence there achieves a much-desired consummation for Naomi and the dead ones with whom our kitty has been keeping faith. It may even be that the feline Ruth is a tacit inversion of the imagery of the harvest/fertility demoness,[59] often imaged with wings and bird's feet, thought to pray upon those men who had opened the earth and later had the poor sense to fall asleep in the

58. I.e. *Beth-lehem*.

59. I.e. Lilith, in her less child-oriented guise. Note that the mystical treatise *The Book of Raziel* composed by Eleazar b. Judah b. Kalonymos in Worms during approximately the time of the Maḥzorim (1176–1238), contains an amulet against Lilith for women and children during childbirth. This amulet features crude bird figures (Raphael Patai, *The Hebrew Goddess* [Detroit, MI: Wayne State University Press, 3rd edn, 1990], pp. 237-39).

cultically fertile and occultly charged arena of the threshing floor.

It must be noted that Ruth's depiction marks her as both different from the Jewish *males*, who have normal human heads, but also as different from *Jewish* women, who are portrayed throughout the zoocephalic manuscripts primarily with bird's heads. Does this iconographic reading view Ruth as a 'cat among the pigeons', an implicitly predatory female of an essentially different order from the appropriate bird-headed women of one's own community? Is Ruth a cat who hopes to swallow the canary? For the male illuminator, it certainly seems that our Ruth bears the markings of double 'other'-ness: female and foreign, forever relegated to the outer court of the true insiders. Yet like the ubiquitous domestic cat, a dedicated mother and protective housekeeper, Ruth the Cat has value for this community, even in her Otherness. Given the veiling of Jewish brides during this period and others (see Fig. 8), from the male point of view, who knows just *what* one might be marrying?[60] After all, as the saying goes, 'All cats are grey at night'.[61]

---

60. Note also the cat/mouse/other intermarriage motif played out in the postmodern context in Art Spiegelman, *Maus II, a Survivor's Tale: And Here my Troubles Began* (New York: Pantheon Books, 1991), pp. 11-12. In this cartoon where all the Jews are mice and the Nazis are cats, the child of two Holocaust survivors ponders how to draw his Gentile wife (a bunny? a frog?) who has converted to please his father. Although the wife is French, she argues strenuously that she must be drawn as a mouse, too.

61. My thanks to my husband Craig for assisting me in the preparation of this manuscript, as well as my MIS, Lee Parsons, and Jean Sangster, my research assistant.

Fig. 8 Bridal Couple from thirteenth-century Germany (Metzger, *Jewish Life*, Illus. 335, p. 224)

RUTH AND NAOMI: TWO BIBLICAL FIGURES
REVIVED AMONG RURAL WOMEN IN GERMANY

Ursula Silber

1. *The Frame: 'Educational Days for Rural Women'*

In the winter season, when cold and snow are master, the farmers have less to do. At present, the German 'Catholic Farmers' Movement'[1] offers traditional classes and seminars for the women of the farms, and the 'Educational Days for Rural Women' is one variation. For an entire day, 30–50 women from various villages meet in one house and work with a leader-expert on a selected theme. For the winter of 1996/97, a preparation group selected the general theme 'Discovering my Potential: To Be a Woman in a Varied World'.

2. *Two Different Worlds of Women Meet:*
'the Urban Flower' and 'the Country Bloom'

I was invited to serve as consultant for the first time. As an 'urban flower', I had spent my entire life living, studying and graduating in a large city. 'Country life' was familiar to me only through stories in my own family's history, tales about friends and acquaintances and, not to be forgotten, anecdotes from my husband's family. Nevertheless, village life remained a foreign world to me. The dialect that was spoken in the countryside, the physical work—especially the increased pressure of the farming season, the social rules of the village and the tight net of relatives and neighbors—everything was 'exotic': simultaneously fascinating and foreign.

---

1. The Catholic Farmers' Movement (c. 12,000 members in Bavaria) was conceived as 'the association for people in the countryside': not just for farmers but increasingly for the people who live in rural areas. They may work in crafts or go to work in industry or services. Besides the support of families and assistance in religious matters, the association has also recently recognized ecological and development politics.

The 'Educational Days for Rural Women' were announced, organized and also heavily financed by the office of the association.

The women who come to 'Educational Days for Rural Women' generally originate in small villages and towns. Because of the high economic pressure on farmers, only a handful of especially large or specialized farms survive. Frequently the farms are maintained as a secondary occupation, mostly by the women, while the men take paid work in the city. The increasingly worsening economic situation of farming, the loss of many family businesses and the pressure on the yet existing farms is part of the background of most country women.

For the majority of these women, the current situation is (at the minimum) a second experience of economic crisis and emergency. Dependent upon age—the majority are between 55 and 70 years old, rarely under 40—most of these women lived through World War II and the difficult years after the war. As country farmers, they learned about hunger through communicating with evacuated or bombed-out city-dwellers, refugees and exiles. The present situation is for many of them an even more threatening experience: in spite of the relative affluence in Germany and basic social insurance, an agricultural enter-prise is often insufficient to support a family. The prices for agricul-tural products have fallen and it is not considered economically viable to engage in farming[2]—and this in a very fruitful and productive agricultural area.

Most of the women know each other. In a village they know each other anyway. Often they are familiar with the background of gener-ations of relatives and neighbors. This knowledge of each other and about each other offers significant social control;[3] on the other hand, such an atmosphere of trust and solidarity also acts like an inter-woven net. In working with such a group, I attempted to utilize and strengthen the solidarity among the women as a basis of dialogue. It was also necessary to facilitate discretion in order to insure that the women could continue to speak to each other in the village without embarrassment and shame.

3. *The Motivation: To Have a Beautiful Day for Yourself*

For many women, the dominant motivation for participating in an educational day is simply 'to have one beautiful day for myself'. It

---

2.   A farmer's wife said that more is paid for the removal of a tonne of waste than is paid for the production of a tonne of wheat.

3.   This also means that deviation from the social norms may be sanctioned: church attendance, Sunday rest, the organization of family celebrations, etc., are controlled by more or less strict rules.

begins with getting out of the house and the farmyard and going away, even if it is only for a little distance, and continues with the possibility of chatting with other women. A less important issue for almost all the women is to feel cared for, taken care of. Just not having to cook and clean up is for many woman a luxury that they can appreciate. Correspondingly, the women arrive with expectations of the contents of the day's work and of the leader-expert, who will take care of them and offer them a beautiful experience. Many women prefer to just listen; they are used to 'spiritual lectures' in such days for themselves. Others also seek food for thought through stimulation and conversation. The readiness to engage in something 'difficult' and 'strenuous'—and that includes themes like 'kinds of work'—is not very high. They do not want to do more work than they do at home! On the other hand, most of the women arrive in the morning in a good mood, they come willingly and are ready (within limits) to respond to that which I offer them.

One important and not unproblematic expectation is that of a 'spiritual day'. Traditionally, the rural women are led by Catholic priests and conclude their day with a sacrament of the Eucharist. For many women it was a switch, even a disappointment, when I—*only* a woman—and unordained, could only celebrate a spoken service with them. Many educational processes among the women take place in an atmosphere of scepticism, resistance and pain—but the women do learn. For some women it is a positive experience, perhaps even a key experience, to encounter a woman as leader-expert and to celebrate a religious service (without man/priest) that liturgically includes all the women had experienced during their day.

4. A Story of Hopes: My Access to the Book of Ruth

The wisdom novella of Ruth is a story of hope for an Israel threatened with extinction.[4] It is an everyday story of ordinary country people as the protagonists, with everyday events like harvests and threshing, legal transactions and family life. Indeed, this normal, everyday reality of the simple people conceals—despite the apparently idyllic setting—experiences of suffering and great misfortune, hunger and death, for the main characters of the story. The wonderful part of the story is 'that they do not collapse under their tribulations but instead

---

4.   Cf. Erich Zenger, *Das Buch Ruth* (ZBK, 8; Zürich: Theologischer Verlag, 1992), pp. 25, 121.

become subjects of their own life stories'.[5] The original novella,[6] in the form of a wisdom narrative, depicts how God redeems Naomi through the *ḥesed* (goodness, devotion and love) of Ruth and Boaz. Naomi is led from death to life through love, first in the form of grains, the bread of life, and finally in the form of a child.[7] In the sense of a narrative of ethics, the tale seeks to promote these qualities of *ḥesed*, which redeems the living and the dead. It also

> makes the model of Ruth three-dimensional and familiar…the solidarity, without exception, with someone in need, is a way of God and leads to a good end. It is a way of life for those who serve God, who leave bread and life up to God.[8]

The later, Davidic-messianic revision (in the second century BCE) extended the genealogic line of 4.17-22. With the Ruth novella as the prehistory of King David, it simultaneously conveys the hopes for a new messianic kingdom, no longer based on dynasty and political might but grounded instead on solidarity and justice.[9]

Christians have already met Ruth on the first page of the New Testament, not only as the great-grandmother of David but also as the progenetrix of the messiah-king Jesus, whose story begins where the Ruth book ends, namely in Bethlehem.

The message of the Ruth narrative is a promise: where people seek life with one another and for one another, God gives his blessing. 'Rabbi Eliezer said, "Boaz did for his, Ruth did for hers, and Naomi also did for hers; so will I, said God, also do for mine".'[10]

5. *The Course of the Day: Single Building Blocks*

In a single day (from 09:00 to 16:00) it is not easy to follow the path of Ruth and Naomi, with all its highs and lows. Initially, it takes time to adjust oneself to the entirely different world of the narrative, despite certain similarities. For contemporary women, Ruth is also foreign at first.

---

5.   Zenger, *Ruth*, p. 121.
6.   Zenger differentiates vv. 1, 1a and 7, 17-22 as secondary. See Zenger, *Ruth*, pp. 13-14.
7.   Zenger, *Ruth*, p. 14. Cf. Monika Fander, 'Die Geschichte einer Freundschaft', in Angelika Meissner (ed.), *Und sie tanzen aus der Reihe: Frauen im Alten Testament* (Stuttgart: Verlag Katholisches Bibelwerk, 1992), pp. 94-104 (99).
8.   Zenger, *Ruth*, p. 122.
9.   Cf. Zenger, *Ruth*, p. 28.
10.   *Ruth R.* 4.1, as quoted by Zenger, *Ruth*, p. 127.

Within the frame of these possibilities, established by the institutional requirements as well as those concealed by the participants, I attempted to read and to consider the entire book of Ruth together with the women. At any one time, I would read a unit of the book as it is given in the Bible.[11] With cloths, objects and symbols, I explained passages difficult to understand merely by hearing them and thus made the story visible and comprehensible. Then, through differing kinds of tasks, the women were invited to re-discover and recognize correspondences between the events of the story and their own lives. Conversations in 'Murmur Groups', a fantasy trip, a meditation image or a prayer of intercession were typical elements of concretization. With the termination of each sequence came a period of silence, a time in which each woman could privately paint her design for life by imagining a mandala. In this way, *one* image developed for each woman, an image that she began and could further develop in the course of the day. A frame for the day was provided by a painting by Lucy D'Souza, who depicted a scene with Ruth, Naomi and Boaz on the harvest field for a Lenten veil.[12] In the morning, this picture was the 'entrance door' to the narrative and also closed the thematic work. The cloths and symbols had their places in the spoken service that we celebrated at the end of the day, representing the paths of Ruth and Naomi. In the middle of the cloths, the mandalas of the women were laid out. They represented the entirely different, often unfinished, colorful and unique life designs of the women. In the following discussion I will describe more closely the sequence of the day and my experience.

a. *When Death Breaks into Life (1.1-5)*
The narrative begins suddenly with a series of difficult occurrences, with famine and migration, with childlessness and early death. At the end of only five verses the female characters of the narrative, whom we have barely met, find themselves at the depths of their existence.

---

11. Cf. also the concept of the Projektgruppe 'Ruth' (ed.), *Das Buch Ruth: Eine Weg-Beschreibung mit Texten Liedern, Tänzen und Gebeten*—a path description with text, songs, dances and prayers—published as manuscript by the Beratungstelle für Gestaltung von Gottesdiensten und anderen Gemeindeveranstaltungen (Frankfurt, 1994).

12. Cf. Misereor, Bischoefliches Hilfswerk e.V. (ed.), *Das Misereor-Hungertuch: Biblische Frauengestalten—Wegweiser zum Reich Gottes* (Aachen: Misereor-Vertriebsgesellschaft, 1989; Reihe: Arbeitshefte zum Hungertuch).

*I lay a large black cloth out on the ground. The story begins on the dark side
of life, even if it does not remain there.*

In Bethlehem and in the entire land of Judah, famine reigns. As always,
including today, when famine and desolation are masters, when there is no
work and no bread, the people arise in order to flee and seek the necessities of
life somewhere else.[13] In this way, an entire family tore itself loose: hunger
refugees, we would say.

The Bible presents the people to us with names, and these names speak for
themselves. They tell us about the people who carry them, about their characteristics and behavior. The father of this migrant family was called 'Elimelech', which means 'my God is King'. Thus he is presented to us as a
religious man who honors his God above everything and who carries his
dedication to the royalty of God in his name. His wife, called Naomi, is
depicted as 'lovely, delightful'. With this name, we imagine a beautiful
woman, delightful to see and perhaps also a woman who is much loved by her
husband.

When, in the narration, these two go forth with their two sons from the
desolate land of Judah to the green land of Moab, I lay a green cloth beside the
black cloth. Green is the color of hope: there the country is still fruitful, there
something still grows, there one can find bread and thereby life, also for
refugees.

For a time, the family prospers in the foreign country. The sons marry
local women. But then the land of green, the land of life for the family,
becomes the land of death. First Elimelech dies—a hard blow for the family,
especially for Naomi who remains as a widow. Then it gets even worse: one
after another both sons, Machlon and Kilion, die. In Hebrew, the names are a
rhyming play on words: they translate loosely as 'weak' and 'fragile'. Weak
and fragile: whoever hears these names knows that the sons hold no promise
for a great future in the story. They die like their father. For them I lay three
large stones on the green cloth.

There remains three women, three widows: Naomi, who is already old, and
the two young daughters-in-law. Three women without even one man: that
was in those times almost a catastrophe. Without a man, a woman was not
only poor, without work and without substance, she was also practically
without any rights. Above all, she belonged nowhere. In a world in which
women are recognized only as daughters, mothers and wives, a childless
widow is practically nothing and no one. Socially she is as good as dead.
Without children any future is threatened, for only children can continue the
family name. If no sons can carry the name, the family is forgotten and

---

13. Cf. as realization for the Brazilian context: Carlos Mesters, *Rute: Una historia
da Biblia* (Sao Paolo: Ediçoes Paulinas, 1985).

thereby dead. To be a widow without sons is to be quasi-dead to the world. There is no future, there is nothing more to expect. How did these three women feel?

It probably occurs to you that such experiences didn't only happen then. Yes, the life conditions of women have changed; widows are at least provided for today. But even today women find themselves in difficult conditions: women are thrown off the tracks of life through serious illness, through lack of work or through divorce. Even today women are foreign workers, seek asylum or are evacuees in our country. They have difficulties with the language where they live. Even today, sometimes women do not know if they will manage to survive.

Perhaps you know women in your villages, in your neighborhoods, who have had experiences similar to those of Naomi and her two daughters-in-law. Sit down with some of your neighbors and consider what women have in common today with Naomi.

You have probably spoken about women who have had difficult times like those of the women in our story. It is good not to forget them but to think about them and let them be memories for us. Therefore I invite you to a communal prayer of intercession for these women. They should not be alone; they should be carried and supported by our thoughts. And we will appeal to God for them, that God will give them strength.

I invite you to join me: tell us about whom you have thought and lay a stone for that woman on the cloth. If you do not want to speak, feel free to lay a stone in silence. We will all join you in your thoughts and ask God for a blessing for her with a call for mercy.

You can still take a little time to follow your thoughts, to be with your feelings. In order to assist you, I can offer a little assistance: a mandala. The mandala originates in Indian traditions: it means 'circle'. It is an image of life, lines arranged around a middle to create a design. This design is open, but one can paint it, give it color and thereby involve oneself in the lines and structure. You have time to begin a mandala in this quiet period.

The introduction of the path with Naomi and Ruth is difficult—difficult also for the women, who have come to have a wonderful day and are immediately confronted with hunger and need, sickness and death. It was important for me, as leader, to be aware of the difficult beginning and also to be aware that it would not remain thus; above all, to anticipate the concern of the women that it would be an entire day of sorrow and death. 'We have enough of that at home', said one participant, a woman who found it difficult to get involved. Defense against the dark aspects of the life design also calls up resistance to the tasks and even to the narrative. Therefore, it is necessary to monitor individual women's threshholds of perception and experience, and to make it clear that the discussion with these dark aspects of the life design is not directed at their own selves, that nothing is intended to be self-torture. It is intended that these aspects be seen in relationship to others, to be accepted and interwoven into the entire design.

I have always been impressed by the similarity between many of the women in the group and the two women in the narrative, especially in this initial segment. Many of the mostly elderly women are already widowed, and in each group mothers tell of the death of a child through accident or disease. Many of the women have taken care of others in their homes—their parents, parents-in-law or elderly relatives—until death. For many it is their husbands or a crippled child who still require their constant attention and confront them with the boundaries of life. The dire need of the war and postwar time is still current for many of these women. I often encounter as self-portrait of this generation: 'We are those who had it hard.'

At the same time, these women speak more readily of the sorrows and grief of others than about their own problems. Disaster and disease is a constant encountered by the women in the village. In addition, the situation of a Rumanian-German family or a Philippine wife who does not feel at home in Germany brings new kinds of grief. Much of the pain and grief is kept at a superficial level in these conversations and in the following communal prayer of intercession. First of all, a profound confrontation would not accord with the expectations these women bring with them in the morning. However, it is important to accept the dark aspects of life in order to consider a design of life. During the course of the day, in their journey with Naomi and Ruth, other threads in other colors are introduced. The women are able to experience with Naomi and Ruth how they turn poverty into blessing. For me, this is sufficient justification for asking them to endure this difficult beginning.

b. *Female Relationships with Stumbling Blocks: Mother-in-law, Daughter-in-law (1.6-19)*
In our culture the image of the mother-in-law is still a cliché that frequently recalls the evil witch in fairy tales: envious, controlling, quarrelsome. In January 1997 a German airline advertised in a southern German newspaper with the headline: 'Good for you: Your mother-in-law is finally moving to Hamburg'. And on the next page— with a picture of a mischievous, somewhat eccentric-looking older

woman—'Good for your mother-in-law: We have eight flights daily between Munich and Hamburg'.

The reality is more colorful and more diverse than the cliché image. However, the impressive power of such stereotypes remains, as evidenced by pictures, anecdotes and witty sayings. Current participants in the 'Educational Days', the generation now 50–60 years old, are often especially familiar with the problems from both perspectives: they are simultaneously daughters-in-law and mothers-in-law. As young women, they married into a rural and farming life style and frequently found themselves under the regimen of the mother-in-law. As mothers-in-law, they now experience their own children beginning families and the development of their grandchildren, often under the impression that 'nowadays everything is different'. The change in gender roles in professional and personal lives, the altered conceptions of child raising and also the divorce rate in the younger generation impose great demands on the women. Nevertheless, the generations of women living together and helping one another are often taken for granted—and necessary. Perhaps they did not choose one another, but they can hardly extricate themselves from the relationship. One participant made the point: 'Mother-in-law and daughter-in-law are two women who, by chance, love the same man'.

This theme is very difficult to address, especially among women who live in a close relationship in one village. All the family relationships are known by the others in the community. In respect for this situation, I broadened the scope during the tasks: widened the horizon to relationships between women in general.[14]

The narrative continues:

The women remaining in the family persevere with their lives, their way. Naomi has nothing more to expect. However, she still has one wish, and it requires that she makes an important decision: she wants to return to her own country, to Bethlehem. The poverty and hunger there have gone, 'God had given the land bread again'. For this passage I lay a brown cloth down, with one border thrown over that of the green cloth representing Moab. The contrast suggests the figurative border that Naomi must cross to make her decision, and that Naomi takes the initiative. On their path, Naomi remains

14. In a mixed, more urban-influenced women's group, I worked explicitly on the daughter-in-law and mother-in-law relationship. This was complicated because the experiences of individual women diverged dramatically, and the mothers-in-law were often either idealized or damned. In general, the pain involved in this tense relationship appears to be significant to me.

standing and confronts her daughters-in-law with their futures: What do they want from the remains of their lives? This question, in this decisive moment, reveals the differences between the two young women, and we come to understand their names: 'Orpah' refers to 'neck', and Orpah turns her neck, her back, to Naomi, gives her the 'cold shoulder', as we say. The name 'Ruth' means 'friend'. With her decision to remain with Naomi, Ruth reveals herself as friend.

Actually, Orpah's decision is reasonable. By returning she has a chance to find a husband, have a family and achieve security. Ruth's decision is contrary to reason. Naomi is already old; Ruth has no other relatives in Judah, she will be a foreigner there, and thereby it will be more difficult to find a husband. To go with Naomi is risky.

Each of the three women must make descisions about herself, each of which will affect not only herself but the others. Can you understand how Naomi, Ruth and Orpah each made their decisions? How would you have decided?

The names of the three women have been printed on three large paper placards: Naomi, Ruth, Orpah. Think about what would you like to say to the three women. What questions would you like to ask them? You can write your questions and your opinions on the placards. You can also read what the other women have said and asked and enter into a written dialogue with them.

It is good to have a woman as friend—that was Naomi's experience with her daughter-in-law, and we experience that in our own lives. For many Catholic women, this friendship among women is not limited to this earth; many know of a holy woman in heaven with whom they have a special relationship, who helps them and with whom they may sometimes have conversations.

Now I will introduce you to several holy women and hang a placard in the room with their names or their pictures on it: Maria, Rita, Thérèse von Lisieux, Hildegard von Bingen... I invite you, to present yourselves to the holy woman who seems to 'speak' to you and is important to you. Discuss among yourselves what this holy figure means and why she is important to you.[15]

---

15. Another variation to elicit the theme of tense female relationships in their own lives is a guided fantasy trip through their own memories: Who are the women have I encountered in my life? Who has proven herself as friend to me?

In both forms of actualization the accent is not on 'in-law relationships' in a narrow sense, but on the differences between women, on solidarity and tension in female relationships. The relationship between mother-in-law and daughter-in-law is only an example of how women can interrelate.

Identification with the three women of the narrative and their different decisions is easy for most of the women. The groups always find speakers for both decisions, for Orpah's as well as for Ruth's. In the process, the women raise questions that are *not* part of the biblical narrative: What was the relationship between the mother-in-law and her two daughters-in-law? Was it different, and was it not as good with Orpah as with Ruth? Did one daughter-in-law have more alternatives than the other? These plays of thought made it clear that, for most of the participants, the decision was dependent on a myriad of factors; and the the most important was the quality of the relationship. Almost always, Naomi's behavior was admired because she allowed her daughters-in-law the freedom to decide for themselves. 'I wish I had a mother-in-law like her', the participants said among themselves; or, 'I would like to be a mother-in-law like her'.

The search for one's own woman friend among the holy women accorded with the spirituality of many older women, while the younger women were often helpless. Overwhelmingly, the majority always sought Maria—no wonder in an area heavily influenced by Catholic popular religion. What was more astonishing to me was the basis: Maria is important for many women 'because she had a difficult time in her life'.[16] It is less the beaming representation or the powerful help that is dominant; it is the ability to share sorrow. Because Maria had also suffered difficulties, women turn to her for an understanding and supportive friendship.

c. *Solidarity and Loving Kindness: Bread of Life (Chapter 2)*
At the end of the first chapter, *Mārâ*—the bitter one—is the name Naomi suggests the women in Bethlehem call her by. Naomi's bitter fortune takes a turn in the scene in Boaz's field. Ruth, Boaz and Naomi herself contribute to the possibilities of life that appear for the 'deceased'. It was important to keep the aspect of mutual assistance in this section in the foreground. When natives and foreigners, old and young, men and women work with one another instead of against one another, the harvest is abundant.

Naomi and Ruth return to the place where the story began. In the beginning, the flight from Bethlehem was a flight from hunger and poverty. The two women return to that place because there is bread there again. This is evident in the name of the place, a name carries an important message: Bethlehem,

16. This basis is valid also for Holy Rita, who is buried in Würzburg and is greatly honored.

'house of bread'.[17] *To represent the grain that is harvested, I lay a yellow cloth in the middle of the others.*

The time when the two women arrive is a special one: it is harvest time. It is a critical time that determines whether or not a year of hunger will follow. The time of harvest is also a time of abundance, a time when there is more than enough to satisfy oneself.

Nevertheless, not all can profit from an ample harvest! The poor people, who do not have their own fields, do not have a harvest. Such people have the rights of the poor in Israel: whoever does not have a field has the right to glean the fields after they have been harvested, to collect what has been left behind. There is even instruction in the Bible not to harvest the field thoroughly. Instead, something should always be left for the poor. This 'second harvest' reflects not just the generosity of the wealthy but the right of the poor.[18] In this situation, the friendship between Naomi and Ruth is proven. The two women work together, not only on the path but also in daily life in Bethlehem. They help each other in order to improve their difficult situation: without a man, without property and without profession.

Naomi is at home in Bethlehem and is familiar with the legal system of Israel. She knows of the rights of the poor—that they have the possibility to glean—and she makes Ruth cognizant of those rights. On her side, Ruth is younger and stronger; and she is willing to go to work in the fields. By means of this work, she can do something to insure their survival in the immediate future.

Ruth is led to glean by chance, in a field belonging to the third main character, who now makes an appearance. With Boaz, a man reappears in the story. 'Boaz' means 'strength is in him', and he presents a contrast with the other men, the 'weak' and the 'fragile'. Boaz is a powerful man, perhaps generous to the poor, but certainly a man with a great heart, as the following events reveal.

Boaz sees Ruth in the fields, and he sees in her not only a foreigner but also an energetic woman who helps provide for another woman. He speaks to her and supports her in a simple way: he permits her to remain in his fields as long as there is harvesting. This provides security for Ruth and Naomi. He even informs his workers not to glean too thoroughly, to leave something for her to harvest, so that she can glean more and her harvest will be somewhat more ample. Finally, he invites her to eat and drink with his employed workers, and he instructs the men not to bother her. This is an important

17.   On the character of this translation and the relevance of 'mythology' and symbolic names to the period of formation of the tale of Ruth, cf. Zenger, *Ruth*, pp. 31-32.

18.   Lev. 19.9-10; Deut. 24.19. Cf. Zenger, *Ruth*, pp. 48-49.

protection for a single and foreign woman, a protection she certainly needs.[19]

The results are predictable: *Ruth puts energy into the arduous work of harvesting, the beating and the hand–threshing until, at the end of the day, she has a full measure of barley—probably about 20–40 pounds.*[20] *With such a quantity of grain two women have enough to bake bread for a good week. For a short while life will be secure. Bread is made from grain, and is a basic form of nourishment here in Germany. We eat it morning and evening, the children take it with them to school and the adults to work. Nowhere in the world are there so many different kinds of bread as there are here in Germany. Grain is thus symbolic for everything that we need for life, everything that nourishes us and gives us strength. Among those things that we need are the help of and the solidarity with other people.*

I hold out a handful of grain and ask the women to take one for themselves, to look at it, to feel it between their fingers, perhaps to bite and taste it. In the middle, I place a bowl of earth. Each woman who wishes to can put her grain into the earth and, as she does so, say aloud in what situation she has received help, and from whom.

Lucy D'Souza filled the center of her Lenten veil[21] *with a picture of a woman sitting on the floor and kneading bread dough. All around her ears of corn are growing, and they create for her an area that also takes the shape of a grain of wheat. The artist wrote that this picture presents the traditional rite of Indian women: sitting on the ground with covered head, kneading the dough for bread. And the wisdom of the people adds: 'Only bread that has been baked with love can really satisfy'.*[22]

I invite the women to look at the picture and to let it involve them. Bread is essential for us: a sacrament of life, a symbol for everything that we consider as necessary as bread. Solidarity and friendship, loving kindness and generosity are among those qualities.[23]

With this section of the narrative it becomes most clear to me how strongly the experiences of the participants in the story are reflected in the story. Many older women remember gleaning grains in their own childhood.[24] Either the native children had to glean in the fields or the refugees and exiles from the war went to collect grain. From

19. In contrast to Zenger, who emphasizes the obedience aspect: see Zenger, *Ruth*, p. 56.

20. Cf. Fander, 'Die Geschichte', p. 97; Zenger, *Ruth*, pp. 58-59.

21. Cf. Misereor (ed.), *Biblische Frauengestalten*.

22. Cf. Misereor (ed.), *Biblische Frauengestalten*, pp. 19-20.

23. Cf. The Impulse text by Hubertus Halbfas, 'Sakrament Brot', in Misereor (ed.), *Biblische Frauengestalten*, p. 47.

24. Cf. Misereor (ed.), *Biblische Frauengestalten*, pp. 19-20.

time to time they had bad experiences associated with gleaning, as
when less generous farmers chased them out of their fields or preferred to drive their pigs onto the fields. With modern mowing/
threshing machines, the women say, it is no longer possible to glean.
It is not that 'waste' is not there—on the contrary! It is just that the
already-threshed grains are not collected any more. Why should they
be, in a society of abundance, in which grain farming is subsidized
and nevertheless hardly covers the cost of farming? For many of the
women the kernel of grain was a trusted symbol for the reality of their
lives, a piece of the earth and of its fruitfulness, the fruit of hard work
and unearned blessings, a simultaneous memory of hunger and a
calling for justice.

d. *Conclusion: Blessed Life (Chapters 3–4)*

The end of the narrative was not surprising to the participants. 'Ruth
marries Boaz and they have a child' was always the prediction when I
asked how the story would develop. Too good to be true? The
deliverance of Ruth and Naomi through marriage and the birth of a
son was always a bone of contention for me: it was too much like a
fairy tale; the solution seemed locked in the gender politics of a patriarchal society. It took me a while to discover the 'subversive potential'
of the narrative. That Naomi and Ruth reached their goal in a a very
unconventional way, that they consciously skirted the boundaries of
social game rules, that they cancelled the taboos delineating the
possible and appropriate behavior for women demanded my initial
and developing respect. For the participants it was (astonishingly, I
thought) no problem to accept this solution. That a woman is defined
by her husband/son, and finds her completion and value only
through them, was a foregone conclusion for many. Furthermore, that
there is little discussion of love between Ruth and Boaz, and the
action is more practical than romantic, is normal for the older women.
In this generation, 'to be taken care of' was and remains an existential
question and not an expectation.

The participants were particularly attentive to the manner in which
Ruth and Naomi become active in order to reach their goal. The
women easily became involved with the rustling tension on the night-
time threshing floor: they smiled at one another knowingly, or whis-
pered among themselves. For women of that generation the erotic,
sexual initiative of Ruth and Naomi showed best the outrageousness
of this united action. And that the Bible did not brand the action as
'unseemly' and 'scandalous', but gave God's blessing to it, moved
many of the women to an 'Aha!' experience they could go home with.

Initially Ruth says to Naomi, 'Everything you shall say, I will do' (3.5); exactly these words are later spoken by Boaz to Ruth (v. 11). To really listen to one another, to give one another their attention and to respond generously are behaviors that promote relationships between different kinds of people—between strong and weak, between men and women—to more fairness and equality. At the conclusion of the story hunger, loneliness and death have metamorphosed. Blessings in the form of bread and child are the fruit of righteousness and goodness. God himself is at work.

6. *Reflections*

a. *God Is Revealed in the Lives of Women: Then and Now*

The book of Ruth tells of women who encounter tragedy and famine, women who have a difficult time in a patriarchal society, women who wrangle with God. Above all, the book tells how the two women, Ruth and Naomi, take the outcome of their lives into their own hands. They form a female bond of friendship that enables them to go beyond the constraints of behavior established for females. Through female solidarity and independent action the women find the value and opportunity that were not in their lives before. With courage and persistence, sometimes also with cunning, and together, they find means for turning from social and factual death back to life. They are even able to restore a portion of life for the dead. In so doing they extend the limits of feminine roles in their patriarchal context a bit further. They do the unexpected with cleverness and panache. In seeking a way to live, the experience the blessing of God. Thus the friendship and devotion of individuals shows the goodness and loyalty of God.

It was out of personal interest that I chose the Ruth narrative as a thread for the 'Educational Days for Rural Women'. First of all, during the time the two—that is, the old story, women of the past— came together, it occurred to me how closely we, the rural women and also I myself, are related to Ruth and Naomi. The bond with the earth and the land; the work and the gratitude for the harvest (and also the experience of bad harvests); even the archaic elements of the story, such as the gleaning of grain or in-law marriage customs, belong—as I was surprised to discover—to the expectations of most rural women. I encountered very similar experiences in the stories and life histories of simple rural women: tales of hunger and death, of being foreign and marginalized, of friendships with women that were full of tension, of the (sometimes unexpected) combined assistance of friends and neighbors so that someone can master a life-threatening situation. Ruth and Naomi are two of them; their story is preserved in the Bible. The life stories of the rural women are therefore a secondary, smaller 'holy script'. In them, life experiences and God experiences grow together. The stories' wisdom is a living source of revelation that can be read anew each day. This is what I learnt in my meeting with both the biblical and the contemporary women.

b. *Finding Yourself: Putting Oneself in Words*
A motive was encapsulated within the delineated general theme—'Discovering my Design for Life': to discover an exemplary female figure and to experience her being in the narrative. One's own design for life often appears like a tapestry or carpet which is still being worked on. The design is complicated and, furthermore, unfinished, so that it cannot be identified as complete. It can be recognized only as an entity; how the many colored threads run and develop a design can be understood only when the reverse side is studied. In our own lives that is seldom possible. However, the female characters in the Ruth novella can be offered as figures for identification.

The rural women could find themselves in Ruth and Naomi: they could relate to their path and its stations in hunger and blessings, to their acting with cleverness and female solidarity. By this identification the rural women found it possible to see and interpret their own lives anew. In this process, the contrast between the world of the biblical Ruth novella and the daily lives of the women in the here-and-now was overcome in a way that was fruitful in many respects. The women re-examined their own lives, the unreasonable demands those lives encompass and the structure of the suppression they have experienced. They also found possibilities for actions that are grounded in solidarity with women (and men), actions that can lead to blessing. They discovered thereby a bit of the Bible as a female tradition. The largely unknown, unconsidered and foreign narratives of women, narratives that could have developed a theological tradition, found life and color and faces. The women became involved through the reversible mirrors of Bible and life. They could say, 'That happened to us; that shows our lives and our experiences'. Thus women's traditions were not only (re)discovered, but also imagined and thereby advanced further. The women learnt to tell their own stories, to tell their concealed experiences of God, to share those with one another. Women could raise their voices and put their lives into words. Therein lies the feminist-theological relevance of this project for me.

c. *The Story of Ruth and Naomi: A Parable for Feminism*

Phyllis Trible interpreted the book of Ruth entirely as a parable of feminism:

> As a whole, this human comedy suggests a theological interpretation of feminism: women working out their own salvation with fear and trembling, for it is God who works in them. Naomi works as a bridge between tradition and innovation. Ruth and the females of Bethlehem work as paradigms for radicality. All together they are women in culture, women against culture, and women transforming culture. What they reflect, they challenge. And that challenge is a legacy of faith to this day for all who have ears to hear the stories of women in a man's world.[25]

This story was heard among rural women, and not only the biblical women became alive thereby. The women assumed the inheritance of Ruth and Naomi in the here and now of their lives, to be friends and witnesses of the blessings of God's goodness.[26]

---

25. Phyllis Trible, *God and the Rhetoric of Sexuality* (Philadelphia: Fortress Press, 1978), p. 196.

26. Translated by Lillian R. Klein.

'WOMEN OF THE NEIGHBORHOOD' (RUTH 4.17): INFORMAL FEMALE NETWORKS IN ANCIENT ISRAEL[*]

Carol Meyers

Imagine for a moment that you are able to visit a farmer in a small village in the East Mediterranean in the Iron Age. One of the farmer's children falls ill, and a health care consultant is summoned. Shortly thereafter, it being a dry year, the household runs short of some basic commodities; a small supply to meet the shortfall is procured from a somewhat more fortunate neighbor on the other side of the village. Then, the oldest son having reached puberty, kin in the next village are contacted about a suitable bride.

If you are like most people reading this account, you will assume that all the characters, except the bride, are men. But you would be mistaken. Some could equally have been women—the farmer, for example, because roughly 40 per cent of the productive labor in agrarian communities in the highlands of Palestine was contributed by women.[1] Others were likely to have been women—the health care consultant, for one. The rest were almost certainly women: the neighbor providing aid, the distant kinsperson with the marriageable daughter. In fact, only the eligible groom in the household need be a male in this scenario, which depicts inter-household and inter-village activities involving both the formal and informal roles played by women as members of a variety of social groups. In this paper, I shall focus on women's informal associations, or networks, in Israelite agrarian communities.[2]

[*]   This essay is adapted from a larger article, 'Guilds and Gatherings: Women's Groups in Ancient Israel', in P.M. Williams, Jr, and T. Hiebert (eds.), *Realia Dei: Essays in Honor of Edward F. Campbell, Jr* (Scholars Press Bible and Archaeology Series; Atlanta: Scholars Press, forthcoming). The editors of that volume have graciously granted permission to reproduce portions of that paper.
   1.   See C.L. Meyers, 'Procreation, Production, and Protection: Male–Female Balance in Early Israel', *JAAR* 51 (1983), pp. 569-93.
   2.   By agrarian communities I mean not only small hamlets and villages but also larger settlements called *'ārîm* (cities) in the Hebrew Bible. See below, n. 15.

1. *Theoretical Considerations*

Assumptions about male dominance in the group life of traditional as well as contemporary societies are common. Associations formed by men for military, economic and political purposes have long garnered the lion's share of the attention of social scientists examining human cultures, both ancient and modern. Indeed, in many cases men's organizations and structures are the only supra-domestic associations to be afforded legitimacy in the eyes of observers and scholars. The result has been that the varied, and often powerful, connections forged by women have largely gone unnoticed. The contributions of women's groups to the social, political and economic aspects of their communities have thereby been rendered invisible or, at best, trivialized. Certainly such is the case for ancient Israel. Although feminist biblical scholarship has drawn attention to formal or professional women's groups,[3] the existence and function of women's informal networks have been hitherto overlooked.

The failure to take note of women's informal groups in biblical Israel is part of a wider androcentric bias that exaggerates the juridical and political spheres by focusing on formal or national structures in which men are the major participants. Concomitantly, female activities in informal and local settings are ignored or discounted. There are additional reasons for Israelite women to have been left out of much of the discussion of group life. One factor is that the major source of information about Israelite society, the Hebrew Bible, is itself relatively silent about women's activities in general and their corporate behavior in particular. The Bible represents the viewpoint of high status males, and using it as the only source for information about women's social relationships entails blindness to significant areas of women's behavior patterns.[4] For informal associations of women, the book of Ruth is virtually the only source, although there are other scattered clues and references that can be helpful.

---

3.   Examples of professional women's groups (or 'guilds') are: mourning women, wise women, health care practitioners (midwives and probably sorcerers/witches), musicians and other performers, popular prophets. These professions are discussed in Meyers, 'Guilds and Gatherings'. See also C. Meyers, 'Mother to Muse: An Ethnoarchaeological Study of Women's Performance in Ancient Israel', in A. Brenner and J.W. van Henten (eds.), *Recycling Biblical Figures: NOSTER Conference 1997* (Leiden: DEO, forthcoming).

4.   Cf. S. Allen and D.L. Barber, 'Sexual Divisions and Society', in D.L. Barber and S. Allen (eds.), *Sexual Divisions and Society: Process and Change* (Explorations in Sociology, 6; London: Tavistock, 1976), pp. 1-24 (3).

But it is not simply the relative invisibility of women's groups in the Hebrew Bible that is the problem. Western ideological constructions are also implicated. The Western patriarchal interpretive stance of biblical scholarship is characterized by assumptions, based on post-biblical traditions and experiences, about women's roles in public affairs that occlude the perception of women's participation in Israelite community life. The stay-at-home full-time wife-and-mother pattern, which emerged with the industrial revolution and contributed to the family's success in making the transition to industrialization, has created distorting preconceptions about women's roles. The radical functional shifts in family life in the West in the nineteenth century were accompanied by ideological shifts that reinforced the reconfiguration of the family and took away the opportunity or need for women's economic productivity, except for those in the poorest sectors of society. A woman's role, limited to the reconfigured family, became that of non-producing housewife and mother. The home became 'private', and the Cult of Domesticity effectively kept women out of the 'public' sphere. Child rearing and housekeeping were the woman's household domain; and religion in America and on the continent contributed to the development and maintenance of the ideology of a distinct woman's sphere. Separate spheres meant that, at least for Christian women, the avenue to God was only through submission to husbands.[5]

The theological power of such ideas permeated critical biblical scholarship as it emerged in the nineteenth century. Female autonomy and male dependence on women (and vice versa) for economic survival could not be recognized as essential aspects of life in the biblical world. Biblical women were invariably compared to men and inevitably pronounced subordinate and inferior possessions of men.[6] Male biblical scholars, reading the text with their own presuppositions and often with their own claims to authority at stake, saw women through distorting interpretive lenses. Even the development of feminist biblical scholarship, which in its early stages sought to rescue women mentioned in the Hebrew Bible from obscurity, tended to think of women primarily in 'wife–mother' terms, which are difficult to sepa-

---

5.   So K. Rudy, ' "Haven in a Heartless World": The Historical Roots of Gendered Theology', in *idem*, *Sex and the Church: Gender, Homosexuality, and the Transformation of Christian Ethics* (Boston: Beacon Press, 1997), pp. 15-44.

6.   E.g. O.J. Baab, 'Woman', *IDB*, IV, p. 865; R. DeVaux, *Ancient Israel* (trans. J. McHugh; New York: McGraw–Hill, 1961), p. 39.

rate from their Western connotations even when the productive roles of Israelite women are noted.[7]

All told, these two factors—the relative paucity of information about women in the Hebrew Bible and the modern ideological creation of the idea of women's separate domestic sphere—have influenced consideration of Israelite gender roles and made it difficult to see women as other than subservient wife–mothers. Although public figures such as Deborah and Miriam are regularly noted, they appear more as exceptions that prove the rule that women's lives were circumscribed by activities in their immediate households and by the authority of men. But the legitimacy of such claims, whether proposed by the supporters or the critics of patriarchal patterns, can be contested. In recent decades, social science research has provided new perspectives on women's lives in marginal agrarian societies like that of ancient Israel. Such perspectives enable us to shed some light on the lives of Israelite women.

To begin with, advances in contemporary social science have meant radical revisions in general notions about women's status in premodern farming households. The conventional wisdom that saw women as passive and powerless in virtually all pre-industrial cultures is now known to be deeply flawed. That idea is seldom borne out by newer studies of such societies, which rely on information gathered from within households and from female as well as male informants rather than on the 'public' information given by male informants to earlier generations of social or cultural anthropologists.[8] The work patterns and authority structures that characterize the reality of daily life in pre-modern societies are rarely hierarchical along gendered lines, even if such hierarchies exist in certain political or jural aspects of the

---

7.   P. Bird, in her pioneer article on 'Images of Women in the Old Testament', in *Religion and Sexism: Images of Women in the Jewish and Christian Traditions* (ed. R.R. Ruether; New York: Simon & Schuster, 1974), pp. 41-88, puts it this way: 'Central to most [references in the historical and prophet books] ... and underlying all are the images of wife and mother (or wife-mother) ... These two primary roles defined most women's lives' (p. 69). And in her analysis of women in legal texts she concludes that women, where mentioned, are dependent and usually infirm (p. 56).

8.   N. Quinn, in the 'Introduction' to her article ('Anthropological Studies on Women's Status', *Annual Review of Anthropology* 6 [1977], pp. 181-225), reviewing the impact of the women's movement on anthropology, highlights the biases and distortions of traditional male-oriented ethnography and its readiness to see gender asymmetry as signifying male privilege, dominance or superior status.

society.[9] A rich assortment of recent studies of the family and household in traditional societies is especially cognizant of the range of women's contributions to and also control of household economic functions. Such research helps to 'strip away ideological blinders to women's actual economic contributions'[10] at the household level and beyond.

Such studies of the family and household reveal otherwise unacknowledged aspects of women's work and also of male dependence on female productivity, thereby contesting traditional views of female dependency. They also examine the articulation of the household with wider community functions. In other words, the modern conceptual separation between domestic and public, although widely used in cross-cultural studies of the position of women with some value in assessing women's roles, cannot hold up to nuanced evaluations of women's supra-domestic activities. The consideration of separate spheres, popular several decades ago,[11] has now given way to a more integrated approach.[12] The two spheres, it is now understood, are not necessarily separate. Public and private are not uniformly two distinct kinds of social units, the first society-wide and the second consisting

9.   A pioneering theoretical piece on this subject, based on fieldwork in rural Greece, is E. Friedl's 'The Position of Women: Appearance and Reality', *Anthropological Quarterly* 40 (1967), pp. 97-108. See also C. Cronin's study of 'Illusion and Reality in Sicily', in A. Schlegel (ed.), *Sexual Stratification: A Cross-Cultural View* (New York: Columbia University Press, 1977), pp. 67-93, and S.C. Rogers, 'Female Forms of Power and the Myth of Male Dominance: A Model of Female/Male Interaction in Peasant Society', *American Ethnologist* 2 (1975), pp. 741-54.

10.   K.S. March and R.L. Taqqu, *Women's Informal Associations in Developing Countries* (Women in Cross-Cultural Perspective; Boulder, CO: Westview Press, 1986), p. viii.

11.   Classically expressed by M.Z. Rosaldo, 'Women, Culture, and Society: A Theoretical Overview', in M.Z. Rosaldo and L. Lamphere (eds.), *Women, Culture, and Society* (Stanford, CA: Stanford University Press, 1974), pp. 17-42. See also P.R. Sanday, 'Female Status in the Public Domain', in M.Z. Rosaldo and L. Lamphere (eds.) *Women, Culture and Society* (Stanford, CA: Stanford University Press, 1974), pp. 189-206.

12.   See the essays in D.O. Helly and S.M. Reverby (eds.), *Gendered Domains: Rethinking Public and Private in Women's History* (Ithaca, NY: Cornell University Press, 1992); and in J. Sharistanian (ed.), *Beyond the Public/Private Dichotomy: Contemporary Perspectives on Women's Public Lives* (Contributions to Women's Studies, 78; Westport, CT: Greenwood Press, 1987). In a later essay, 'The Use and Abuse of Anthropology: Reflections on Feminism and Cross-cultural Understanding', *Signs* 5 (1980), pp. 389-417, Rosaldo herself questions the validity of some aspects of the binary construction of public/private as expressed in her 1974 essay (cited above, n. 11).

of small family units. In most village-based societies the lines between such hypothetical spheres are blurred. Connections between domestic groups often entail larger or community-wide interests, with needs or issues arising in family units being dealt with by the larger community. The private *is* the public when the interests of individual households are reflected in the collective actions of larger groups. In traditional societies it is not an 'either/or' matter of private versus public; rather, many issues are 'both/and'. To put it another way, activities in the household or family have implications for the broader social world. Women's roles in domestic ('private') life often have consequences in the wider community (the 'public' sphere).

Public and private are thus overlapping and integrated domains in many aspects of family and community life in traditional societies. Nonetheless, there is some heuristic value in considering them separately. When doing so, it is important to remember that the two domains are not necessarily hierarchically related, with the public valued more than the private. The tendency in the West to devalue women's unpaid housework in urban settings has unconsciously and unfairly colored considerations of women's labor in traditional agrarian ones. Our Western eyes often blind us to the possibility that women's productive labor carried out in household units in premodern societies can be valued as highly as men's leadership tasks in community-wide structures. Similarly, female (domestic) status cannot be judged in relationship to male (public) status, as has often been the case. Cross-cultural studies of traditional societies indicate that it is impossible to characterize women's status, in some global way, as either 'high' or 'low' in comparison with men's. Greater male visibility in public life is not equivalent to higher male status in all aspects of daily life. The idea of a fixed relationship between genders—men superior, women subordinate—cannot be demonstrated for *all* inter-gender interactions.[13] Indeed, status itself is not a unitary condition; it involves many variables, often causally independent of one another. The implication of such findings is important in biblical studies, for example, in looking at differentials in Pentateuchal law that seem to privilege Israelite males; such differentials cannot automatically be treated as an indicator of an overall inferior status for Israelite females.

Studies of household dynamics in traditional societies are relevant for biblical studies in more ways than in helping us to recognize and

---

13. M. Strathern, *Women in between: Female Roles in a Male World* (Seminar Studies in Anthropology, 2; London: Seminar Press, 1972), p. 290.

correct the biases of Western scholarship. Our intent here is to recognize and understand women's informal groups. To do so, we shall draw upon the plethora of recent ethnographic studies informed by critiques of androcentric research strategies. Such studies show how women in traditional societies connect with other women across family boundaries in ways that have consequences for community as well as domestic life. That is, the existence and function of informal associations of women have been so well documented across cultures all over the globe that there can no longer be any doubt about their significance. Relations forged by women outside of formal public structures, and usually overlooked by older investigations because of their absence from formal cultural productions, are often essential to supra-household community life even when they are grounded in household activities.[14] In looking at women's groups in ancient Israel, the focus on the agrarian population means that we will be considering the social settings in which up to 90 per cent of the people would have resided.[15]

2. *Women's Informal Groups or Networks: Linking Communities*

Decades of ethnographic research, informed by feminist anthropological sensitivities to the male biases of traditional cross-cultural research, have shown that women in peasant societies are invariably connected to each other in a series of informal relationships. Such relationships are designated 'women's networks'.[16] These alliances are not some hypothetical web of acquaintances or sets of friendships among women. Rather, informal as they are and even as invisible as

14. March and Taqqu, *Women's Informal Associations*, p. 16.

15. The great majority of the population in agricultural societies consists of peasant farmers in rural settings, with city-dwellers constituting only a tiny minority—never more than 10 per cent and perhaps as little as 5 per cent. See G. Lenski, *Power and Privilege: A Theory of Social Stratification* (Chapel Hill, NC: University of North Carolina Press, 1984), pp. 199-200. Many of the Iron Age settlements called 'cities' in the Hebrew Bible did not actually have the features and functions associated with the urban life of their Bronze Age precursors. Most had no public buildings and were little more than fortified villages ('residential cities') inhabited by farming families (peasant farmers) that worked the surrounding lands. See F.S. Frick, 'Cities: An Overview', *OEANE*, II, pp. 14-19, and V. Fritz, 'Cities of the Bronze and Iron Ages', *OEANE*, II, pp. 19-25.

16. So V. Maher, 'Kins, Clients, and Accomplices: Relationships among Women in Morocco', in D.L. Barber and S. Allen (eds.), *Sexual Divisions and Society: Process and Change* (Explorations in Sociology, 6; London: Tavistock, 1976), pp. 52-75 (52-53.)

they may be to a casual observer, women's networks actually function as institutions that provide critical social linkages. Hence they carry considerable weight in traditional societies. Although women's networks are informal structures, they should not be viewed as supplemental either to formal public ones or even to domestic units. The tendency to relate 'formal' with 'important' and 'informal' with 'unimportant' does not do justice to the dynamics of informal alliances; and it occludes the way women's networks perform essential social and even economic tasks.[17]

In considering women's alliances in ancient Israel it is important to note that marriages were usually parentally arranged and involved patrilocal residence: the newly wed couple resided near or with the husband's parents. The incest prohibitions of Leviticus (18.7-9; 20.11-14, 17, 19-21), while perhaps not the same as marriage regulations, would have insured that the eligible spouses for a man would come from beyond his residential family. By forbidding sex within the immediate family incest taboos necessitate out-marriage, thereby creating alliances among families of neighboring villages. Such webs of kinship—perhaps the equivalent of the Israelite *mišpāḥâ*, which functioned as a 'protective association of families'[18]—helped maintain peace among contiguous settlements and increased the likelihood that related families would come to each other's assistance in times of economic or personal troubles.[19] The resulting cooperation and reciprocity among families was essential for the survival of family units in the uncertain agrarian world of the Israelites, for whom there were no government agencies to provide the kind of services, in economic or other emergencies, that we take for granted in the modern world.

The groundwork for inter-family and inter-village mutual aid was laid by the marital ties of the Israelite villagers and/or by the fictional ties created by genealogical constructions of lineages. The actual mechanisms for carrying out the socio-economic functions of allied groups were likely to have been women's networks. Women in Israelite society were well situated to play such a role. When a woman married *into* a family she had affiliations with *two* descent groups: the residential household of her husband—her marital affiliation; and the

17. Maher, 'Kins, Clients, and Accomplices', pp. 52, 71.

18. See N.K. Gottwald, *Tribes of Yahweh* (Maryknoll, NY: Orbis Books, 1979), pp. 257-84.

19. F. Zonabend, 'An Anthropological Perspective on Kinship and the Family', in A. Burghière, C. Klapisch-Zuber, M. Segalen and F. Zonabend (eds.), *A History of the Family*. I. *Distant Worlds, Ancient Worlds* (trans. S.H. Tenison, R. Morris and A. Wilson; Cambridge, MA: Harvard University Press, 1996), pp. 25-39.

family into which she was born—her natal affiliation.[20] Because of Israelite marriage customs, women had two sets of family ties—with their own kin and with their husband's kin. Women, rather than men, were therefore uniquely positioned to facilitate intergroup relationships.

The Hebrew Bible provides virtually no information about the dynamics of mutual assistance and reciprocity involved in the *mišpāḥôt*. Similarly, the role of women's networks in activating such alliances is not indicated. Cross-cultural evidence, however, suggests that women are the ones who effect cooperation between settlements inhabited by affinals (people with kinship ties created by marriage). In virtually all traditional peasant societies, women maintain relationships with their natal kin that prove vital to various aspects of their lives in their marital communities. Women in ancient Israelite settlements were likely to have been part of similar relationships. A hint of the maintaining of ties with one's natal community appears in the tragic story of the Levite's concubine in Judges 19. Discussion of this narrative inevitably focuses on the sexual outrage and the violence. Yet the tale does reveal that, when marital difficulties arise, the unnamed secondary wife returns to her natal household (Judg. 19.2).

The ongoing relationship between women and their families of origin also functioned in the matter of arranging marriages for their sons with daughters from nearby villages. The mothers of eligible sons typically retain or obtain knowledge about eligible mates from their natal community. The formal negotiation of marriage arrangements may be done by men, but the information obtained from women's networks is often decisive in selection of mates for offspring.[21] The bride prices or dowries involved in Israelite marriages should not be conceptualized as the buying or selling of brides but rather as exchanges or gifts that contributed to or helped maintain connections between two family groups.[22] Such marriage customs created mutual obligations that increased the likelihood that families connected in this way would offer economic or other assistance. The marginal subsistence level for most Israelite villagers, and the great

20. Strathern, *Women in between*, pp. viii-ix, 130.
21. March and Taqqu, *Women's Informal Associations*, p. 39.
22. Cf. March and Taqqu, *Women's Informal Associations*, p. 41. This is a good example of how the male-oriented analysis of bride prices or dowries, which looked at them as part of traffic in women, must be revised; from other perspectives, those exchanges are important in establishing family ties as the basis for mutual aid.

variation in ecosystems, meant that crop disaster in one village could be mitigated by aid from affines living in a nearby settlement.[23]

3. *Women's Networks: Ruth and the Residential Community*

As important as natal ties were for Israelite women, most of their daily interactions were with members of the marital community to which they had moved. Alliances among women who lived near each other included the women in their husband's extended family household and also the women in the larger residential community. Several biblical passages provide evidence that such informal associations were part of community life. Two of these passages are in the book of Ruth. Although Ruth is more of a folktale than the authentic record of an historical event, most critics agree that certain aspects of Israelite society are reflected in the plausible details of the narrative.[24] The author may have taken liberties with legal niceties and cultural expectations in order to serve plot development, characterization and dramatic interest. Yet, because the narrative assumes familiarity with certain practices, the social customs and interactions in Ruth are likely to be authentic.

The book of Ruth lends itself magnificently to consideration of female relationships. Whether or not it is evaluated as valorizing women's autonomy or as portraying women trapped in patriarchal modes,[25] it is clearly a 'woman's story'.[26] Virtually all discussions of

23. It was functionally more adaptive to have men farm the land of their patrimony than to move to another area (i.e. their wife's village) with a subtly different ecosystem. Successful strategies for working the marginally productive zones of the Palestinian hill country were thus ones that men learned from the fathers, whereas successful completion of women's tasks, in the division of labor by gender in ancient Israel, was less dependent upon location contingent knowledge. This functional aspect of family structure is discussed in C. Meyers, 'The Family in Early Israel', in L. Perdue, C. Meyers, J. Blenkinsopp and J.J. Collins, *Families in Ancient Israel* (Family, Religion, and Culture Series; Louisville, KY: Westminster/John Knox Press, 1997), pp. 1-47 (22-32).

24. E.g. E.F. Campbell, Jr, *Ruth* (AB, 7; Garden City, NY: Doubleday, 1975), pp. 8-10; J. Sasson, *Ruth: A New Translation with a Philological Commentary and a Formalist-Folklorist Interpretation* (Baltimore: The Johns Hopkins University Press, 1979), pp. 228-30.

25. Examples of the various readings of Ruth appear in A. Brenner (ed.), *A Feminist Companion to Ruth* (Feminist Companion to the Bible, 3; Sheffield: Sheffield Academic Press, 1993).

26. P. Trible, *God and the Rhetoric of Sexuality* (Philadelphia: Fortress Press, 1978), p. 166.

female relationships in Ruth examine the interactions between the major characters, the Ephratite woman Naomi and her Moabite daughter-in-law Ruth; and, to a lesser extent, between Naomi and Orpah, the Moabite daughter-in-law who chooses to remain in Moab. There are other female characters in Ruth, however, and their presence in the story provides an opportunity to consider some otherwise unexamined aspects of women's social relationships and roles.

The story of Ruth's sojourn in her mother-in-law's community, Bethlehem, is framed by the mention of women's groups. In Ruth 1.19 'the whole town' is happily aware of Naomi's return, but 'the women' of Bethlehem are specifically mentioned as the ones who greet her. At the end of the tale, in 4.17 (cf. 4.14) immediately before the genealogical appendix, the 'women of the neighborhood' appear at the occasion of the birth of Ruth's son (and Davidic ascendant) Obed. Coming together for this important occasion, this group of women—uniquely in the Hebrew Bible—names the infant; in so doing the women signify solidarity with the new mother.[27] The two references in Ruth to local women, which form an inclusio around the Ruth-in-Bethlehem story, depict the behavior of women in informal groups. Women join together to greet Ruth and Naomi and perhaps to help them establish themselves in Naomi's marital community; later they participate in the ceremonial event, a naming, connected with an important life event, childbirth.[28]

In addition to emphasizing that an informal women's network is visible in these texts, it is also important to look at the close relationship of Naomi and Ruth in anthropological terms. It is an instance of bonding between female members of a marital household. The incoming bride is always in a precarious position as the newcomer in an established household. Although that is not quite the case for Ruth, nonetheless the notion that female family members in the husband's household can act in concert to achieve results that will serve the

27. Mothers, more often than fathers, give names to newborns in the Hebrew Bible. In 17 instances names are provided by men; in 27 cases the name-givers are female. See I. Pardes's discussion of naming in 'Beyond Genesis 3: The Politics of Maternal Naming', in *Countertraditions in the Bible: A Feminist Approach* (Cambridge, MA: Harvard University Press, 1992), pp. 39-59.

28. It is possible that the name-giving ceremony, coming at birth, was an extension of the midwife's role; cf. the naming of Tamar's twins in Gen. 38.27-30 and the discussion in C. Meyers, 'Midwife (Gen 35.17; 38.28)', in C. Meyers, T. Craven and R. Kraemer (eds.), *Women in Scripture: A Dictionary of the Named and Unnamed Women in the Hebrew Bible, Apocryphal/Deuterocanonical Books, and New Testament* (Boston: Houghton Mifflin, forthcoming).

entire household is part of the message of the book of Ruth.

The term used in Ruth 4.17 for the group of women who participate in the birth ceremony, by offering a blessing as well as a name for the newborn, deserves comment. The term is literally 'neighbors' (NRSV, 'women of the neighborhood'), Hebrew šᵉkēnôt, a feminine plural participle (absolute) of the verb škn, 'to settle, dwell'. This feminine form is found in only one other place in the Hebrew Bible: in Exod. 3.22, where, in anticipation of the exodus, the women are instructed to collect valuables from their (female) Egyptian neighbors and from any women living in their (female) neighbor's houses. These items of movable wealth become 'plunder' in the eyes of the narrator. Yet that exploitative outcome depends on the existence of the solidarity of women in residential proximity. Note that the Israelite women 'ask' for the valuables; they do not steal them. The text assumes that the Egyptian women who are 'neighbors' participate in a women's network with a high enough degree of solidarity and cross-group identity that the Egyptian women would accede to the request of the Israelite women.

In addition to the two instances (Ruth 4 and Exodus 3) of 'neighbor' in its female form, the several places in which it is used in the masculine form probably represent instances of inclusive language, with the term referring to both men and women. In Exod. 12.4 neighboring households are instructed to share a lamb for the Passover feast if they are too small to consume a whole lamb by themselves. All the family members are included in that designation of neighbors (cf. Exod. 12.21). The same can be said for Jer. 6.24, where the four male nouns (father, son, neighbor, friend) represent close family groups and close non-kin associations that will die in God's punitive acts. Proverbs 27.10 proclaims the value of friends, and of 'neighbors' who live nearby, over distant kin; associations, male or female, involving residential contiguity can be more important at times than kinship connections. Finally, 2 Kgs 4.3 provides evidence of a widow receiving economic aid from 'neighbors'. The aid is in the form of household containers for the storage of oil; and the masculine form 'neighbors' must surely include the female members of the neighbors' families, for the women were likely the ones who dealt with domestic food supplies and their containers. Neighbors of either gender constituted networks of people sharing residential space and similar life styles. Such associations based on locational proximity were important in the economic and cultural life of the community.[29]

29. Relevant here are a group of terms denoting friends or companions: several

The textual glimpses, in Ruth and elsewhere, of women's groups in residential communities, and also of the esteem in which they were held, evoke questions about how such groups functioned. What were their specific activities, other than the ones revealed in the Ruth story? Again, ethnographic data are invaluable. Informal women's networks in residential communities have been observed in many traditional societies. Their importance is greatest in societies existing at the sub-sistence level, where labor and material resources are limited,[30] as was the case in Israelite villages.

Women's networks in small agricultural communities function in several important economic and social ways. The nature of women's daily routines, given the division of labor by gender,[31] and also the spatial organization of Iron Age villages, with domestic clusters adjoining each other,[32] meant that Israelite women had more access to each other than men did to other men. Many repetitive household activities performed by women, such as certain food preparation tasks, would have been done in each other's company.[33] Such regular and intimate contact creates familiarity; and the shared tasks, problems and experiences create a sense of identity. Familiarity and identity foster the solidarity of the women of a community—the neighborhood associations visible in the Bible.

The existence of regular female contact across households allows women's associations to be information sharing groups. Women

---

substantives found in both feminine and masculine forms and derived from the root *r'h*, 'to associate with'. The term *ra''yâ* seems to indicate age cohorts, as in the companions of Jehpthah's daughter (Judg. 11.37) and of the maiden of Canticles (where it is used nine times); and in Exod. 11.2, which parallels the text about Egyptian neighbors discussed above, *r''ût* overlaps with *š'kēnôt* as a designation for someone living nearby.

30. March and Taqqu, *Women's Informal Associations*, pp. 20, 58.

31. The nature of farm family life and of the division of labor by age and gender is treated in Meyers, 'The Family in Early Israel', and also in C.L. Meyers, 'Everyday Life: Women in the Period of the Hebrew Bible', in C.A. Newsom and S. Ringe (eds.), *The Women's Bible Commentary* (Louisville, KY: Westminster/John Knox Press, expanded edn, 1997), pp. 251-59.

32. See L.E. Stager, 'The Archaeology of the Family in Ancient Israel', *BASOR* 260 (1985), pp. 1-36.

33. The recent discovery of an Iron I (late twelfth–early eleventh century BCE) installation, made of mud brick, and covered with mud plaster, at Tel Dor has been interpreted as a communal trough in which women kneaded bread dough in light of models of such communal troughs known from later Aegean terracottas. See E. Stern, J. Berg, A. Gilboa, I. Sharon and J. Zorn, 'Tel Dor, 1994–95: Preliminary Stratigraphic Report', *IEJ* 47 (1997), pp. 47-56, and especially Figs. 11 and 12.

quickly become aware if there are acute labor needs in an individual household because of the illness or absence of one or more family members. Because of their solidarity, they rally to provide assistance, perhaps creating informal labor pools or other non-hierarchical structures for rotational mutual aid.[34] These adaptive procedures, in which all households ultimately benefit, in turn increase the solidarity among the women. The character and location of women's tasks as distinct from men's means that women are far more likely to participate in such informal association,[35] which can be critical to the viability of individual households given the risk factors for agricultural subsistence in the Palestine highlands.

One other significant aspect of women's groups in Israelite villages was undoubtedly their role in religious or ritual activities. Biblical texts present males in the leadership roles and also in most of the secondary roles of national and public cultic life. Yet the biblical references to women engaging in forbidden cultic practices or in the service of forbidden deities suggest that only as Yahweh and Jerusalem became dominant did women's participation in the official cultus become circumscribed. Even so, to focus only on the relative participation of females and males in the national cult delineated in the Pentateuch, in which women's roles are quite restricted, would be to miss the activities of women in village and domestic rituals and celebrations. Such activities are often viewed as secondary or of less value than the formal public events. That notion, however, is an invalid perspective, based as it is upon some of the false assumptions about the domestic–public dichotomy as noted above. Religious activity in household or village settings can represent the most accessible and most significant experience for the majority of people in isolated agrarian communities. For Israel, this would have been especially true following the centralization of the official cult in Jerusalem in the seventh century BCE.

Just what was the nature of women's cultic activity in Iron Age Israel? Again, ethnographic studies of traditional societies are extremely useful in reconstructing the religious life of Israelite households.[36] Women probably organized and participated in a variety of

---

34. March and Taqqu, *Women's Informal Associations*, pp. 54-58.

35. March and Taqqu, *Women's Informal Associations*, p. 59.

36. Such an approach has been used to good effect by P. Bird, 'The Place of Women in the Israelite Cultus', in P.D. Miller, P.D. Hanson and S.D. McBride (eds.), *Ancient Israelite Religion: Essays in Honor of Frank Moore Cross* (Philadelphia: Fortress Press, 1987), pp. 397-420.

domestic and community ritual events. Some may have been connected with female biological processes, such as the childbirth and
child naming that appear at the end of the Ruth story, and may have
excluded males. But most events centering on the life cycle events,
such as marriage and death, would have been gender-inclusive family
or 'neighborhood' events. Groups of village women probably developed traditions of sacral behaviors for which they, not the men, were
experts. Women's roles in creating feasts, in maintaining shrines or
tombs of ancestors, and in making and paying vows are widely
attested aspects of women's religious practice.[37] From the perspective
of agricultural village women rather than that of male urban priests,
women's ritual behaviors are extraordinarily meaningful in sacral-
izing their lives and in helping them feel that they are contributing to
the well-being of their families and their community.

Clearly, the corporate behavior of Israelite women in their residential communities represents an area of activity that transcended their
domiciles and that contributed to the welfare of the larger settlement
in which they resided. Although they maintained their ties with their
natal villages, for those ties facilitated the mutual interests of Israelite
villages sharing a larger territorial setting, most of the productive
lives of Israelite women were lived in their marital communities. It
was within those villages that their participation in informal networks
constituted a vital aspect of their daily lives and of the community's
well-being.

4. *Discussion: Women's Groups and Women's Lives*

The focus on the jural-political sphere in Western historiography has
meant, until recently, that men were the main actors in reconstructions of past times. The role of roughly half the population—women—
in the production of both subsistence goods and cultural forms was
minimized or ignored. The second wave of American feminism,
emerging from the civil rights movement of the 1960s, brought about
important changes in the goals and methods of historical research.
Women began to be visible as significant members of the societies in
which they lived—not only by occasionally appearing as political or
religious leaders or as performers or creative artists along with the
plethora of males in public life, but also as persons whose efforts in

---

37. See, e.g., S.S. Sered's sensitive study of Jewish women from Kurdistan and
the Yemen: *Women as Ritual Experts: The Religious Lives of Elderly Jewish Women in
Jerusalem* (New York: Oxford University Press, 1992).

the domestic economy and in informal social networking had a profound and pervasive impact on the course of community life.[38] In short, women were becoming visible on the broad landscape of human history.

It has taken some time for a similar shift to occur with respect to the emphasis on the public jural-political domain that dominates the Hebrew Bible.[39] The relative invisibility of women in the biblical text has led feminist as well as sexist commentators to minimize the informal aspects of community life in general and to ignore women's relationships across families and villages in particular.[40] This study is an attempt to redress the imbalance caused by the exaggeration of the importance of formal or public life in both the biblical text and the interpretive tradition. Considering scattered biblical references together with ethnographic data has brought visibility to women's informal networks in ancient Israel. It remains for the social dynamics of such groups to be examined.

The informal associations of village women in ancient Israel, as well as their links with women in other settlements, represent a more diffuse and thus more elusive form of female power than that of women in formal or professional groups (i.e. musicians, mourning women and others).[41] Yet these women's groups were no less real and

38. A landmark publication marking the shift from political history to a more inclusive social history is R. Bridenthal and C. Koontz (eds.), *Becoming Visible: Women in European History* (Boston: Houghton Mifflin, 1977). This volume, which includes prehistoric, North African and Near Eastern societies as well as historical European ones, was completely revised in a second 1987 edition.

39. Ironically, the chapter in *Becoming Visible* that includes a discussion of ancient Israel fails to step out of the androcentric perspective of the Bible in its discussion of women in Israelite society. The author (B. Lesko) of 'Women of Egypt and the Ancient Near East' is thus misguided in her claims (p. 73) that 'men controlled the religious life of the community', that women were 'economically and socially' subordinate to men, and that the general female population had 'little space for creative self-development' with their 'singular contribution' being the reproductive one.

40. For example, P. Bird recently (in 'Women [Old Testament]', *ABD*, VI, pp. 951-57 [955]) asserted that women's roles 'outside their households' were of two types: (1) assistance in productive agricultural tasks, and (2) specialized services. Perhaps influenced by the idea of household as the domicile itself she fails to see productive tasks as *part* of the household economy, and she misses completely the *informal* supra-household dynamics of women's associations and networks.

41. The social dynamics of formal groups, 'guilds' of female professionals, are discussed in Meyers, 'Guilds and Gatherings'.

important than were the more visible public organizations.[42] The very informality of Israelite women's networks gave them great flexibility to respond in innovative, situation-specific ways to human needs. Women's alliances in agrarian communities were hardly casual affairs with little relevance to the overall processes of social existence.[43] Though rarely recognized as such, they performed essential functions without which the economic survival and social stability of small premodern communities such as existed in ancient Israel would not have been possible.

The value of informal networks lay not only in what they provided to community life but also in what they contributed to the lives of women. As for more formal groups, hierarchies within village networks provided leadership roles for women, based variously on seniority (and wisdom), expertise (in certain household tasks) or charisma (in organizing labor or commodity exchanges). In short, the dynamics of women's gatherings expanded and enhanced women's lives; and the informal connections of women with each other across family boundaries empowered them as community members.

The solidarity of women in informal groups was not simply a psychological or social strategy of defense devised by women in vulnerable circumstances, although female solidarity can indeed provide collective female power over abusive or controlling males. More important, the quasi-autonomy of women's networks in ancient Israel would have empowered women by virtue of the positive contributions such alliances made to the overall social fabric. Women became part of the public domain by virtue of their informal linkages within communities and between communities. The accessibility of women

42. The ubiquity of informal women's networks and the way they exert effective power in their communities may actually be characteristic of female primates in general, not only of humans. Primatologists have noted that many primate groups are 'female-bonded', with the females having very close relationships with each other; see R.W. Wrangham, 'An Ecological Model of Female-Bonded Primate Groups', *Behaviour* 75 (1980), pp. 262-300. Alliances formed along both kinship and non-kinship lines provide social power to the females in primate communities; so M.F. Small, *Female Choices: Sexual Behavior of Female Primates* (Ithaca, NY: Cornell University Press, 1993), p. 144.

43. March and Taqqu, *Women's Informal Associations*, pp. 9-11. The highly significant role of women's networks in traditional societies is similar in many ways to the powerful though little-heralded role of women's voluntary associations as a distinctly American form of public life. See S.M. Evans, *Born for Liberty: A History of Women in America* (New York: Free Press; New York: Macmillan, 1989), pp. 1, 2-3; cf. C. Lambert, 'Leadership in a New Key', *Harvard Magazine* 97 (March–April 1995), pp. 30-31.

to such extra-household alliances and activities represents a little-recognized form of female power; it would have compensated for the asymmetry of gender power that otherwise seems to have prevailed in Israelite public life.

Recognizing the participation of Israelite women in informal groups means acknowledging that they led more complex and probably more interesting lives than is generally assumed. In the process of contributing to the collective family and community welfare, their daily undertakings as well as their occasional ones were replete with opportunities for self-expression and self-fulfillment.

B.

RUTH PAPERS, ORPAH PAPERS: PAPERS DELIVERED AT THE
'SEMIOTICS AND EXEGESIS' SESSION, AMERICAN SOCIETY OF
BIBLICAL LITERATURE, NOVEMBER 1997

THE SIGN OF ORPAH: READING RUTH THROUGH NATIVE EYES

Laura E. Donaldson

Prologue: Reading in the Contact Zone

This was no party
how the house was shaking.
They were trying
to nibble my bones, gnaw
my tribal tongue.
They took turns
pretending they had the power
to disembowel my soul
and force me to give them
my face to wear
for Halloween.
They like to play
that I want to change,
that I don't mind ending myself
in their holy book.
They think they can just twist till the blood has drained
and I am as white
and delightsome
as can be.

(Wendy Rose, 'The Mormons Next Door')[1]

The act of reading the Bible has been fraught with difficulty and contradiction for indigenous peoples. On the one hand, the translation of God's Book into Native vernacular comes with a high price: the forcing of oral tongues into static alphabets and its context of a colonizing Christianity. All too often, biblical reading has produced traumatic disruptions within Native societies and facilitated what we now call culturecide. On the other hand, this depressingly long history of victimization should not obscure the ways in which Native peoples have actively resisted deracinating processes by reading the Bible on

---

1.   In Wendy Rose, *Going to War with All my Relations: New and Selected Poems* (Flagstaff, AZ: Entrada Books, 1993).

their own terms.[2] As Rigoberta Menchú (Quiché Mayan) notes in her moving *testimonio*, *I, Rigoberta Menchú*:

> We accept these Biblical forefathers as if they were our own ancestors, while still keeping within our own culture and our own customs... For instance the Bible tells us that there were kings who beat Christ. We drew a parallel with our king, Tecún Umán, who was defeated and persecuted by the Spaniards, and we take that as our own reality.[3]

Whether Menchú and the Quiché Mayan people scan a printed page or learn the stories by heart, they claim the Bible's 'reality' as their own and thus exceed the bounds of imperial exegesis. A vivid example of this dynamic emerges from the way Menchú and other women of her community learned to negotiate the biblical narratives of liberation.

As Menchú remarks, the Quiché began their reading process by searching the scripture for stories representing 'each one of us'. While the men of Chimel village adopted Moses and the Exodus as their paradigm text of liberation, the women preferred the tale of Judith, who 'fought very hard for her people and made many attacks against the king they had then, until she finally had his head'.[4] Here, the distinct hermeneutic tradition of Mayan women begins to emerge— one that does not indoctrinate the reader with the colonizer's values but, rather, helps them understand and respond to their own historical situation (in this case, the brutal war being waged against them by the Guatemalan regime of García Lucas). Menchú rejects the belief that the Bible, or the tale of Judith and Holofernes, themselves effect change: 'It's more that each one of us learns to understand his reality and wants to devote himself to others. More than anything else, it was a form of learning for us.'[5] Through this statement, she articulates a process of reading practiced by many of the world's Native peoples— a process that actively selects and invents, rather than passively accepts, from the literate materials exported to them by the dominant Euro-Spanish culture. For Menchú, this transculturation of meaning emerges from the act of biblical reading in the contact zone.

In her book *Imperial Eyes: Travel Writing and Transculturation*, Mary Louise Pratt defines a contact zone as the space of colonial encounters

---

2.   'Deracination' comes from the Latin word meaning 'to uproot or to alienate'.

3.   Rigoberta Menchú, *I, Rigoberta Menchú: An Indian Woman in Guatemala* (ed. E. Burgos-Debray; trans. A. Wright; London: Verso, 1984), p. 80.

4.   Menchú, *I, Rigoberta Menchú*, p. 131.

5.   Menchú, *I, Rigoberta Menchú*, p. 135.

where people who are divided both geographically and historically come into contact with each other and establish ongoing relations, usually involving conditions of severe inequality and intractable conflict.[6] She coins this term, instead of borrowing the more Eurocentric 'colonial frontier', because she wants 'to foreground the interactive, improvisational dimensions of colonial encounters so easily ignored or suppressed by diffusionist accounts of conquest and domination'.[7] For Pratt, a 'contact' perspective treats the bonds among colonizers and colonized (for example, Quiché and *Ladinos*) as implying co-presence, mutual influence and interlocking understandings that emerge from deep asymmetries of power. In this essay I will read the biblical book of Ruth through just such a contact perspective forged by the interaction of biblical narrative, the realities of Anglo-European imperialism and the traditions of Cherokee women. This re-reading is marked not only by the colonial history of Indian–white relations but also by the persistence of American Indian traditions; not only by Anglo-European genocide but also by Native 'survivance';[8] not only by subjugation but also by resistance.

Scholars have traditionally regarded the book of Ruth as one of the Hebrew Bible's literary jewels: 'a brief moment of serenity in the stormy world'.[9] According to Herman Gunkel, for example, Ruth represents one of those 'glorious *poetical narratives*' that exhibits 'a widow's love lasting beyond death and the grave'.[10] Feminist biblical critics have persuasively challenged this view by exposing its masculinist and heterosexist bias. For these interpreters, Ruth's love embodies the love of a woman-identified woman who is forced into the patriarchal institution of levirate marriage in order to survive. It is here—with this struggle over the meaning of women in the text—that I wish to begin my own articulation of the difficult and often dangerous terrain charted by the contact zone. Like Menchú, I hope that my reading of Ruth will function as a form of learning that will enable

6.   Mary Louise Pratt, *Imperial Eyes: Travel Writing and Transculturation* (London: Routledge, 1992), p. 6.

7.   Pratt, *Imperial Eyes*, p. 7.

8.   The term 'survivance' is used by Gerald Vizenor (Chippewa) to describe the complicated gestures of Native survival in the contact zone of contemporary American culture.

9.   Danna Nolan Fewell and David M. Gunn, *Compromising Redemption: Relating Characters in the Book of Ruth* (Louisville, KY: Westminster/John Knox Press, 1990), p. 11.

10.   H. Gunkel, *What Remains of the Old Testament, and Other Essays* (trans. A.K. Dallas; New York: Macmillan, 1928), p. 21.

Native people both to understand more thoroughly how biblical interpretation has impacted us, and to assert our own perspectives more strongly. It seems fitting, then, that this journey begin with a crisis: the journey of Naomi and her husband Elimelech into Moab, the scandalous country of Lot's daughters.

The Daughters of Lot

> Thus both daughters of Lot became pregnant by their father. The first-born bore a son, and named him Moab; he is the ancestor of the Moabites to this day (Gen. 19.36-37, NRSV).

> While Israel was staying at Shittim, the people began to have sexual relations with the women of Moab. These invited the people to the sacrifices of their gods, and the people ate and bowed down to their gods. Thus Israel yoked itself to the Baal of Peor, and the Lord's anger was kindled against Israel (Num. 25.1-3, NRSV).

There was a famine in the house of bread—the literal meaning of the name 'Bethlehem'—and only the threat of starvation motivated Elimelech, a god-fearing Israelite, to forsake his home for the country harboring the sexually promiscuous and scandalous Moabites. Even worse, once he and his family arrive there, their two sons defy the Hebrew proscription against foreign marriage by taking the Moabite women Orpah and Ruth as wives. Indeed, for centuries the Israelites had reviled this people as degenerate and, particularly, regarded Moabite women as the agents of impurity and evil. Even the name 'Moab' exhibits this contempt, since it allegedly originates in the incestuous liaison between Lot and his daughters. According to the biblical narrative in Genesis 19, Lot's daughters devise a plan to get him drunk on succeeding nights so that they can seduce him. Both women become pregnant through this relationship and both have sons. Lot's eldest daughter openly declares her son's origins when she calls him Moab, or 'from my father'. We glimpse the result of their actions in Deuteronomy which declares that, even to the tenth generation, 'no Ammonite or Moabite shall be admitted to the assembly of the Lord' (Deut. 23.3).

As Randall Bailey notes in his fascinating essay on sex and sexuality in Hebrew canon narratives,

> the effect of both the narrative in Genesis 19 and the laws in Deuteronomy 23…is to label within the consciousness of the reader the view of these nations as nothing more than 'incestuous bastards'. Through

the use of repetition in the narrative in Genesis 19…the narrator grinds
home the notion of *mamzērîm* [bastards].[11]

Further, according to Bailey, this dehumanization through graphic
sexual innuendo enables one to read other parts of the Deuteronomic
history—David's mass slaughter of the Moabites in 2 Sam. 8.2 or the
ritual humiliation of the Ammonites in 2 Sam. 12.26-31—as warranted
and even meritorious.[12]

The belief in Moabite women as a hypersexualized threat to Israelite men prophetically augurs the Christian attitude toward the indigenous women of the Americas. Indeed, as early as 1511, an anonymous
Dutch pamphleteer vouched that 'these folke lyven lyke bestes without any reasonablenes… And the wymen be very hoote and dysposed
to lecherdnes.'[13] Significantly (and, I would add, symptomatically), no
less a personage than Thomas Jefferson, the second President of the
United States and a framer of its Constitution, forges an important
link between the Israelite attitude toward the Moabites and the
Christian attitude toward American Indians in his own discourse on
the book of Ruth. After finishing his *Notes on the State of Virginia*
(1787)[14]—one of the most important influences upon Euramerican
attitudes toward Native peoples—Jefferson submitted the manuscript
for comments to Charles Thomson, then Secretary of Congress. Thomson's remarks were included in the published version because, as
Jefferson enthused, 'the following observations…have too much merit
not to be communicated'. In his response to the section that describes
the nation's 'Aborigines', Thomson observes that an alleged lack of
'ardor' in Indian men most probably originated in the forwardness of
their women:

> Instances similar to that of Ruth and Boaz are not uncommon among
> them. For though the women are modest and diffident, and so bashful
> that they seldom lift up their eyes, and scarce ever look a man full in the
> face, yet being brought up on great subjection, custom and manners

11. Randall Bailey, 'They're Nothing but Incestuous Bastards: The Polemical
Use of Sex and Sexuality in Hebrew Canon Narratives', in Fernando F. Segovia
and Mary Ann Tolbert (eds.), *Reading from This Place*. I. *Social Location and Biblical
Interpretation in the United States* (Philadelphia: Fortress Press, 1995), pp. 121-38
(131).

12. Bailey, 'They're Nothing', p. 132.

13. As cited in Robert F. Berkhofer, Jr, *The White Man's Indian: Images of the
American Indian from Columbus to the Present* (New York: Random House, 1978),
p. 10.

14. T. Jefferson, *Notes on the State of Virginia* (ed. William Peden; New York:
W.W. Norton, 1982).

reconcile them to modes of acting, which, judged of by Europeans, would be deemed inconsistent with the rules of female decorum and propriety.[15]

Jefferson endorses Thomson's remarks by locating the relevant biblical passage: 'When Boaz had eaten and drank, and his heart was merry, he went to lie down at the end of the heap of corn: and Ruth came softly, and uncovered his feet, and laid her down. Ruth iii.7'.[16] Although cloaked in the rhetoric of Enlightenment gentility, the statements by Thomson and Jefferson nevertheless disseminate a cautionary tale that is quite similar to the one concerning the Moabites: both American Indian and Moabite women exist as agents not only of evil and impurity but also of men's sexual frigidity. Given such negative representations, we need to investigate why the biblical author of Ruth chooses to foreground precisely this ideological nexus by consistently identifying the protagonist as 'Ruth of Moab'.

Ruth 2.6 provides an insightful glimpse into this process. After Elimelech and his two sons die, Naomi and Ruth return to Bethlehem. Naomi subsequently, and recklessly according to some critics, sends her daughter-in-law into the fields of Boaz, a relative of her late husband, who notices the young widow and asks his servant to whom she belongs. 'The servant who was in charge of the reapers answered, "she is the Moabite who came back with Naomi from the country of Moab".' The redundant doubling of ethnic markers in this passage—the Moabite from the country of Moab—emphasizes the text's construction of Ruth not only as a *gērāh*, or resident alien, but also as an alien who comes from a despised and barbaric country. However, the significance of this particular repetition has been construed in widely variant ways.

For example, the rabbis who wrote *Ruth Rabbah* believe that it reinforces Ruth's role as a paradigmatic convert to Judaism who 'turned her back upon wicked Moab and its worthless idols to become a God-fearing Jewess—loyal daughter-in-law, modest bride, renowned ancestress of Israel's great King David'.[17] The *Iggereth Shmuel* expands this view and suggests that the quality of Ruth's faith even surpasses that of Abraham since, unlike Ruth, he only left home after God

15. Jefferson, *Notes*, p. 201.

16. Jefferson, *Notes*, p. 297. Since in Hebrew 'feet' is often used as a euphemism for a man's genitals, Ruth is clearly initiating some sort of sexual encounter with Boaz.

17. Kathryn Pfisterer Darr, *Far More Precious than Jewels: Perspectives on Biblical Women* (Louisville, KY: Westminster/John Knox Press, 1991), p. 72.

commanded him to do so.[18] For more contemporary critics the message of Ruth's identity is not one of conversion, but rather of 'interethnic bonding' that parallels the gender bond established when Naomi's daughter-in-law 'clings' to her husband's mother instead of returning home.[19] William Phipps articulates this position when he argues that the repetition of 'Ruth the Moabite' connotes 'vital religion and ethics in a time of bigotry and mayhem',[20] and acts as an antidote to the xenophobia of the postexilic Jewish community. Rather than rejection of the Moabites and acceptance of the Israelites, then, Ruth's story conjures a vision of ethnic and cultural harmony through the house of David, which claims her as a direct ancestress.

While the presentation of Ruth as a character manifesting the virtues of tolerance and multiculturalism is appealing, Robert Maldonado's attempt to develop a *malinchista* hermeneutics[21] complicates this view by exposing its political and historical ambiguities. For Maldonado, a theologian of Mexican and Hungarian descent, the biblical figure of Ruth foreshadows the existence of *La Malinche*, or Doña Marina, the Aztec woman who became a consort of, and collaborator with, the conquistador Hernán Cortés. *La Malinche*'s legacy endures not only in historical Mexican consciousness but also in its linguistic vernacular: '*Malinchista* is a common term for a person who adopts foreign values, assimilates to foreign cultures, or serves foreign interests... The usage ties the meaning of betrayal in Mexican Spanish to the history of colonialism and Indian White relations...'[22] Yet *La Malinche* harbors deeper and even more personal levels of betrayal, since she was sold as a young girl to some Mayan traders—an experience that generated the bilingualism so crucial to her equivocal

18. Darr, *Far More Precious*, p. 72.

19. The verb 'to cling' is particularly revealing here, since its customary usage involves the relationships of husbands to wives and of humans to Yahweh. Both womanist and feminist critics have used this linguistic turn to argue for Ruth's status as a woman-identified woman. Or, a woman who embodied the capacity 'to care passionately about the quality of another woman's life, to respect each other's choices, and to allow for each other's differences' (Renita Weems, *Just a Sister Away: A Womanist Vision of Women's Relationships in the Bible* [San Diego: Lura Media, 1988], p. 34).

20. William E. Phipps, *Assertive Biblical Women* (Contributions in Women's Studies, 128; Westport, CT: Greenwood Press, 1992), p. 67.

21. R. Maldonado, 'Reading Malinche Reading Ruth: Toward a Hermeneutics of Betrayal', *Semeia* 72 (1995), pp. 91-109.

22. Mary Louise Pratt, '"Yo soy la malinche": Chicana Writers and the Poetics of Ethnonationalism', *Callaloo* 16 (1993), pp. 859-73 (860); as cited in Maldonado, 'Reading Malinche', p. 99.

status. After she had been acquired by Cortés she was 'given' to one of his officers and subsequently married to another conquistador. We begin to glimpse at least some of the complex and disturbing elements underpinning *La Malinche*'s collaboration with her colonizers. The similarities between the story of Doña Marina and the actions of Ruth lead Maldonado provocatively to ask: 'Could Ruth be a Moabite Malinche'?[23] Maldonado answers his own question with a strong 'maybe'—precisely because of the redundant identification of Ruth described above as well as his own investment in *mestizaje*, or the resistant discourse of racial and cultural mixing.

American Indians have a much more suspicious attitude toward the privileging of mixedness, be it *mestizaje*, *métissage* or life in the border-lands. After all, 'mixing' is precisely what Thomas Jefferson proposed as the final solution to the seemingly irresolvable 'Indian problem'. To a visiting delegation of Wyandots, Chippewas and Shawnees he confidently predicted that 'in time, you will be as we are; you will become one people with us. Your blood will mix with ours; and will spread, with ours, over this great island.'[24] And what better way to accomplish this commingling than with the paradigm of intermarriage that we glimpse in the book of Ruth? Indeed, one could argue that this 'moment of serenity in the stormy world of the Hebrew Bible' exists as the prototype for both the vision of Thomas Jefferson and all those who facilitated conquest of indigenous peoples through the promotion of assimilation.

This social absorption prophetically evokes the fate of many American Indian women and children. In the historically matrilineal Cherokee culture, for example, Jefferson's vision of 'mingling' and the realities of intermarriage wreaked havoc upon tribal organization and development. Wives now went to live with their white husbands—a practice that was contrary to the ancient custom of husbands residing in their wives' domiciles. Further, according to Wilma Mankiller (the former Principal Chief of the Cherokee Nation), the children of these relationships assumed their fathers' surnames and became heirs to their father's, rather than their mother's, houses and possessions.[25] Intermarriage between whites and Indians severely disrupted the traditions of Cherokee women, since a genealogy that had for time

---

23. Maldonado, 'Reading Malinche', p. 101.

24. T. Jefferson, *The Writings of Thomas Jefferson* (ed. A.E. Bergh; Washington, DC: Thomas Jefferson Memorial Association of the United States, 1907), p. 464.

25. Wilma Mankiller with Michael Wallis, *Mankiller: A Chief and her People* (New York: St Martin's Press, 1984), p. 26.

immemorial passed from mother to son or daughter now shifted to the father and drastically curtailed women's power. In contrast to Maldonado, I would argue that the book of Ruth similarly foregrounds the use of intermarriage as an assimilationist strategy.

Soon after Ruth marries Boaz, the text states that she conceives and bears a son.

> Then Naomi took the child and laid him in her bosom, and became his nurse. The women of the neighborhood gave him a name saying, 'A son has been born to Naomi'. They named him Obed; he became the father of Jesse, the father of David (4.13-17).

As Danna Nolan Fewell and David Gunn note, through this announcement Ruth effectively disappears into the household of Boaz, and the legacy of the future king David closes the door upon her story.[26] In other words—although Fewell and Gunn do not use these terms—Ruth's assimilation becomes complete through Obed's transfer to Naomi, the proper Jewish woman, and to Boaz, the Israelite husband. The issue then becomes, What motivates this effacement and what ideological ends does it fulfill?

Even to begin answering this question, however, we must first understand how Ruth is linked to two seemingly disparate female icons—one from the Hebrew Bible and the other from the annals of American Indian history: Raḥab and Pocahontas. Both of these women have played important roles in the construction of national narratives and both, like *La Malinche*, have been mythologized as facilitating conquest through their relationships with colonizing men.

The Anti-Pocahontas Perspex

> You made a decision. My place is with you. I go where you go.
> (Stands With A Fist to John Dunbar in *Dances with Wolves*)

Raḥab, of course, is Ruth's other mother-in-law and the Canaanite prostitute who gave birth to Boaz (see Mt. 1.5). The events leading to this remarkable transformation of status are memorialized in the book of Joshua, ch. 2, and can be briefly summarized as follows. Joshua, who was leading the Israelite invasion of Canaan, sends two spies to reconnoiter the city of Jericho. These two men 'entered the house of a prostitute whose name was Raḥab and spent the night there' (2.1). When the king of Jericho hears of the spies' presence, he orders Raḥab to surrender them. She refuses and hides them under stalks of flax

---

26. Fewell and Gunn, *Compromising Redemption*, p. 105.

that she had laid out on the roof. After nightfall she visits the men and requests that, since she has dealt kindly with them, they might in turn spare her and her family 'and deliver our lives from death'. Jericho does indeed fall: 'But Raḥab the prostitute, with her family and all who belonged to her, Joshua spared. Her family has lived in Israel ever since' (Josh. 6.25). Further, she is extolled in the Greek Bible as a paragon of faith and granted a high status as the ancestress of David and Jesus. Like her daughter-in-law Ruth, Raḥab embodies a foreign woman, a Canaanite Other who crosses over from paganism to monotheism and is rewarded for this act by absorption into the genealogy of her husband and son—in this case, into the house of Salmon and, ultimately, of David. And, like Ruth, she represents the position of the indigene in the text, or of those people who occupied the promised land before the invasion of the Israelites.

However, the narrative figures of Raḥab and Ruth conjure not only the position of the indigene in the biblical text but also the specific cultural and historical predicament of American Indian women. Cherokee scholar Rayna Green has identified this predicament as 'the Pocahontas Perplex'—one of Euramerica's most important master narratives about Native women. It is named for the daughter of Powhatan and the mythology that has arisen around one of the most culturally significant encounters between Indians and whites. In this version of the story Powhatan Indians capture Captain John Smith and his men while they are exploring the territory around what is now called Jamestown, Virginia. After marching Smith to their town, the Indians lay his head on a large stone and prepare to kill him with their clubs. Precisely at that moment, Pocahontas—the favorite daughter of Powhatan—uses her body as a human shield and prevents Smith from being executed. She then further intercedes on behalf of the English colonists, who were starving after a long winter, and consequently saves not only the colonists but also the future of English colonization.[27]

---

27. While most Americans still believe in the myth that Pocahontas loved John Smith, a growing body of scholarship has significantly revised this tale of their encounter. Rayna Green and Kathleen Brown are among those who have persuasively argued that Smith's own account of his captivity, near-execution and rescue by Pocahontas eloquently testifies to yet another example of misrecognized and misinterpreted cultural difference. Brown, for example, contends that Smith's recording of Pocahontas covering his body with her own was most probably part of an adoption ritual in which Powhatan defined his relationship to him as one of patriarchal dominance ('The Anglo-Algonquian Gender Frontier', in Nancy Shoemaker [ed.], *Negotiators of Change: Historical Perspectives on American Indian Women*

As a master narrative with an ideological function, the Pocahontas Perplex construes the nobility of Pocahontas and other Indian women as a 'princess' who

> 'must save or give aid to white men'. As Green notes, 'the only good Indian—male or female, Squanto, Pocahontas, Sacagawea, Cochise, the Little Mohee or the Indian Doctor—rescues and helps white men'. But the Indian woman is even more burdened by this narrow definition of a 'good Indian', for it is she, not the males, whom white men desire sexually.[28]

A consequence of this desire is that the 'good' feminine image also implies the 'bad' one. She is the Squaw whose degraded sexuality is vividly summarized in the frontier song 'Little Red Wing': She 'lays on her back in a cowboy shack, and lets cowboys poke her in the crack'.[29] The specter of the Squaw—also known as a daughter of Lot—retroactively taints Raḥab and Ruth; after all, the former earns her living as a prostitute and, according to Thomas Jefferson and company, the latter's behavior in the biblical counterpart of the cowboy shack was shockingly immoral. Such a debased starting point enables the scriptural stories to proclaim even more stridently the metamorphosis of Raḥab and Ruth into the Israelite version of the Pocahontas Perplex. In this scenario, Salmon and Boaz stand in for John Smith. The result, however, remains the same. An indigenous woman forsakes her people and aligns herself with the men whom Yahweh had directed to 'break down their altars, smash their pillars, burn their Asherah poles with fires, and hew down the idols of their gods, and thus blot out their name from their places' (Deut. 12.3).

From an American Indian perspective, then, the midrashic interpretation of Ruth as the paradigmatic convert who 'turned her back upon wicked Moab and its worthless idols to become a God-fearing

[London: Routledge, 1995], pp. 26-48 [39]). Unfortunately, 'Smith understood neither the ritual adoption taking place nor the significance of Powhatan's promise to make him a werowance and to "for ever esteeme him as [he did] his son Nantaquoud"' (p. 40). Green (in 'The Pocahontas Perplex: The Image of Indian Women in American Culture', *Massachusetts Review* [autumn 1975], pp. 698-714) provides a further gloss. She notes that, as the daughter of the tribe's leader and a woman of considerable status, Pocahontas served as Smith's 'mother', for he had to be reborn, after a symbolic death, as one of the tribe. Thus, Pocahontas was not delaying Smith's execution and thwarting her own people when she threw her body over his. She was in fact acting on behalf of her people (p. 35).

28. Green, 'The Pocahontas Perplex', p. 703.
29. Green, 'The Pocahontas Perplex', p. 711.

Jewess'[30] seems a much more accurate description of the text's actual function than Robert Maldonado's appeal to some undecidable state of *mestizaje*. Indeed, even Ruth's name affirms the hermeneutic acumen of the rabbis, since it derives from the Hebrew root *rwh*, meaning 'watering to saturation'.[31] However, whereas the success of this ideological irrigation inspires rejoicing on behalf of the Israelites, it is an instance of mourning for American Indian women. Yet another relative has succumbed to—been filled up by and 'saturated' by—a hegemonic culture.

Is there no hope in the book of Ruth? Is it nothing but a tale of conversion/assimilation and the inevitable vanishing of the indigene in the literary and social text? In fact, there does exist a counter-narrative—a kind of anti-Pocahontas—whose presence offers some small hope to the Native reader: the sign of Orpah, sister-in-law of Ruth and the woman who returned to her mother's house.

'They broke once more into loud weeping. But while Orpah kissed her mother-in-law goodbye, Ruth clung to her' (Ruth 1.14, translation by Sasson). The figure of Orpah is only mentioned twice in the book of Ruth—1.4, which names her as one of the 'Moabite wives', and 1.14, which describes her decision to part ways with Naomi and Ruth. Unfortunately, however, most contemporary scholars mimic the biblical text by leaving her to return home unattended, both literally and critically. Traditionally, Orpah generated much more scrutiny, although much of it was negative. According to midrashic literature, for example, her name allegorically connotes the opposite of Ruth's, since it originates in the root '*orep* that is, the nape of the neck, and describes how she turns the back of her neck to Naomi when she decides to return to Moab. 'That the sages name Orpah for this moment in her history indicates that they also consider it the most important part of her story'[32]—and it explicitly charges her with the ⟩

---

30. Darr, *Far More Precious*, p. 72.

31. In *The Feminine Unconventional: Four Subversive Figures in Israel's Tradition* (Minneapolis: Fortress Press, 1990), Andre LaCocque observes that most biblical exegetes 'stubbornly propose' the Syriac translation of 'Ruth' as an abbreviation of *Re'uth*, or female companion. Like other scholars who have carefully studied the book of Ruth, LaCocque persuasively argues that, philologically, the name 'Ruth' has nothing to do with *r'h* (to be a companion), but rather is a cognate of *rwh* (to water to saturation). See his discussion, pp. 115-16.

32. Leila Leah Bronner, 'A Thematic Approach to Ruth in Rabbinic Literature', in A. Brenner (ed.), *A Feminist Companion to Ruth* (Feminist Companion to the Bible, 3; Sheffield: Sheffield Academic Press, 1993), pp. 146-69 (155).

narrative role of abandoner.[33] Some writers even suggest that she later becomes the mother of Goliath, the famous enemy of Israel, and that Goliath himself was 'the son of a hundred fathers'.[34] But what else could one expect from a 'daughter of Lot?'

William Phipps expresses a more current and enlightened view of Ruth's sister-in-law:

> Orpah displays wrenching ambivalence, deciding first one way and then another. She finally takes Naomi's common-sense advice and, after an affectionate goodbye, returns 'to her people and to her gods'. Her life is difficult enough without taking responsibility for an older widow in a land presumed to be governed by a deity different from the ones she worships (the Moabite Stone refers to Chemosh and to goddess Ashtar, or Ishtar)... She does the prudent thing and heads for her family home to await an arranged remarriage.[35]

While I do not disagree with Phipps's summary, I also believe that he fails to recognize what is perhaps the most important element of Orpah's decision. She does not just take the path of least resistance— the path of prudence, freedom from responsibility and passivity. Rather, Orpah returns to *bêt 'immāh*, 'her mother's house'.[36] Carol Meyers observes that the use of *bêt 'êm* is quite rare in the Hebrew Bible and indicates a family setting identified with the mother rather than the father.[37] In fact, she notes, each biblical passage using this phrase shares a similarity with all the others: a woman's story is being told; women act as agents in their own destiny; the agency of women affects other characters in the narrative; the setting is domestic; and finally, a marriage is involved.[38] Meyers further concludes that all biblical references to 'the mother's house' offer female perspectives on issues that elsewhere in the Bible are viewed through a predominately androcentric lens. I would argue that the female perspective offered by 'the mother's house' in Ruth is a profoundly important one for Native women, since it signifies that Orpah—the one whose sign is the back of her neck—exists as the story's central character.

---

33. M. Bal, *Lethal Love: Feminist Literary Readings of Biblical Love Stories* (Bloomington: Indiana University Press, 1987), p. 74.

34. Bronner, 'Thematic Approach', p. 155.

35. Phipps, *Assertive Biblical Women*, p. 53.

36. 'But Naomi said to her two daughters-in-law, "Go back each of you to your mother's house"' (Ruth 1.8).

37. Carol Meyers, 'Returning Home: Ruth 1.8 and the Gendering of the Book of Ruth', in Brenner (ed.), *A Feminist Companion to Ruth* (Feminist Companion to the Bible, 3; Sheffield: Sheffield Academic Press, 1993), pp. 85-114 (91).

38. Meyers, 'Returning Home', pp. 109-110.

To Cherokee women, for example, Orpah connotes hope rather than perversity, because she is the one who does not reject her traditions or her sacred ancestors. Like Cherokee women have done for hundreds if not thousands of years, Orpah chooses the house of her clan and spiritual mother over the desire for another culture. In fact, Cherokee women not only chose the mother's house, they also owned it (along with the property upon which it stood as well as the gardens surrounding it). Husbands customarily went to live with their wives; the woman's family, rather than the husband's, became the primary caretakers of any children. Read through these eyes, the book of Ruth tells a very different story indeed.

Ojibway poet Kimberly Blaeser illuminates this transformative process of reading through a concept she describes as 'response-ability'. In her essay, 'Pagans Rewriting the Bible', Blaeser defines response-ability as the need of American Indian people to 'reconsider, reevaluate, reimagine what [religious] terms might mean or have meant to Indian people as well as what they might come to mean to all people'.[39] This is precisely what Rigoberta Menchú accomplishes in her choosing of Judith over Moses and in her insistence that the meaning of any biblical text reflect her people's reality. It is also what I have tried to effect in my own re-reading of Ruth through a Native perspective and, more particularly, through the perspective of Cherokee women. I have reconsidered the dominant exegesis of Ruth as either a paradigm of conversion or a woman-identified woman. I have reimagined this literary jewel of the Hebrew Bible as the narrative equivalent of a last arrow pageant.

During the implementation of the Dawes Act,[40] the 'last-arrow pageant' was a public ritual that marked the translation of American Indian identity into its more 'civilized' white counterpart. Etymologically, the word 'translation' means 'carried from one place to another', or transported across the borders between one language and another,

---

39. Kimberly M. Blaeser, 'Pagans Rewriting the Bible: Heterodoxy and the Representation of Spirituality in Native American Literature', *Review of International English Literature* 25.1 (1994), pp. 12-31 (13).

40. Passed in 1887 and named for its sponsor, Massachusetts senator Henry L. Dawes, the Dawes Act attempted to detribalize American Indians by privatizing communally held Indian lands and partitioning reservations into 160- and 80-acre lots subject to sale or lease by the government. Between 1887 and its end in 1934, the Dawes Act reduced the total land base of American Indian peoples by two-thirds.

one country and another, one culture and another.[41] In the context of last-arrow pageants, participants performed and acknowledged their own translation into the idiom of Euramerican culture:

> This conversion of Indians into individual landowners was ceremonialized at 'last-arrow' pageants. On these occasions, the Indians were ordered by the governments to attend a large assembly on the reservation. Dressed in traditional costume and carrying a bow and arrow, each Indian was individually summoned from a tepee and told to shoot an arrow. He then retreated to the tepee and re-emerged wearing 'civilized' clothing, symbolizing a crossing from the primitive to the modern world. Standing before a plow, the Indian was told: 'Take the handle of this plow, this act means that you have chosen to live the life of the white man—and the white man lives by work.' At the close of the ceremony, each allottee was given an American flag and a purse with the instructions: 'This purse will always say to you that the money you gain from your labor must be wisely kept.'[42]

For 'Ruth the Moabite', the translation from savagery to civilization (or from Asherah to Yahweh) similarly involves the relinquishing of her ethnic and cultural identity. For Orpah, it necessitates a courageous act of self and communal affirmation: the choosing of the indigenous mother's house over that of the alien Israelite Father.

In this interpretation, my response-ability as a person of Cherokee descent and as an informed biblical reader transforms Ruth's positive value into a negative and Orpah's negative value into a positive. Such is the epistemological vertigo inspired by reading in the contact zone. Indeed, paraphrasing Blaeser, response-ability recognizes that life—or meaning in the book of Ruth—cannot be for easy consumption. Chinese feminist theologian Kwok Pui Lan echoes a similar sentiment in her statement that 'these attempts at indigenization [of the Bible] show clearly that biblical truth cannot be pre-packaged, that it must be found in the actual interaction between text and context in the concrete historical situation'.[43] I can only hope that my indigenization of Ruth has located new meaning in the interaction between biblical text and American Indian context—a meaning that resists imperial exegesis and contributes to the empowerment of aboriginal peoples everywhere.

---

41. J. Hillis Miller, *Topographies: Crossing Aesthetics* (Stanford, CA: Stanford University Press, 1995), p. 316.

42. Ronald Takaki, *A Different Mirror: A History of Multicultural America* (Boston: Little, Brown & Co., 1993), pp. 235-36.

43. Kwok Pui Lan, *Discovering the Bible in the Non-Biblical World: The Bible and Liberation* (Maryknoll, NY: Orbis Books, 1995), p. 11.

THE UNPUBLISHED LETTERS OF ORPAH TO RUTH

Musa W. Dube

How I Came to Find Orpah's Letters to Ruth

We were sitting outside, around the fire, during the night. We were discussing many world events as they appear on TV, in newspapers and books. The lively discussion concerned the image of Africa in these sources. Young Lesedi had just returned from abroad. Lesedi explained why she returned, in spite of the fact that her school had offered her an attractive scholarship to pursue anthropology to the highest level. In her words, 'I kissed my professor goodbye and returned to my homeland, for I found the humanity of African people portrayed in less than human terms. In anthropological books African people, and other non-Western or non-Christian people, were described as savage, childish, lazy and sexually immoral. I just could not read anthropology anymore without insulting myself and all my people. That is why I quit my degree and returned to my mother's house here in Botswana, to my Gods.'

'But you know it does not stand for us', said Grandmother. 'Our people have always been strong, disciplined, hard working and wise in their thinking. Long before the white people sold us their dresses, their schools and their religions, we wore short skirts and plenty of jewels. Young men wore very short, tight leather shorts around their loins; yet rape, incest, sex outside marriage, teenage pregnancy and divorce were very rare, if not unheard of. I am not saying we had a perfect world then. But we had a world, our world. Now that we are all Western dressed, Christianized and educated, sexual and sins of all kinds have befallen us. The foreign institutions that were introduced to replace our institutions were undoubtedly inadequate. The anthropologist who writes these terrible things that you mention, my daughter, should tell our story well: a story of wise, kind, strong, responsible and disciplined people.'

There was quiet following the authoritative voice of Grandmother. She is well over a century and her head is as white as cake flour.

'But, Grandmother, why should anyone wish to characterize a

whole people and their lands in a totally negative light?' persisted Lesedi.

'Lesedi, Grandmother has hit the tip of a cow's horn', said Kabo. 'That is, they "should tell our story well", but it is not their story. They do not know, understand or appreciate it. Besides, they wanted to sell us the story of their dresses, their education, their religion, their culture. I believe everyone must tell the beauty of their own story.'

'All my life', insisted Grandmother, 'I have not ceased to tell the beautiful stories of our people. I have recited all the poems of our heroes and heroines, poems of our origin, of our brave battles of survival in drought and in good rains. I have told stories of the intelligent Sechele, Semane, Kgama and Kgamane, Mantatis, Lobengula, Shaka, Nandi, Mbuya Nehanda, Joshua Nkomo, Seretse Kgama, Bessie Head, Kenneth Kaunda, Nelson Mandela and the like. I have written these stories in your ears and hearts.'

'Yet, Grandmother', said Kabo, 'that is just the problem. None of your beautiful stories have been written on paper and published in a book. None of these good stories are read at school. Only the derogatory stories are in the library and are read.'

'That is a role I leave to you', said Grandmother. 'I speak these stories to your hearts and ears. You must write them on paper, publish them and make the books available to all our reading kids and communities.'

'That's true. It is a role that I have taken up with all vigor', said Lesedi. 'I have returned to write our stories. I spend all my days and nights writing, but there is no publisher. There is no publisher who accepts my version of our stories. They will only take what matches the version of the anthropologists. In short, there is "no publisher".'[1]

The fire was dying down, darkness was gathering very fast around us, but the discussion was far from dying down. Many other people from history, literature, archeology, geography, travel narratives, photography and religion were beginning to tell of their struggles with the image of Africa in these disciplines. So I stood up and went inside the house to find some old newspapers to keep the fire going. I entered Lesedi's room, for I knew she is a woman of letters. She reads so much, writes so much and keeps so much material. I came upon a box in the corner of her room. 'NO PUBLISHER' was written on it in big bold letters.

---

1. For the idea of 'no publisher' see a footnote in Obery O. Hendricks, 'Guerilla Exegesis: A Post-Modern Proposal for Insurgent African-American Biblical Interpretation', *Koinonia* 7.1 (1995), pp. 1-19 (1).

I was digging for old newspapers in Lesedi's numerous unpublished writings and some related collections, when something caught
my eye. It was an article entitled 'The Unpublished Letters of Orpah
to Ruth'. I picked it up immediately, remembering that I had been
invited to write a paper on Ruth from the perspective of my own
culture. I do not like to write, since, in my culture, we do not write.
We speak, listen and hear. In my culture some write, but they have no
publisher. I do not know from where Lesedi picked these letters. Yet
the fact that these letters are among her collections attest to the fact
that Orpah is one of us: most of her stories have been written for her,
and the stories she writes end up in the 'No Publisher' box. I believe,
therefore, that these attached four letters are signed with Orature—
the culture of speaking, hearing, re/writing and finding no publisher.

The Unpublished Letters of Orpah to Ruth

To Ruth, Our Youngest Moabite Sister. From Orpah Your Eldest
Moabite Sister. I am Orpah, the one who returned to her mother's
house and to her Gods.

I am writing to tell you the story of our origin. I know you were
young when you moved into Naomi's household and you have never
heard about the origin of the Moabites. I am writing that you may
know the true story, as my mother passed it to me. I am also writing
so that your children should not grow up ignorant of the true story of
the Moabites.

Long ago our people lived in the fertile valleys of Sodom and
Gomorrah. But the fertility of these areas became their end, for their
rich soils were products of active volcanoes and earthquakes. One day
there was a big festival in the town square. There was dancing, sing-
ing and food. All the townspeople were there when a big earthquake
triggered a volcanic eruption that decimated all the people except for
Lot's family.

Lot, his eldest son, his daughter-in-law and his youngest daughter
had gone to their farm outside town early that morning to bring food
for the feast. They were carrying fruits from their farm and journeying
back to town when, suddenly, there was a big earthquake and an
explosion that sent a cloud of hot ash into the sky. Fire then erupted
from one of the oldest mountains. Lava poured down the valley and
buried the town and all its people. Lot, overcome by disbelief and
thinking of his wife, who was in the town, ran towards the town and
was immediately engulfed by the ashes and turned into a hill of salt.

Lot's children fled and sought refuge in Zoar, a small town in the southern end of the Dead Sea. There they lived and multiplied into a people called Moabites, meaning those who survived a painful disaster. This is the true story of the Moabites. And these are the words of Orpah, the one who returned to her mother's house and to her Gods.

To Ruth Our Youngest Moabite Sister. From Orpah, Your eldest Moabite Sister. I am Orpah, the one who returned to her Mother's house and to her Gods.

In this letter I am going to tell you about Naomi and Elimelech, and how they came to live in the country of Moab. It was during the strong rule of King Eglon, when the country of Moab was blessed with rain, peace and plenty, that a severe famine struck Judah. Elimelech, who had just married his young bride Naomi, left Bethlehem with others in search for food. Many of them were in distress, many were in debt, and many were quite discontented by the severe drought. Those who were with him numbered four hundred. They came to rest in the cave of Adullam. Elimelech went from the cave of Adullam to King Eglon, saying, 'Please, give some food to my young wife and our company so that we can continue with our journey until we know what God will do for us.'

King Eglon replied, 'Bring your wife and company to me, so that I may give you the best land of Moab and you may enjoy the fat of the land.' And when Elimelech brought his wife and travelling company to King Eglon, the king instructed his servants to give them bread and water. And when they had all eaten, washed their feet and rested from their long journey, the king said to his councilors, 'Elimelech, his wife and his travelling company have come before you. Their homeland has been struck by severe famine. Settle them therefore in the best part of your country. And find out if some of them are skilled keepers of livestock, and put them in charge of my livestock.'

Elimelech was a skilled husbandman and bred the best livestock for the king. Thus Elimelech came to dwell in the king's court as one of his outstanding servants. Soon after Elimelech's wife, Naomi, gave birth to two sons, Mahlon and Chilion. At about the same time, you and I were born to the king. And the king called us Orpah and Ruth. Balak was the last and only son to be born to our father.

War came upon Moab, and Elimelech went forth to fight for the country that he loved, and he died. King Eglon vowed to bring up Mahlon and Chilion as his own sons; he vowed that he would ensure that the seed of Elimelech will not die. Thus the king expressed the wish that I should marry Mahlon and you marry Chilion. Naomi continued to live in the royal court with us, as she had always done.

We all grew up together in the king's court, but before we were ready to marry the king died of old age. Our only brother Balak became the king. And you and I married the husbands that our father had chosen for us, the sons of Elimelech. These are the true words of Orpah, the one who returned to her mother's house and to her Gods.

To Ruth Our Youngest Moabite Sister. From Orpah Your Eldest Moabite Sister. I am Orpah, the one who returned to her mother's house and to her Gods.

In this letter I am going to tell you how disaster struck the house of Elimelech, indeed in our family, for we all lived in the royal court. When Balak became the king, no one knew that both Mahlon and Chilion harbored dreams about the throne of Moab. So one evening, as they reclined with King Balak, who regarded them as his own brothers, they drew swords and murdered him. They tried to escape to their rooms, first locking the door of the king's chamber behind them as they left, but some of the king's guards had witnessed the murder from behind a secret window and attacked them. Both brothers were killed.

When the deaths of the King, Mahlon and Chilion were reported to us, Naomi and all of us were struck by sorrow. Naomi decided to return to her country. At this point the king's guards had not yet disclosed what happened. You and I could only do the right thing, that is, accompany our beloved mother-in-law in her grief and old age. Indeed, Naomi was more than a mother-in-law to us; she was a mother who had brought us up and loved us. You, in particular, were Naomi's child from the time you were two years to the time when you married her son. So in the fields that morning, when you vowed to Naomi saying,

> Where you go, I will go; where you lodge, I will lodge;
> your people shall be my people, and your God my God.
> Where you die, I will die—there will I be buried.
> May the Lord do thus and so to me, and more as well, if even
> deaths parts me from you.

I knew you were doing the right thing. I would have done the same thing myself, but I took heed of Naomi's advice to go back to my mother's house. For, as much as I loved Naomi, it was wise that we should not all depart from Moab. It was important that you go and take care of Naomi, an old childless widow. It was also right that you travel with her and live with her people since, indeed, Naomi herself had done the same thing: she left her people and lived in the country of Moab.

But I had to return to my old widowed mother who, like Naomi, did not have any son or husband left. It was also right that I should return to my people and religion, for Naomi herself was returning to her people and religion. I have continued in this court, serving my mother and my country as the regent queen and priestess. I am telling you all these things because by the time you left, the guards who witnessed the murder of the king and who killed our husbands had not yet disclosed in full what had transpired that evening. These are the true words of Orpah, who returned to her mother's house and to her Gods.

To Ruth Our Youngest Moabite Sister, From Orpah Your Eldest Moabite Sister. I am Orpah, the one who returned to her mother's house and to her Gods.

I often wonder what became of you and Naomi in Bethlehem. Sometimes I wish I could see you. Did you have a safe journey? Were you well received? How are you surviving now? Did you remarry and bear daughters and sons? Or did you cleave to Naomi and Naomi only?

I married a certain priest called Balaam. He helps me to officiate in the religious duties of protecting the nation against all foreign invaders. We have a son and a daughter. The son was named Lot, after the founding father of the Moabites; the daughter was named Ruth, after you. For, in this land, you shall never be forgotten.

I know you pledged to cleave to Naomi, but I know you will always be Ruth the Moabite, for this is the only way you can be. Since you pledged to cleave unto Naomi, to go where she goes, to lodge where she lodged, to die and be buried where she died, I hope you bear children only to our beloved Naomi. And when you have borne children, you should tell them these stories of the Moabites: of their origins, of their kindness, of their hospitality and of their struggles for survival.

These are the true words of Orpah, your eldest Moabite Sister, the one who returned to her mother's house and to her Gods.

A SON IS BORN TO NAOMI: A HARVEST FOR ISRAEL

Judith E. McKinlay

The book of Ruth—that idyllic tale of love and devotion. Told by? Told to? Told for? Take these questions seriously and there is a sharpness not only in the tale/tail of Ruth but in the very body.

Imagine the storyteller beginning and the listeners settling down. Listen carefully. Do you remember *the days when the judges ruled* (1.1)? Have you been to Egypt, Gerar perhaps, with Abraham, and Isaac, and the brothers of Joseph when there was *famine in the land*? Then this is your story. But listen further: *a certain man of Bethlehem* called Elimelech is forced to flee, not to Egypt, not to Gerar, but to Moab.[1] You, as Israelite, remember a Mosaic instruction that no Moabite, even down to the tenth generation, is to be admitted to the assembly of God (Deut. 23.3). What is this storyteller up to? Ask what is an Israelite and the biblical answer is not a Moabite. But settle down again. Moab for these God-fearing, life-seeking Israelites is deathly, only a woman is left as survivor. Listen as the storyline is replayed in reverse: in the days when there was death in the land of Moab, a woman sets out, but now to Bethlehem, where there will be bread from God for God's people. And for Moabite daughters-in-law?! Can they be included? But Naomi attempts to dissuade them. The phrase *mother's house* (1.8) points to the crux of the matter; these are not Naomi's daughters, these women have Moabite mothers. One Moabite listens, weeps, kisses Naomi and leaves the narrative; the other weeps but clings, and edges forward into the storyline. Naomi the Israelite now names the hurdle, which is not only kinship but a matter of the divine. *Your sister-in-law has gone back to her people and to her gods* (1.15). Can a Moabite Ruth enter this Israelite story with integrity? That is the question. The audience waits—will they be reassured by her speech, *your people shall be my people and your God my God* (1.16)? I

---

1. For a discussion of the significance of this setting see Danna Nolan Fewell and David M. Gunn, ' "A Son Is Born to Naomi!": Literary Allusions and Interpretation in the Book of Ruth', *JSOT* 40 (1988), pp. 99-108 (103).

do not think that this confession 'blunt[s]' the issue of Ruth's foreign-ness', as Katrina Larkin suggests.[2] On the contrary, I see its implica-tions setting the basis for what follows. Naomi may be resoundingly silent now, but there is certainly more to be said. For the Moabite herself there will be no return; her bones will not lie in the soil of Moab. *And so the two of them went on* (1.19)—the two of them. Naomi returns; Bethlehem, *home of plenty*, is home to Naomi, but Ruth, despite her speech, is explicitly Ruth the Moabite, daughter-*in-law*. No recognition yet of the Israelite transformation; tension remains for the Israelite audience, relieved only by the final sentence that tells of the beginning of the barley harvest with its hint of gathered blessing in the plural *they came*—the two of them.

Chapter 2's talk of wealth, of Naomi's kinsman, keeps *the Moabite who came back with Naomi from the country of Moab* (1.22) as the outsider. The audience stirs. Ruth's question, *Why have I found favor in your sight...when I am a foreigner* (2.10), is theirs. Listen for the answer. She has *left father and mother, and native land* (2.11); therefore, she may justifiably hope for a *full reward* from the God of Israel, *under whose wings* she has sought refuge (v. 12), a wing somewhat fused with that of Boaz in ch. 3 (v. 10). The redeeming Israelite God and the solidly human Israelite redeemer Boaz are apparently acting together. The Moabite, however, is not yet fully gathered, so the Bethlehem elders sit in the town gate to sort out publicly the redemption rights—of property, of family name and of the outsider woman now part of an Israelite inheritance (ch. 4). Once acquired with the land rights, she is no longer Ruth the Moabite but the woman *coming into the house* of Boaz (4.11). The prayer of all the people announces to the audience—in case they have missed the full significance of this insider/outsider dealing—that Ruth is joining the line of Rachel, Leah and Tamar to become, like them, a mother in Israel. But does Ruth perhaps still have something of the Moabite about her that not even the exagger-ated perfection of the 'seven' can wholly eradicate? The storyteller reassures with the cry *a son has been born to Naomi* (v. 17). Ruth may be allotted an Israelite husband but not his child. The Israelites stretch with satisfaction. All is well. The story that began with famine and death for Israelites has ended with birth; promise leads not only to hope for Israel but to that archetypal Israelite, David. It is good to be Israelite in the storyteller's world, good to have one's cultural identity so warmly affirmed.

2.   Katrina J.A. Larkin, *Ruth and Esther* (Old Testament Guides; Sheffield: Shef-field Academic Press, 1996), p. 53.

Yet textual clues are not so much decoded as teased out for fit by readers who not only bring but are enfleshed and enmeshed in their own cultural assumptions. I am clearly not an ancient Israelite. I am a twentieth-century woman reader from Aotearoa New Zealand, who comes from a country that purports to live by a bicultural treaty that would guarantee rights and respect to two cultures.[3] The treaty itself was written in the languages of each culture, English and Maori, but each with significantly different wordings and interpretations, the consequences of which are part of the contemporary context.[4] There continues to be a dominant culture that still lives in a colonial, albeit postcolonial, twilight zone, where the rhetoric and the reality, despite current government moves and legislation to restore treaty rights, belies a dominant set of cultural norms and unequal access to resources.[5] So I read with a very shaded if not shady lens. But if my decodings make the text a world that I inhabit, it is a world of ambiguities. While as *Pakeha*, non-Maori, I am part of the dominant culture, my place as woman in a culture which continues to privilege one gender over another means that I read with suspicion and hear with an ear attuned to the silences. So, while as a New Zealander for whom land rights signify a crux of bicultural relationships and con-flict, I note the pivotal place that acquiring Israelite land occupies in

3.   The Treaty of Waitangi was signed in 1840 between Queen Victoria and the Chiefs and Tribes of New Zealand, whereby the Chiefs ceded to the Queen all the rights and powers of Sovereignty (in the English version), Governship or *Kawana-tanga* (in the Maori version) of their lands, while being guaranteed the full exclu-sive and undisturbed possession of the Lands and Estates, Forests, Fisheries and other properties under their possession.

4.   The most significant of these concerns the difference in understanding of Sovereignty and Governship (*Kawanatanga*).

5.   New Zealand is now an independent state within the Commonwealth, recognizing Queen Elizabeth as head of state. Anne McClintock, 'The Angel of Progress: Pitfalls of the Term "Postcolonialism" ', in Francis Barker, Peter Hulme and Margaret Iversen (eds.), *Colonial Discourse/Postcolonial Theory* (Manchester: Manchester University Press, 1994), pp. 253-66, includes (pp. 257-58) New Zealand among those countries she designates 'breakaway settler colonies...distinguished by their formal independence from the founding metropolitan country, along with continued control over the appropriated colony (thus displacing colonial control from the metropolis to the colony itself)'; and which, as such, 'have not undergone decolonisation'. Claudia Orange, *The Treaty of Waitangi* (Wellington: Allen & Unwin New Zealand Ltd, 1987), p. 5, comments that 'the European record in the last century and a half has shown a determination to dominate. In many respects New Zealand, in spite of the treaty, has been merely a variation in the pattern of colonial domination of indigenous races.'

this story—as a woman I also note the acquiring of the woman with the land. As Aotearoa New Zealand is a country in the Pacific, which people from the Pacific Islands have entered in considerable numbers, to become New Zealanders, I am not only *Pakeha* but also *Palagi*, the term that sets me as non-Pacific Islander but, again, one of the dominant culture. So, as a New Zealand *Pakeha/Palagi* I attempt, though all too falteringly, to read against my own cultural positioning and look for telltale signs of an ideology of domination, for the contradictions that flag the cover-up of asymmetrical power relations.

And so I go back to the very beginning of the tale, to *the days when the judges ruled*. At first reading this is a simple matter-of-fact, context-providing statement. But who were these judges? Surely none other than those military deliverers raised up to deliver the would-be Israelites from the peoples of the land, and from the rule of Moab? So this is a tale told in the context of land wars; I know such a history well, and its ways of telling. For in my childhood education the land wars in my country were called the Maori wars, and the telling was all from one side.[6]

That beginning signals: Be alert. Note, for example, the curious God ambiguity in ch. 1. Naomi may recognize a difference in kinship but she clearly does not afford religious difference the same respect. Ruth herself later chooses to leave her Moabite gods, but as early as v. 8 Naomi is heard invoking the Israelite Divine Name for daughterly blessing. But read the whole tale again and ask that most basic of questions: who is this Ruth to whom we are introduced? Is she not the Moabite who speaks the language of Israelite covenant theology, the Moabite who knows the requirements of Israelite family law? The Moabite who knows that the *kānāp* of the god of Israel can materialize in the *kānāp* of the worthy Israelite benefactor? The Moabite who acts not so much for herself but for the promise to Israel, the Moabite who will bear the son anticipating the golden age of David? This is Ruth who once was Moabite but now is Israelite, denying her own language, denying her own spirituality, denying her own kinship claims. Even burial on home ground, on the tribal *marae*,[7] for the land acquired with Ruth is not her land at all. The choice of returning

6.   James Belich, *The New Zealand Wars and the Victorian Interpretation of Racial Conflict* (Auckland: Auckland University Press, 1989), p. 15: 'The New Zealand Wars of 1845–72 were ... bitter and bloody struggles, as important to New Zealand as were the Civil Wars to England and the United States ... they were examples of that widespread phenomenon: resistance to European expansion'.

7.   The *marae* is the tribal meeting ground, where bodies lie in state and the funerals take place; the burial grounds themselves usually lie close by.

home or going forward with Naomi, posed by the storyteller, turns out to have been no choice at all but a textual strategy to promote the model of Israelite faith; Orpah was the literary foil. This is an Israelite metamorphosis framed by intertextual allusion. Not only does Ruth *cleave* to Naomi (1.14), but she also is directed by Boaz in ch. 2 to *cleave* to his Israelite women workers (v. 9); the language of Gen. 2.24 transformed from marriage relations to ethnic relations. But can a Moabite Ruth be a model Israelite heroine? Again, the text shows its ideological colors. Ruth on the threshing floor (ch. 3) is a questionable adventuress. A chorus of intertextual allusions to other sexually questionable foreign or outsider women, including that ancestral daughter of Lot,[8] can be all too clearly heard. Boaz is, of course, an honorable redeemer.

And who is Naomi? On the surface level working to provide husband, security and Israelite identity for Ruth, but more significantly serving the 'hidden transcript'[9] of the text, the underlying goal of assimilation, transforming Moabite into Israelite. And yet I am not sure. Perhaps Naomi did respect difference. Perhaps Naomi and the narrator had different views. Perhaps she genuinely wanted both her daughters-in-law to return home because that was culturally appropriate, so that Orpah's action followed Naomi's wish; but what can a mere character achieve against the powerful ideology of a narrator's text? Do I wish to be reminded yet again of the powerlessness of those whose views are silenced by the overwriting of the public text? The Israelite Naomi playing her set role is uncomfortable for a *Pakeha* reader, although questions of reading continue to arise. Consider the final scene (4.15-17): is it a powerfully silent, or powerlessly silenced, Naomi who takes and nurses the child born by Ruth? If read through the lens of traditional Maori custom, where the first grandchild was commonly claimed for its upbringing by the grandparents, this might be heard as Naomi's formal recognition of Ruth as her daughter. Or is it the Moabite producing the child for the Israelite, a *rediviva* Hagar? For the consequence is that the Moabite's child is now truly Israelite, assimilation complete, with Israel the winner.[10] Which raises that

8. Noted by Danna Nolan Fewell and David M. Gunn, 'Boaz, Pillar of Society: Measures of Worth in the Book of Ruth', *JSOT* 45 (1989), pp. 45-59 (48).

9. A phrase used by James C. Scott, *Domination and the Arts of Resistance: Hidden Transcripts* (New Haven: Yale University Press, 1990).

10. Ellen van Wolde, 'Texts in Dialogue with Texts: Intertextuality in the Ruth and Tamar Narratives', *Biblical Interpretation* 5.1 (1997), pp. 1-28, read since this paper was written, also raises the question of the requirement of assimilation in this text.

other knotty question, whether the hidden transcript throughout was the working of the divine.

The Bethlehem women, however, almost pre-empt the final ideological climax. Or does the text waver under the weight of its claims? They have already given the child a name (4.17) before the narrator sets the text firmly in the direction of Israel's Davidic history, adding the Israelite genealogy, the authenticating *whakapapa*,[11] the ancestral authority, with its final erasure of Moabite maternity. The covenant vow of Ruth so memorized, quoted and sung over centuries as a model of devotion and faith, but now heard as a speech of ethnic and religious rejection, was a significant hint of the direction ahead.

Not a good story for Moabites. While I cannot read as an ethnic Moabite, although colonizers have a long history of presuming to be surrogate indigenous readers, women of both races are, at least to some degree, Moabites. Mothers, and Moabite mothers even more so, know of daughters taken off by the powerful and the consequences of that. Young women creeping among the gleanings, in danger of rape, promised rewards by older power-holding men who may or may not deliver; who if they do, will make sure the deed is done secretly at night, with all that that implies—this is not a story, this is known experience. And yes, I know that according to the text it is Naomi who suggests the threshing floor strategy, but I am reading with suspicion even here.

Among the voices of the underside there are those who tell this as a story of resistance, as the story of an outsider woman who infiltrates for gain under cover of darkness. Turn the lens and it is Naomi's actions that are suspect. For can one trust a woman who has shown such ambivalence to her daughter-in-law, who both incites her to resistance and yet exposes her to danger and the charge of cultural dishonor? Is it not a case now of daughter beware, and daughter be on guard against power-wielding woman as well as power-wielding man?

Many marginalized voices of women tell this story, and tell it differently. Some tell it as a story of a woman driven to survive, of a woman heard through submissive speech, *I am Ruth your servant* (3.9), through male-validated relationship, *and now my daughter* (3.11), through marriage, through male property rights, through the birth of a male heir. These are voices whose readings resist the invitation to

11. The Maori term for genealogy.

enter the narrative world for warm embraces with role-modeling biblical ancestors.

What has happened to that idyllic tale of love and devotion? Am I only to read it that way under the bedclothes at night? For my own mental and emotional health, and perhaps even for the strength to confront the truths presented in these other readings, I need to hear Ruth in more than one key. I need to hear of Ruth and Naomi as strong women, as part of the scriptural blessings. But a text that begins in Moab and whose last word is David (cf. 2 Sam. 8.2) not only concerns women; its canonical setting in the Septuagint-Christian tradition, after the book of Judges and before 1 Samuel, only serves to make its political agenda the more overt.[12] As I have reread the book for this paper I have become fearful of its place as sacred scripture in my country, for racial politics are alive and well in Aotearoa New Zealand. I am mindful of the point made by Victor Matthews and Don Benjamin that 'culture is always a delicate blend of story and daily living, of mythos and ethos'.[13] My fear is that there is a seemingly coherent insider mythos of the book of Ruth that all too easily reinforces a sadly persisting and pervading colonial ethos. Moabite mothers beware! *Pakeha/palagi* women read very carefully.

Colonial ethos in Ruth?

12. See the comments made by David Jobling in 'Ruth Finds a Home: Canon, Politics, Method', in J. Cheryl Exum and David J.A. Clines (eds.), *The New Literary Criticism and the Hebrew Bible* (JSOTSup, 143; Sheffield: Sheffield Academic Press, 1993), pp. 125-39 (139).

13. Victor H. Matthews and Don C. Benjamin, 'Introduction: Social Sciences and Biblical Studies', *Semeia* 68 (1994), pp. 7-21 (19).

RUTH AS A FOREIGN WORKER AND THE POLITICS OF EXOGAMY

Athalya Brenner

Temporary, hopeful migration of workers from underprivileged locations to more developed locations sometimes results in the workers'
settling in the host location and a permanent or semi-permanent abandonment of the source community. A cluster of cultural issues—
economic, religious, linguistic, and more—either contributes to the
integration of the foreign worker in the host culture/location or hin-
ders it. In this essay I shall examine some of such foreign workers'
issues in modern Israel in light of the Ruth narrative while, simultaneously, rereading the Ruth narrative in light of those foreign
workers' situation.

Modern Israel imports workers, chiefly from eastern Europe and
the far east (for the purposes of the present paper, I shall not look at
Israel's employment of Arab workers from the occupied territories).
The importation of foreign workers is dictated by the country's
fluctuating needs and human resource shortages and is subject to
relatively stringent rules and quotas. Foreign workers sign a contract
of employment. They generally do menial jobs, are often underpaid
and badly treated by their employers. Presumably, however, they
would fare even less well in their source communities economically;
this is their prime motivation for coming and for staying for a while.
Fifty-six foreign workers died in Israel in 1996, according to a report
in the newspaper *Ha'aretz* from the end of August 1997, in spite of
their legally enforced access to health and social care.

Foreign work in modern Israel is decidedly gendered. In sociological analyses, any line of employment whose practitioners are over 50
per cent females is feminized, and vice versa. To follow this broad
definition, the gendering of foreign workers is as follows. The majority of male workers will do construction and agriculture, a minority
basic health care for the physically handicapped and other services.
The majority of female workers do care work for the young, elderly or
disabled, a minority agricultural work and other services. Female foreign workers are much in demand. Their stereotyped image is: young,

positive, modest, trustworthy, industrious. Male workers have a stereotyped image of troublemakers and drunks.

There is no question of widespread integration into Israeli society: the work permit is valid for a fixed and short period; cultural and religious differences are too great; there are language barriers; Israeli society is, by and large, snobbish and insular, suspicious of strangers and xenophobic; personal isolation and workers' group dynamics, not to mention specific living arrangements, contribute to their isolation. And yet, for financial gain and perhaps for other motives, foreign workers keep on coming back to Israel. And yet again, against all odds, some integration occurs in the form of cross-cultural marriages (although not all workers are single). In Israel of the 1990s such unions will be less problematic if the local spouse is a woman, ostensibly because any offspring of this union will still be considered Jewish according to orthodox *halakhah*; however, both combinations are known to have happened.

It is possible, perhaps illuminating, to read Ruth's story against this background. Some similarities between her situation and that of single, female foreign workers in modern Israel are apparent—although dissimilarities obtain as well they will not be discussed here. In the following discussion, I'm heavily indebted to Jack Sasson's commentary, whose results I view from this specific angle.[1]

Ruth comes from another culture, another language, another place. She is a *zārāh* woman (see Prov. 1–9). It is customary to idealize Ruth's decision of following Naomi to the strange land into a decision primarily motivated by her love for her mother-in-law, thus filling an obvious gap in the text: this is how I have read it, too. *Point One* of the present cross-cultural, cross-everything reading: Ruth might have had less of a free choice than we fondly imagine, as is the case with many a foreign worker nowadays.

Sasson points out in his commentary that Ruth binds herself to Naomi by verbal contract (1.16-17). The concept of 'love' that is applicable here, as in the slave's love for his master in Exod. 21.2-6 [5], is a legal rather than an emotional concept: it indicates intent as well as consent. *Point Two*: Ruth has a contract implying that she has to work for Naomi, she has to take care of the older woman—see ch. 2— as is true of many contracted female foreign workers. Questions concerning Naomi's inability or ability to fend for herself are thus made

---

1.   J.M. Sasson, *Ruth: A New Translation with a Philological Commentary and a Formalist-Folklorist Interpretation* (Baltimore: The Johns Hopkins University Press, 1979; The Biblical Seminar, 10; Sheffield: JSOT Press, 2nd edn, 1989).

redundant: she has somebody contracted to do it for her.

The only one to notice Ruth at the end of ch. 1, the homecoming scene, is the narrator. Neither Naomi nor the Bethlehem women acknowledge her existence. *Point Three*: foreign workers are invisible to the dominant culture.

Ruth decides to glean in Boaz's field. It can be argued that she thus becomes a lowly agricultural worker. The laws, or customs, or utopian demand to make gleaning of agricultural produce accessible to the poor are codified in Lev. 19.9-10 and 23.22, Deut. 24.19 (see also *b. Pe'ah* and *Gittin*). One could argue that Ruth is *not* an agricultural worker, since she is not employed by Boaz and does not receive wages for her activities. However, from *her* implied viewpoint, she *is* self-employed; does work in the field for her livelihood; does support Naomi by it. In that HB world, wages were probably in kind anyway. And, as will be seen, she does aspire to become a contractually recognized worker of Boaz's economic family (next point). *Point Four*: most foreign workers work as menial laborers; their livelihood depends to a large extent on seasonal changes and market demands.

Ruth is noticeably industrious. *Point Five*: a foreigner's—a foreign worker's—way to becoming visible is to try harder.

Boaz notices Ruth in his field, awards her some privileges but refuses to grant her a more solid footing among his local workers (ch. 2). *Point Six*: hard work is noticed; so is devotion. However, these are not enough for a female foreign worker if she seeks integration into the host society.

Naomi recommends that Ruth create a situation of seduction (3.1-4). Ruth apparently knows that seduction alone will not mean integration and asks Boaz to marry her (3.9). Irrespective of what precisely happens on the *goren*—did they? did they not?—Ruth is well aware of *Point Seven*: integration into the host community, if at all possible, can be achieved only by marriage. And of *Point Eight*, of which Boaz is also aware (3.14): a foreign (working) woman should be especially mindful of her reputation; she has an image to protect as well as an image (the *zārāh*) to shun. And if she wants to be accepted by the host community, a foreigner—particularly such a female worker—ought to maintain a stereotype of apparent modesty and reticence. Hence, Ruth is silent and invisible through the negotiations in ch. 4 (vv. 1-10).

When Boaz declares his intention to marry Ruth she is compared to Rachel, Leah and Tamar (4.11-12); these verses are usually read as a special blessing conferred on a foreigner, thus concluding her integration into Judahite society. This can undoubtedly be so read. The mention of those female forerunners has a sting, however—and perhaps also a veiled sub-textual threat or warning. Those female figures constructed 'the house of Israel', true; all three entered exogamous marriages with 'our' men; all three produced children, future leaders and heirs. However, none is portrayed as an exemplary figure. The Leah and Rachel of the obvious intertext, Genesis 29–30, bicker and compete and their sons imitate their behavioral patterns. Tamar (Gen. 38) stretches sexual norms beyond the utmost limits. If the world of the Bible, if the world-vision of Ruth is of a world inhabited by just desserts and earned rewards, then Rachel's early death, Leah's death before Jacob and Tamar's non-marriage to Judah are relevant asides on their behavior. It is futile to ask why no other ancestress is mentioned in this string of 'foreign women'. Nevertheless, a suspicion of ambivalence can and should be retained. *Point Nine*: can foreignness (Moabite in this case) and class (worker) be overcome, even when the foreigner conforms to a positive stereotype and embraces the local culture?

Much has been written about Ruth's disappearance from the last narrative scene of 'her' story, the child's name-giving scene (4.14-17), in the story that bears her name. It seems unwarranted that, immediately upon fulfilling her duty as set out in the 'blessing' and bearing a male child, immediately upon following in Rachel and Leah and Tamar's footsteps, Ruth is rewarded by becoming as invisible as she is at the end of ch. 1. Several explanations for her disappearance from the final stage of the narrative have been offered. One solution is the traditional viewing of Naomi as the baby's caretaker or adoptive mother. Another is the understanding of the word *bēn* (v. 17: 'a *bēn* is born unto Naomi') as 'child, offspring' rather than the straight forward 'son'. Yet another explanation is to view the story's ending as a final fusion into one finale of pretextually separate Naomi and Ruth stories.[2] Another possibility is to draw yet another analogy to the plight of female foreign workers in Israel today. *Point Ten*: a female foreigner can perhaps be integrated into Judahite, or Israelite, or Israeli society through marriage—if and when the additional issue of class does not occur. Cultural, religious, linguistic, ethnic and similar variables can be overridden: this is the basis for royal political marriages, for instance. Stereotypes of foreign femaleness can be either negative or positive or in between. But ultimately the factor of class, of social background and wealth or its lack and the resultant

---

2. A. Brenner, 'Naomi and Ruth', in A. Brenner (ed.), *A Feminist Companion to Ruth* (Feminist Companion to the Bible, 3; Sheffield: Sheffield Academic Press, 1993), pp. 70-84.

personal status involved, is the decisive determinant. Hence, finally, Ruth might be a prime example of this reality: a low-class foreign woman, a worker without property, will become invisible in the host community. She will be *absorbed* rather than *integrated*. Her prospects, however virtuous she is, are less than promising.

The book of Ruth can and has been read as an optimistic, idyllic story of integration, of polemic against exogamy and xenophobia (see Ezra and Nehemiah), as a story of love, as a story of duty and *ḥesed*. It has also been read as a story of traditional Jewish conversion. These readings and others are possible, certainly. What marks them is the common denominator of viewing the story as a comedy, the birth of a son being interpreted as a happy ending. But a happy ending for whom? Is it a happy ending for the foreigner, for the working woman Ruth? Read against the reality of foreign female work today, the story may seem different. The *realpolitik* of economics, law, supply and demand, supports the necessity to treat the foreigner reasonably well. However, custom mitigates the possibility of the foreigner crossing cultural boundaries into integration in the host culture. Foreigners may be accepted: less so if they are of the underprivileged classes and women; and full integration, even in the case of Ruth, an exemplary female character in many ways, is in fact impossible. The variables of class, occupation and femaleness usually override those of foreignness and personal excellence—then and now.

CULTURE, ETHICS AND IDENTITY IN READING RUTH:
A RESPONSE TO DONALDSON, DUBE, MCKINLAY AND BRENNER

Roland Boer

One of the many enjoyable dimensions of reading, hearing, and then thinking further about these papers[1] on the book of Ruth is located in the variety of style: there is the concise, clear and lucid argument of Athalya Brenner's paper, the powerful and subversive prose of Laura Donaldson, the lingering oral traces and structures in the stories of Musa Dube, and the questioning lyric text of Judith McKinlay.

However, it seems to me that these papers make their initial moves by means of character, and this is where I would like to begin my response, since it will allow me to question my own position in responding to these excellent papers. The nervousness I have about being a respondent in this particular situation is that I may come across as a Boaz, as the male who appears at the end to resolve all the problems, as the one who redeems Ruth, Naomi and the story as a whole and sets it on its messianic trajectory. I will return to my nervousness later.

The four essays may be conveniently designated as either 'Ruth' papers or 'Orpah' papers. They are, of course, all Moabite essays, since both Ruth and Orpah are, to state the obvious, Moabites. And all of the essays share a deep suspicion that this is an assimilationist text, that there are deep problems with the way Ruth in particular seems to be both assimilated and yet not, to be absorbed and yet rejected. The question here is one of cultural tension and assimilation from one to the other: from Moab to Israel, or not (in the case of Orpah). But these are mediated through the complex cultures of present-day Israel, Aotearoa New Zealand, Native North America and Botswana Africa.

---

1.   Papers initially presented at the session 'Signs of Culture: Reading Ruth' of the Semiotics and Exegesis section of the SBL Annual Meeting, San Francisco, November 1997: Athalya Brenner, 'Ruth as a Foreign Worker and the Politics of Exogamy' (here pp. 158-62); Laura Donaldson, 'The Sign of Orpah: Reading Ruth through Native Eyes' (pp. 130-44); Judith McKinlay, 'A Son Is Born to Naomi' (pp. 151-57); Musa W. Dube, 'The Unpublished Letters of Orpah to Ruth' (pp. 145-50).

And there seems to be no desire, as in more reformist approaches to the text, to retrieve the text as such, although there are some efforts to salvage it in a sort of dialectical reversal that switches the apparent valorizations around.

The two 'Ruth' papers are those of Athalya Brenner and Judith McKinlay. Athalya's 'Ruth as a Foreign Worker and the Politics of Exogamy' places the book of Ruth beside the contemporary Israeli practice of hiring foreigners to carry out a range of unskilled tasks, although primarily domestic and carer roles for foreign women and agricultural and construction work for men. To see the character of Ruth as a foreign worker in this light is very fruitful, and Athalya explores some of the dimensions of such a juxtaposition. Many characteristics of foreign workers in present-day Israel may also be found in the story of Ruth. Ruth's 'choice' to go with Naomi back to Bethlehem is a contract in order to care for the older woman. She is invisible to/by the foreign culture. She does menial labor. She works hard to gain notice; and she finds that an attempt at integration through marriage is the best way to achieve this. Marriage also helps to guard her reputation. The major value of Athalya's paper is that it foregrounds socio-economic questions, especially the question of class, for it is with class that the issue of assimilation arises. To quote, 'But ultimately the factor of class, of social background and wealth or its lack and the resultant personal status involved, is the decisive determinant [of integration]' (pp. 161-62). The question of class thus enables and disables Ruth's integration: the only possibility for Ruth is to become invisible (hence her absence from the final part of the story). Once the process of marriage is under way she disappears.

It seems to me that it is important to read Ruth in terms of class, economics, ethnicity and gender, as well as to read it in conjunction with these and other questions in a contemporary situation, such as that of contemporary Israel. The inevitable issues of historical distance and anachronism do arise in such an effort, especially when closer, point by point, comparisons are made. But what is far more interesting, especially in the light of current theoretical and political concerns over ethnic and national identity, is, Why does Athalya bracket the issue of Arab workers from the occupied territories in present-day Israel? Is it merely because such an issue does not fit the book of Ruth? Or is it that such workers are not 'foreign' in a strict sense?

This might be read in two ways: that Arab workers do not count as 'foreign', that they are as much part of Israel/Palestine as Israelis themselves; or that they do not have a distinct, Palestinian, identity. These two positions may both overlap (the absence of Palestinian identity is part of their belonging to Israel) or be at odds with each other (they have a distinct Palestinian identity and are part of Israel). Apart from this crucial specific question, it is the broader one of ethnic and national identity to which I will return shortly. In the context of the extraordinarily complex situation regarding Palestinian and Israeli coexistence, the whole area of identity insists on being considered a little more extensively. Of course, the book of Ruth has a curious resonance on precisely this issue.

Judith McKinlay's paper, a *Pakeha/Palagi* reading of Ruth, is more tentative and suspicious (in all the best senses of the term) but is a reading that, like Athalya Brenner's, focuses on the character of Ruth. The difference is a profound suspicion of the text that finds expression in the discussion of Naomi and her assimilationist role. I suspect that this is because Naomi comes closest to the *Pakeha/Palagi* identification of Judith McKinlay herself. Naomi serves the 'hidden transcript' of the text, which is the underlying goal of assimilation, of transforming Moabite into Israelite—something that has some parallels with the English colonizers' efforts to assimilate Maori people in Aotearoa New Zealand to European ways. The burning question is, then, how to 'read against my own cultural positioning and look for telltale signs of an ideology of domination' (p. 154). And that cultural positioning is ambiguous, since she—Judith (Naomi?)—is both privileged (as European-derived colonizer) and oppressed (as a woman). It seems to me that Judith does a good job of reading against her own positioning, precisely because of the questions and the suspicions (I counted 21 questions in her paper). She fears for the power of Ruth as sacred scripture in her country, where racial politics thrive, where the insider ethos of the book of Ruth reinforces a colonial ethos in Aotearoa New Zealand. So, while she recognizes the power of a canonical religious text like this one, the desire to retrieve the text for some sort of use is very subdued.

Yet I have some questions regarding Judith McKinlay's essay. There is a Gunkelesque feel to this piece of work, a positioning of the book of Ruth before a group of reconstructed Israelites listening to an oral tale, replete with their ethnic assumptions and moral identifications. They are troubled, it seems, by the story of Ruth, but then reassured as it unfolds and reinforces their own prejudices. Inevitably, such a reconstruction of a campfire storytime is subject to the vagaries of imagination and assumptions—necessary in any contextual refurbishment, but also fraught with Gunkel's romanticism that always attached to his search for the *Sitz im Leben*.

My second question for Judith (and others) is this: Is it possible to question one's cultural positioning? Does the attainment and use of privilege enable or preclude this questioning? In the end this is the old Marxist issue of the ideological formation of ruling and ruled classes. Being a member of the ruling classes permits a distinct perspective on ruling-class ideology (understanding ideology here as the necessary corollary of class formation, as class discourse), but it also closes off other perspectives that might critique such an ideology. As a white woman in Aotearoa New Zealand, Judith McKinlay is uniquely positioned as both a descendant of colonizers and yet a subordinate within such a colonial heritage. Thus, Judith identifies with Naomi.

Ruth is, as Judith McKinlay says, 'not a good story for Moabites' (p. 156). And, apart from Ruth, the forgotten Moabite of this story is Orpah, who features in the two papers by Laura Donaldson and Musa Dube. Both undertake, in their very different ways, significant rereadings of the book through what might be termed 'suppressed narratives': a narrative written by Laura Donaldson through connections with indigenous North American material, and by Musa Dube through the imaginative invocation of story and letter. Laura Donaldson reads Ruth in the 'contact zone' between European invader and North American indigenous peoples, a radically imbalanced zone, but one in which she finds the perpetual appropriation of canonical European texts refreshingly subversive. This is done both by being selective about what is taken over, and then by inventing new ways of reading that which is taken. Laura Donaldson's suspicion is, as with the other papers, concerned at least in part with the question of assimilation, for she feels that the book of Ruth is the narrative equivalent of a 'last-arrow pageant', a final rite whereby Native Americans gave up the visible signs of indigenous identification and took on those of the colonizers. Yet while this applies to Ruth, whose positive value must be significantly deflated, it does not apply to the one who exits the text and thereby refuses such a pageant—Orpah. And it is Orpah who may be read positively from a Native perspective, especially that of Cherokee women. Orpah returns to *bêt 'immāh*, her mother's house, and is therefore one who takes the hard path of not rejecting her traditions and sacred ancestors. She goes back to the house of her clan and spiritual mother, where the mothers control and own the house and its traditions. In doing so, Orpah resonates with the indigenous women, often completely 'out of' the text, who persisted with their sacred traditions.

There is something very powerful about taking the narrative loading in a different direction, about following a character who has left the text at some stage and seeing where her story might lead and how that might alter the text as it stands. What is the fate of a character such as Orpah who leaves the text in haste, hardly before it has begun to unwind its tale? This is a reading that is both profoundly suspicious of the text and yet salvages something from it with the assistance of Orpah. It does so with what might be termed an 'alternative history',[2] an effort to retell a story in a way that has implications for the perception of the present. Such alternative histories are absolutely necessary in order to recover the stories of those who have been silenced—through death, through exclusion, or through an exit from the story before it begins.

But when such alternative histories, the histories of the forgotten and repressed, are written, an ethical question starts to come to the surface. By what criteria are such stories and histories to be valued? On what basis do they claim a much-belated priority over the already existing stories? That many of us do value these alternative stories above the official ones goes without saying, but we need to ask why we do so. Here of course it is the imperative to end oppression and suffering, or at least never to forget their continual presence in the lives of so many people and groups, as a first step to its end. And then the question that arises is whether replacing official histories and stories with other stories merely replicates the existing patterns of dominance and suppression: is it possible to walk away from such a situation by refusing to claim canonical status for these newly recovered and written stories?

Laura Donaldson clearly identifies with Orpah and claims her as her own, as Musa Dube does too. However, whereas Laura Donaldson finds in North American indigenous materials the spark needed to bring the Orpah stories to life, Musa Dube reinscribes Orpah by means of African patterns of story and retelling. Further, whereas Laura, through Orpah, questions the characterization of Moab in the Hebrew Bible (as the result of the incest of Lot and his daughters, Gen. 19), Musa Dube provides an imaginative reconstruction of the whole Moabite context and culture. In this reconstruction—mediated through the established literary device of the 'finding' of hidden manuscripts, documents or letters—Musa presents the alternative history of Moab, and those elements of the story of Ruth that take place in or touch on Moab.

---

2.   See further my *Novel Histories* (Sheffield: Sheffield Academic Press, 1997), pp. 128-32.

Various elements are thus cast in a new light: the story of Lot, who turns into a pillar of salt instead of his wife; the immigration of Elimelech and Naomi to Moab, where they are graciously assisted by King Eglon; the social status of the Israelites, the deaths of Elimelech, Mahlon and Chilion; Naomi's flight; and Orpah's tasks as regent queen and priestess upon returning to her mother's house. Now it is Orpah who does not know what has happened to Ruth. Ruth has left this story in the same way Orpah left Ruth's (biblical) story. What we have in Musa Dube's paper, then, is a book of Orpah.

The key in all of this is the question of the 'image', or the impression, that one culture has of another. For, in Dube's frame story, Lesedi, the student of anthropology, returns to Africa because she could no longer accept the image of Africa in the anthropological literature with which she was dealing. In the same way, Orpah writes to Ruth: 'And when you have borne children, you should tell them these stories of Moabites: of their origins, of their kindness, of their hospitality and of their struggles for survival' (p. 150). The imaginative effort here is stunning, and also somewhat subversive, since Musa Dube draws all of the elements of Orpah's story from texts of the Hebrew Bible (Genesis, Numbers, Judges, 1 Samuel, Nehemiah and Ruth). Now, however, the stories have a particular twist (for example, Lot turns into salt rather than his wife) that claims to be the true account. Here there is a much clearer valorization of the alternative story: it tells the 'truth' about certain things that have been falsely represented in the standard Hebrew text. Once again the canonical question returns. Does the strong claim for the 'true' story seek to replace the existing canonical stories with others that are felt to be better? Is this the best move to make?

I have two smaller questions of detail about the story Musa Dube so skillfully reconstructs. Is the claim for a much stronger moral code—inevitably cast in sexual terms—in Africa before the arrival of Europeans a storytelling device, or does it have some contact with 'real' history? Secondly, why does the action take place in the *royal court* of Moab? Is this also a literary device, part of the total reassessment of the characters in this story? Yet does not this elevation of the characters to royal status raise some problems for the story, given the crucial role of the ruling elite in the construction of ideological hegemony, of the ideological control of the crucial stories of a culture?

Alongside, and generated out of, the particular contributions made and issues raised by these essays, there are four larger questions: culture; how to deal with a text like Ruth; ethics; and then identification and identity.

As for the issue of culture, this seems to have been largely assumed rather than defined in the four essays. Each of these readings of Ruth has undertaken its tasks from a specific cultural situation—be it foreign workers in Israel, white women colonizers in Aotearoa New Zealand, indigenous people in North America or storytelling in Africa. The insights provided by considering Ruth from each cultural situation are very worthwhile, but what is missing is some reflection on what is meant by 'culture' in the first place. How does one understand culture? How is it related to other areas of life, such as the political, the economic, the social? For me, the best way to deal with the issue of culture is through a Marxist frame, where culture shares space with religion, the state, intellectual endeavour and so on, which are then set over against economics, the relationship being mediated by social class (Marx's relations of production). If we understand culture in this sense, then it begins to expand our perceptions of what is relevant. For example, in considering Ruth from Israeli, New Zealand, Cherokee or Botswana African cultural situations, I would like to inquire about the social and economic signals these readings give out in their very act of being cultural readings of Ruth.

And dealing with the text? What, in the end, are we to do with a text like this, a text that has so much that is suspicious, particularly in the assertion of cultural assimilation? For Athalya Brenner and Judith McKinlay, this question is made much more explicit: neither of them likes the assimilationist logic of the text, although they do name it directly. Is the text to be discarded? Does it become, in part at least, a negative example that deserves continued attention? Laura Donaldson and Musa Dube take a different tack, preferring to write alternative histories and stories that will then replace, in some fashion, the flawed text of Ruth.

As I have suggested above, there is also a distinctly ethical feel to the way the biblical text is approached. Athalya Brenner is the exception here, but Judith McKinlay, Laura Donaldson and Musa Dube all make ethical claims with their readings. For all three the text of Ruth is troublesome: a difficult, assimilationist piece of work. Laura Donaldson and Musa Dube provide at least one option for rereading these texts—the construction of an alternative history or story. But I found that even these entail ethical choices about the validity, or otherwise, of what has been created.

Finally, in each paper there is a process of focusing on a character, and then identifying with at least one over against the others.[3] Thus

---

3.   This is a well-tried strategy for reading Ruth. See, for example, Ilona

Athalya Brenner's interest is in the figure of Ruth herself, while Judith McKinlay finds Naomi her enigmatic double. Both Laura Donaldson and Musa Dube identify most strongly with Orpah, seeking to recover her story. While it seems in some ways inevitable that a text like Ruth will often produce such responses—the characters in the text are so strong that they attract the people 'outside' the text to indentify with one of them—I want to ask whether it is possible to resist identifying onself with anyone in these stories.

Yet the impossibility of avoiding such contact and identification with one of the characters brings me to identity (or the essentialist question). What is the relation between identification with particular characters and the way the writers themselves construct their own identities in relation to the text of Ruth? Further, what does ethnic and national identity mean, particularly in the context of Israel, or New Zealand, or the USA, or Africa? Here I want to connect with the debate over essentialism, asking whether there is some incontrovertible essence or core that determines whether one is Israeli, Palestinian, African, indigenous person, Moabite or Israelite. If, by contrast, we understand these as constructed items (ethnicity, nationality), then much more sense may be made of the contested situation in Israel, of the relations between white colonizer woman and Maori worker, of the interaction, the 'contact zone', between indigenous Americans and foreign intruder, and so also of the fluid distinctions between Moab and Israel, between Ruth and Naomi.

Let me close by returning to character identification, for there are some others who rate little mention in most critical reflections. These are the men who disappear even before Orpah. Indeed, as far as this story is concerned, rather than the dangerously patriarchal and messianic Boaz, I would much prefer to be Elimelech, Mahlon or Chilion, killed off early in the story.

Rashkow, 'The Discourse of Power and the Power of Discourse', in Athalya Brenner (ed.), *A Feminist Companion to Ruth* (Feminist Companion to the Bible, 3; Sheffield: Sheffield Academic Press, 1993), pp. 26-41. Also A. Brenner, 'Naomi and Ruth', pp. 70-84, and 'Naomi and Ruth: Further Reflections', pp. 140-45, in the same volume.

Part II

RUTH AND ESTHER:
MOTHERS AND DAUGHTERS

THE INVISIBLE RELATIONSHIP MADE VISIBLE:
BIBLICAL MOTHERS AND DAUGHTERS

Leila Leah Bronner

What does the Hebrew Bible tell us about mothers and daughters? This question is surprisingly difficult to answer because, although we find many interactions between fathers and sons, mothers and sons, and even fathers and daughters in the Bible, it records only a few interactions between mothers and daughters. Moreover, biblical narrators often portray women as yearning to bear sons but do not depict parents as wanting daughters. By so doing the narrators imply that daughters are not as important as sons to the continuation of the nation, and that mothers naturally wish for sons rather than daughters.[1] Is this impression further substantiated or is it contradicted by the traces of mother and daughter relationships in the Bible? By bringing together and focusing on the few instances of mother–daughter interactions, I hope to explore what roles a biblical mother plays in relation to a daughter and how a biblical daughter might be imagined in relation to her mother.

I will begin by looking at the metaphors of 'mother' and 'daughter' as used to describe the relationship between God and Israel. I next discuss the mother in the general statements about parent–child relationships in the Bible. From there, I will consider three daughters whose mothers are named in the Bible: Miriam, daughter of Jochebed; Dinah, daughter of Leah; and Tamar, daughter of Maacah.[2] Finally, I will look at Ruth and the Song of Songs, two books in the Bible that,

---

1.   The confusion of the rabbis on this point is telling. See *b. B. Bat.* 16b, on Gen. 24.1: '[It is written,] *The Lord had blessed Abraham in all things* [*ba-kol*]. What is meant by '*in all things*'? R. Meir said: In the fact that he had no daughter; R. Judah said: In the fact that he had a daughter. Others say that Abraham had a daughter whose name was *ba-kol*.'

2.   I discuss here the Tamar of 2 Samuel who is the daughter of King David and Maacah, not the Tamar of Gen. 38, who is the daughter-in-law of Judah and the mother of his twin sons, Perez and Zerah.

along with the story of Rebekah as daughter, quite unexpectedly provide glimpses of positive mother–daughter relationships.

God as Mother, Israel as Daughter:
A Metaphorical Relationship

On the occasions when the word *bat* (daughter) appears in the Bible, it may refer either to an actual person or to an abstraction (e.g. a nation, a poetic persona).[3] *Bat* is often used in poetic epithets that personify cities and nations—the most commonly occurring combinations are *bat ṣiyyon* (daughter of Zion), *bat yᵉrûšalāyîm* (daughter of Jerusalem) and *bat 'ammî* (daughter of my people).[4] The personification of the people as a daughter has something to do with the structure of the Hebrew language. The gender of the words for countries and cities is feminine, and the prophets capitalized on that fact in their poetry. What does the personified daughter of the prophets do? She cries and rejoices, sneers and minces. She is always embedded in emotions and is shown only in roles expressing the (collective) emotional life of the nation of Israel.[5] In other words, the metaphorical daughter is a pub- lic rather than a private figure.[6] The negative side of this figuring is

---

3.   For example see Barbara Bakke Kaiser, 'Poet as "Female Impersonator": The Image of Daughter Zion as Speaker in Biblical Poems of Suffering', *Journal of Religion* 67 (1987), pp. 164-82. Kaiser demonstrates how the biblical poets used female experience as a metaphor to express joy or agony over Jerusalem's fate or to give voice to other happy or painful experiences of the nation. Kaiser uses the word *bat* in a precise, carefully defined sense, quoting William Lanahan's defini- tion as given in a study of the book of Lamentations. On the word *bat*, see also *EncJud*, XVI, col. 161; A. Even-Shoshan, *A New Concordance of the Old Testament* (Jerusalem: Kiryath Sepher, 1985); Robert Young, *Analytical Concordance to the Bible* (Grand Rapids: Eerdmans, 1970), s.v. 'daughter' and 'son'.

4.   There are many more, of course, but it seems unnecessary to go into them all here, as they all serve essentially the same function. See Young, *Analytical Con- cordance*, for full list.

5.   See, for example, Isa. 1.8 for daughter/Israel abandoned; 2 Kgs 19.21 and Isa. 37.22 for a daughter scorning enemies of Israel; Isa. 3.16 for daughters as vain; Lam. 1.6, 8-9 for fallen Israel figured as daughter/harlot. In the Bible, women seem to play a prominent role in mourning rituals (e.g. Isa. 15.2, 32.11-12; Jer. 7.29, 9.17, 16.6, 41.5, 47.5, 48.37; Mic. 1.16) and in rituals of celebration (e.g. Judg. 21.16-24; Isa. 5.1-7).

6.   Karla G. Shargent comes to the same conclusion from a different starting point: 'Contrary to the gender assumptions of the public/private dichotomy, which would confine daughters to the private sphere, the narrative daughters of the Hebrew Bible are remarkably mobile and can be found in the most disparate locations'. See her 'Living on the Edge: The Liminality of Daughters in Genesis to

that when the nation of Zion falls away from God, the daughter of
Zion is figured as a fallen woman.

The figure of the daughter of Zion and the metaphorical association
of God with the figure of the mother are connected on only one point:
they are both shown as a woman giving birth. In Isa. 42.14, for
example, the prophet has God threaten, 'Now I will cry out like a
woman in travail / I will gasp and pant'; while in Isa. 66.8 the prophet
has God say, 'For as soon as Zion was in labor, / she brought forth
her children'. The one function that the metaphorical God as mother
and metaphorical daughter of Zion share is that of bearing children.
When Moses complains to God about being burdened with the people
of Israel, we gain further insight into the role of the mother. Moses is
crystal clear about God's responsibilities: 'Did I conceive this people,
did I bring them forth?/that Thou should say to me, carry them in
your bosom / as a nurse that carries the suckling child?' (Num. 11.12).
The mother is entirely responsible for her immature children, according to Moses, and he finds mothering a wearisome task. In contrast,
exilic Isaiah puts a positive spin on mothering in its repeated figuring
of God as a mother bearing, caring for, carrying and comforting her
children.[7] For example, in Isa. 46.3 we find:

> All that are left of the House of Israel,
> Who have been carried since birth,
> Supported since leaving the womb:
> Till you grow old, I will still be the same;
> When you turn gray, it is I who will carry;
> I was the Maker, and I will be the Bearer;
> And I will carry and rescue [you].

Over and over in exilic Isaiah God's unfathomable love for his suffering people is figured as motherly love: 'Can a woman forget her baby,
or disown the child of her womb? Though she might forget, I could
never forget you' (Isa. 49.15). And throughout, the motherly image is
an image of steadfastness and care.[8]

---

2 Samuel', in Athalya Brenner (ed.), *A Feminist Companion to Samuel and Kings*
(Feminist Companion to the Bible, 5; Sheffield: Sheffield Academic Press, 1994),
pp. 26-42 (40).

7.   See, for example, Mic. 4.8 versus Isa. 66.8. The female imagery of Isaiah is
treated in more detail in Leila Leah Bronner, 'Gynomorphic Imagery in Exilic
Isaiah (40–66)', *Dor leDor* 12 (1983–84), pp. 71-83.

8.   Elsewhere the Bible describes God's love as fatherly love: 'As a father has
compassion on his children, so the Lord has compassion on those who fear him'
(Ps. 103.13). It is surprising how distinct fatherly and motherly love are, here and

Whenever a feminine role is attributed to God, it is always *mother* but never *wife*.[9] Moreover, the Bible seems to strictly distinguish the √ mothering role for God from any erotic role. God the mother never has any marital dimension, just as Zion the daughter never has any private dimension. In both cases, then, the patterns of the imagery are about how women should act in relation to communal obligations— especially if we recognize that, in biblical terms, the bearing and caring for children is not primarily a fulfillment of private desire but of communal obligation.

Despite the common association of the image of the mother with God and the image of the daughter with the nation of Israel and Zion, I cannot find any place where God the mother is mothering Zion the daughter. This is, in fact, in keeping with most of the Bible. Mothers are mothers of sons; and daughters are daughters of fathers, at least in the stories clearly enunciated in the text. The figurative use of daughter and mother personas can be seen as acknowledging and dignifying female experience; yet, when we turn to daughters and mothers as historical persons, we find a less glorious picture.

Raising a Daughter: Implied Parenting in the Bible

Statements about parenting in the Bible generally concern the discipline and the marriage of children. The mother is included in several of the mandates to children about honoring parents, beginning with the commandment 'Honor thy father and thy mother'.[10] Only two passages mention the mother vis-à-vis her daughter explicitly. One says that the mother of a daughter shall be regarded as unclean for twice as long as the mother of a son (Lev. 12.2-5). The other states that 'the girl's father and mother shall produce the evidence of the girl's virginity' (Deut. 22.13) if a man declares that the girl was not a virgin when he married her. The mother drops out of sight immediately in this case, however, possibly because the biblical narrators recognize

---

throughout the Bible. The former tends toward the contingent, the latter toward the categorical.

9. Jer. 51.5, 'For Israel and Judah were not widowed ['almān]/ Of their God the Lord of Hosts', is the exception to this rule. Many commentators change the reading of the text from 'almān (widower) to 'almānâ (widow) to prevent the possibility of figuring God as the wife with the people as his husband. In 'widow' there is still a certain distancing of the sexual.

10. For example Exod. 20.12, 21.15, 21.17; Deut. 5.16; Lev. 19.3, 20.9; Prov. 1.8, 6.20, 20.20.

the father as a public figure but not the mother.[11] Only the father goes before the elders to provide the proof of the daughter's virginity and, if the daughter is found guilty, she is stoned to death at 'the entrance of her father's house' as she 'fornicated while under her father's authority' (Deut. 22.17, 21). As so often in the Bible, the daughter's fate is placed in the hands of her father and her mother is narratively absent.

Such mandates are occasionally supplemented by more informal instructions to parents and children. For example, in Mic. 7.6, the complete despair of the prophet is communicated through his vision of the disintegration of the family:

> For son spurns father,
> Daughter rises up against mother,
> Daughter-in-law against mother-in-law—
> A man's own household
> Are his enemies.

Note how the daughter is paired with the mother, the son with the father—even in rebellion the Bible divides the sexes. Similarly, the proverb 'Like mother, like daughter' (Ezek. 16.44-45) divides the sexes in order to visit the sins of the mother on her daughter. Proverbs gives importance to the mother's instructions but it admonishes only the son to 'not forsake your mother's teaching'—the daughter goes unmentioned, for reasons we can only speculate about. Here and there, in the general discussions of the parent–child relationship in the Bible, we catch glimpses of the mother–daughter relationship and glimpses of its absence. The daughter is, by implication, under the supervision of the mother and has little to do with the father, but we are given very little sense of the day-to-day interaction of mothers and daughters or of the responsibilities of the mother toward the daughter. For the most part, we have to interpolate and imagine.[12]

---

11. The role of the queen mother (*gᵉbîrâ*) at court is perhaps an exception, in that the king's mother may have held an official position as an advisor to her son. On this see, for example, Niels-Erik A. Andreasen, 'The Role of the Queen Mother in Israelite Society', *CBQ* 45 (1983), pp. 179-94; Zafrira Ben-Barak, 'The Status and Right of the *Gᵉbîrâ*', *JBL* 110 (1991), pp. 23-34.

12. Carol Meyers argues that 'Women in agrarian household settings probably exercised some control over the marital arrangements of their offspring. The Bible calls the household "mother's household" rather than the usual "father's household" in several passages concerned with marriageable daughters (Gen. 24.28; Ruth 1.8; Song 3.4, 8.2).' See Carol L. Meyers, 'Everyday Life: Women in the Period of the Hebrew Bible', in Carol A. Newsom and Sharon H. Ringe (eds.), *The*

Visible Mothers and Daughters: Three Stories

Let us turn now to the three stories that feature a daughter whose mother's name is written down in the Bible. Given that Dinah, Miriam and Tamar—unlike Achsah, Jephthah's daughter, the Levite's concubine and so many of the other daughters in the Bible—have mothers who are named, and given that naming implies importance in the Bible, these stories should give us the rare opportunity to explore the biblical mother–daughter relationship.

The first mother and daughter—Jochebed and Miriam—remain unnamed in the narrative for a long time. This, however, is true for all the participants in the story of Exodus 2: Moses is named first (Exod. 2.10, by the daughter of Pharaoh), then his brother Aaron (Exod. 4.14), then his parents Amram and Jochebed are named together (Exod. 6.20). Pharaoh's daughter is never named,[13] and Miriam is not named until very late (she is left out of the genealogy in Exod. 6.20), after the parting of the Red Sea, when she is called 'Miriam the prophetess, Aaron's sister' (Exod. 15.20). In fact, we must read back from Num. 26.59 that Miriam is the sister who, in Exodus 2, waits to see Moses' fate and brings their mother to Pharaoh's daughter as a wet nurse. The latter is as close as the biblical narrator gets to an interaction between this daughter and her mother. Although we assume that the daughter is acting in sympathy with her mother, even this is guessing. Jochebed and Amram both disappear from the narrative immediately,[14] and neither is shown interacting with their children. All three children have brilliant careers. Although God speaks mostly to Moses and Aaron, Miriam is accorded the role of prophetess and leader, her death is recorded (Num. 20.1), and in Numbers 12 God speaks to her directly—of course, God punishes her but not Aaron for speaking against Moses' marriage, but at least the narrator has God talk to her. The women of Exodus, as has been noted by scholars such as Eileen Schuller and J. Cheryl Exum,[15] are resourceful, wise and defiant in the

Women's Bible Commentary (Louisville, KY: Westminster/John Knox Press, 1992), pp. 244-51 (249).

13. The daughter of Pharaoh is identified by the rabbis with the Bithiah mentioned in 1 Chron. 4.18. The Midrash comments that her name indicates that she was a daughter of God (*bat-Yāh*) and celebrates her defiance of her father; see *Lev. Rab.* 1.3.

14. Amram's name appears 13 times in the Bible and Jochebed's twice—all in the context of genealogical lists.

15. Eileen Schuller, 'Women of the Exodus in Biblical Retellings of the Second Temple Period', in Peggy L. Day (ed.), *Gender and Difference in Ancient Israel*

face of the oppression of their Egyptian overlords. Miriam and
Jochebed are numbered among those women, and we can only wish
that the narrator had seen fit to give us reason to argue 'Like mother,
like daughter'. Jochebed's daughter had the strange luxury of growing up at a time when the birth of a son was a painful and futile event,
for Pharaoh had decreed, 'Every boy that is born you shall throw into
the Nile, but let every girl live' (Exod. 1.22). It is a situation fraught
with gender politics and emotional possibilities that the narrative,
unfortunately, does not explore.

This failure on the part of the biblical narrator to follow up on
extraordinary narrative possibilities occurs again in the stories of
Dinah and Tamar. Both of these stories involve an extraordinary
event—a scandal or a tragedy—that apparently motivated their inclusion in the biblical record. In the stories of Dinah and Tamar the
themes of rape and incest are played out—with visible consequences
in the public as well as the private sphere. Dinah is the daughter of
Jacob, the patriarchal founder of Israel, and his unloved first wife
Leah. She is the last of Leah's children, the only girl and the only one
of Leah's children whose name is not given an etiology (Gen. 30.21)—
all of which augurs an unfortunate future for this child. The next
incident of Dinah's life recorded in the Bible is her rape by Shechem,
the son of the chief of the region (Gen. 34.1-31). Susan Niditch notes
that Dinah is,

> on the one hand, central to the action, the focus of Shechem's desire, the
> object of negotiations between Jacob and Hamor, the reason for her
> brothers' trickery, and the cause of tension between Jacob and his sons.
> On the other hand, she has no dialogue, no voice.... She seems to fade
> out after her brothers retrieve her.[16]

This is an accurate summary of the biblical narrative, down to the fact
that Leah participates neither in protesting nor in revenging Dinah's
rape. Today the story of the rape of a daughter might well include her
mother's reaction, but this is not the case in the Bible. The mother participates only indirectly and in only one way: she has produced the

(Minneapolis: Fortress Press, 1989), pp. 178-94; J. Cheryl Exum, ' "You Shall Let
Every Daughter Live": A Study of Exodus 1.8–2.10', *Semeia* 28 (1983), pp. 63-82.
More ambivalent views about the roles of the women of Exodus can be found in,
for example, J. Cheryl Exum, ' "Mothers in Israel": A Familiar Story Reconsidered',
in Letty M. Russell (ed.), *Feminist Interpretation of the Bible* (Philadelphia: Westminster Press, 1985), pp. 73-85; Drorah O'Donnell Setel, 'Exodus', in Newsom and
Ringe (eds.), *The Women's Bible Commentary*, pp. 26-35.

16. Susan Niditch, 'Genesis', in Newsom and Ringe (eds.), *The Women's Bible
Commentary*, pp. 10-25 (23).

sons, Simon and Levi, who negotiate with their sister's rapist and make sure that he does not go unpunished.

Jacob, when told of the rape, 'kept silent until [his sons] came home' (v. 5), and the narrator says that 'Jacob's sons answered Shechem and his father Hamor' (v. 13). Throughout, Jacob is depicted as acting expediently and diplomatically (v. 30), while Simon and Levi react vociferously and violently. They ask Jacob, 'Should our sister be treated like a whore?' (v. 31), and destroy the nation of the Hivites in retribution for their sister's dishonor. Years later, on his deathbed, Jacob recalls this incident when talking to his sons (49.5-7):

> Simon and Levi are a pair;
> Their weapons are tools of lawlessness.
> Let not my person be included in their council,
> Let not my being be counted in their assembly.
> For when angry they slay men,
> And when pleased they maim oxen.
> Cursed be their anger so fierce,
> And their wrath so relentless.
> I will divide them in Jacob,
> Scatter them in Israel.

As a result of their violent actions, one of which was their response to the rape of their sister,[17] Simon seems to be excluded from having specified tribal territories and Levi is given the singular blessing of service in the Temple instead of land. The consequences of Simon and Levi's response to their sister's rape are far-reaching. But what happens to Dinah? Her name appears in the list of the descendants of Jacob who came into Egypt (Gen. 46.8, 15), but the Bible makes no further mention of her.[18] The biblical story plays out the meaning of her name, 'judged' or 'avenged'—others act on her behalf and make

17. Later, Simon is chosen, from among the ten of Jacob's sons who went for food to the land of Egypt, as the brother who is left with Joseph as a hostage for their return with Benjamin, Joseph's brother (Gen. 42). Is this because Simon is a troublemaker? because Joseph would find him easiest to kill? because his brothers or his father will miss him most or least? It is impossible to tell from the narrative. Note also that Leah does not intercede for Simon and Levi, which might indicate that she supported or was appalled by their response to their sister's rape. Of course, she may have died before this point in the biblical narrative.

18. Interestingly, the rabbis spend some time developing Dinah's relationship to Leah and discussing her fate. For example, they suggest that by going out alone Dinah is imitating her mother's behavior ('Like mother, like daughter', they quote), and they marry her off variously to Job or her brother Simon. See Leila Leah Bronner, *From Eve to Esther: Rabbinic Reconstructions of Biblical Women* (Louisville, KY: Westminster/John Knox Press, 1994), pp. 118-22.

decisions about her—and then she disappears from the narrative.

As in the story of Dinah, in the story of Tamar, brothers rather than parents play the prominent parts. The opening verses set the scene by naming the three most important characters in the story: Absalom, Tamar and Amnon (2 Sam. 13). They share the same father, King David. From information provided elsewhere we know that Amnon's mother is Ahinoam (2 Sam. 3.2), while the mother of Tamar and Absalom is Maacah (2 Sam. 3.3). Seeing that Amnon's infatuation with his half-sister is making him ill, a cousin of all three siblings advises Amnon to feign illness so that when King David comes to visit, Amnon can ask his father to send Tamar to him. King David sends Tamar to Amnon's quarters, where she bakes and serves him cakes. Having sent all his attendants away, he grabs her and says, 'Come lie with me, sister!' She protests, struggles, argues, to no avail. She asks, 'Where will I carry my shame? And you, you will be like any of the scoundrels in Israel!' (2 Sam. 13.13).

After raping her Amnon's feelings for Tamar shift abruptly, from love or lust to hatred and disgust. He tells his attendants, 'Get this thing out of my presence, and bar the door behind her' (2 Sam. 13.17). She walks away, screaming and tearing her clothes. Whereas Shechem's desire for Dinah had in it an element of love, the story of Tamar begins with Amnon's lust and ends with him loathing her. According to Mosaic law, a man was obligated to marry a woman he raped and could never divorce her (Deut. 22.28-29; cf. Exod. 22.16), and it also prohibits sexual relations between siblings with the same father. There is precedent, then, for dealing with the rape of a daughter, if not necessarily the rape of a daughter by her half-brother. But the spanner in the works is Amnon's sudden hatred for his sister and their father's lack of response. Why does Amnon's love—lust—turn to loathing? The narrative in some respects seems to anticipate modern theory about rape as an act of violence rather than love or lust: Amnon hates Tamar for failing to prevent him from harming her, for reminding him of his own weakness and sinfulness.[19] The rabbis seemed to have shared the view that Amnon's behavior was violent and loathsome, and they discuss at length what they consider to be Tamar's understandable desire for revenge. They empower Tamar to punish Amnon by physically maiming him in such a way as to impair his virility,[20] thus providing a physical basis for his hatred of her.

19. See, for example, Ganse Little, '2 Samuel: Exposition', *IB*, II, pp. 1041-1176 (1113).

20. *B. Sanh.* 21a.

Neither the rabbis nor the biblical narrator bring the mother into the narrative to comfort Tamar, as we might expect today. Her brother Absalom is the first and only one to speak to her: 'Was it your brother Amnon who did this to you? For the present, sister, keep quiet about it; he is your brother. Don't brood over the matter.' Clearly, Tamar expected the shame of her rape to affect Amnon as well as herself, but the king does nothing and her mother is excluded from the narrative. There is no direct communication and little warmth between King David and Tamar, especially by modern standards.[21] King David visited his sick son, but to his violated daughter he sends only a message ordering her to go to Absalom. The biblical narrator does not show King David visiting or comforting Tamar and, although as king he has the power to punish Amnon, he does not; his response communicates neither empathy for Tamar nor outrage at Amnon's immorality.[22] Absalom is the one who acts on Tamar's behalf—he advises her, he takes her under his protection when it becomes clear that King David's only reaction will be to be 'very wroth' (2 Sam. 13.21), and two years later he has his servants kill Amnon.

These details combine to make it clear that behind this series of incidents lurks the specter of King David's sin in taking the wife of Uriah. The story of Tamar is the precipitating factor in the fulfillment of Nathan's prophetic curse, 'The sword shall never depart from thy house' (2 Sam. 12.10), and it is this that the biblical narrator is interested in. The Bible deals with the communal ramifications of this rape, rather than the private experience. It deals not with the psychological but with the practical. It never considers rape from the perspective of the female victim. Because the Bible considers rape a matter of public concern—for example, legally, the father or husband, not the woman, is considered the injured party[23]—the mother's reactions, as part of

---

21.   Ben Sira 7.24-25, 22.3-5 (second century BCE) reiterates this lack of warmth and closeness in father and daughter relationships; Warren C. Trenchard, 'Woman as Daughter', in *idem*, *Ben Sira's View of Women: A Literary Analysis* (BJS, 38; Atlanta: Scholars Press, 1982), pp. 129-65.

22.   See Phyllis Trible, *Texts of Terror: Literary-Feminist Readings of Biblical Narratives* (Philadelphia: Fortress Press, 1984), pp. 53-54: 'David's anger signifies complete sympathy for Amnon and total disregard for Tamar. How appropriate that the story never refers to David and Tamar as father and daughter! The father identifies with the son; the adulterer supports the rapist; the male has joined male to deny justice for the female.'

23.   Louis M. Epstein, *Sex Laws and Customs in Judaism* (New York: Ktav, rev. edn, 1967), p. 179: 'Violation of a girl caused great humiliation to the girl herself,

the private realm, are left out of the narrative, and the fathers must act as political patriarchs rather than as agents of violent revenge.

Later the Sages discuss to what extent Dinah's parents were responsible for her rape, noting that Leah was a bit forward and thus perhaps her daughter was too, but more important is their strengthening of the father's responsibility. They argue that Jacob's delay in returning to his own father is the cause of all the bad things that happen to Jacob, and the rape of his daughter is just one of the evils that befall him.[24] By constructing this connection the Sages make Jacob parallel to King David: in both cases the sins of the father are visited upon their children—their daughters are raped and their sons commit terrible sins—and the fathers must bear the all consequences without reacting violently.

What is interesting in the stories of Dinah and Tamar, then, is that the psychological and emotional component is displaced from the daughters and mothers onto the daughter's brothers by her mother. The brothers are neither responsible patriarchs, nor powerless daughters, nor silent mothers—they find themselves free to express outrage and, as male power figures, as sons rather than daughters, they can act on their emotions. In neither case is it clear that the brother is acting in accordance with his sister's (or his mother's) wishes, but their actions are consonant with how the brother acts as a protector for the sister from the same mother (see also Gen. 24.55-59).[25]

Bitterness Turned to Sweetness:
Ruth, the Song of Songs and Rebekah

But what about the relations between women when the sons and the fathers are dead? The scroll of Ruth provides one answer to this question. The widowed Naomi's first impulse after her sons and her husband die is to send her daughters-in-law away. She says to them,

> 'Turn back, each of you to her mother's house. May the Lord deal
> kindly with you, as you have dealt with the dead and with me! May the

constituted an affront to the family, and, of course, meant a loss of value in the defloration of the virgin.'

24. See Avivah Gottlieb Zornberg, *Genesis: The Beginning of Desire* (Philadelphia: Jewish Publication Society of America, 1995), pp. 225-29.

25. Rivkah Harris, 'Independent Women in Ancient Mesopotamia?', in Barbara S. Lesko (ed.), *Women's Earliest Records from Ancient Egypt and Western Asia* (Atlanta: Scholars Press, 1989), pp. 145-56 (153), similarly notes in passing the way brothers play a protective role for their sisters.

Lord grant that each of you find security in the house of a husband!'
And she kissed them farewell. They broke into weeping (Ruth 1.8-9).

Here again we have women in the midst of tragedy, but the contrast
is startling. Tamar and Dinah are surrounded by men who, to put it
baldly, are either silent or violent. Of the few kind words spoken in
their stories, none are spoken by women. Here, at the beginning of the
book of Ruth, we suddenly hear the voice of loving kindness, words
that are spoken between women that both enshrine acts of kindness
and are an act of kindness in themselves.

Ruth is the unique story in the Bible of two women choosing to be
together as mother and daughter even after their formal familial ties
have been sundered. Naomi always calls Ruth 'daughter' and is
always concerned about Ruth's future. She tells Ruth, 'Daughter, I
must seek a home for you, where you may be happy' (Ruth 3.1).
Although Ruth names Naomi neither 'mother' nor 'mother-in-law',
she allows Naomi to function as her mother throughout the narrative,[26] and her devotion to Naomi is unconditional from the start of
the book:

> Do not entreat me to leave you, to turn back from following you. For
> where you go, I will go; wherever you lodge, I will lodge; your people
> shall be my people and your God my God; where you die I will die and
> there I will be buried. Thus and more may God do to me if anything but
> death parts you and me (Ruth 1.16-18).

The loyalty between these women is extraordinary by any standards, and it is particularly notable given that the Bible rarely records
scenes of loyalty or kindness between women.[27] What are we to make
of the fact that the Bible explicitly has these two women play the roles
of mother and daughter? Is it that the Bible can only imagine female
friendship, especially between women of different generations, in
terms of mothers and daughters? Or is it that the Bible is holding up
the mother–daughter relationship as a paradigm of love, namely that

26. The narrator carefully distinguishes that Ruth and Orpah are daughters-in-
law and that Naomi is 'mother-in-law'; Boaz, too, notes that Naomi is Ruth's
'mother-in-law'. Naomi calls Ruth and Orpah 'daughters', Boaz and Naomi both
call Ruth 'daughter', but Ruth calls Boaz only 'my lord'.

27. We find such scenes in Ruth, the Song of Songs and perhaps in Gen. 24,
when Rebecca runs home to 'her mother's house'. Lot's daughters cooperate in
seducing their father, and Jephthah's daughter is comforted by her female companions. In the Bible there are also scenes of cruelty between women as they compete for the love of men (e.g. Sarah and Hagar, Leah and Rebecca, Hannah and
Penenah). It must be significant that, as will be discussed below, the three stories
of cross-generational affection between women include the term 'mother's house'.

at their best humans will care for one another *as if* they were mother and daughter? Before we can begin to answer such questions, however, we have to address another problem: that it is hard to know exactly what comprises 'daughterly' behavior or 'motherly' behavior in the Bible because we see so little of it. Ruth gives us some insight, even if it is impossible to keep our modern understanding of these roles from influencing our perceptions. The dialogue between the women is about mundane matters, and yet to modern ears it seems full of love and care. The mother says: tell me about your day, do this so you will be safer, do that so you can be married. The daughter says: I went to work, I met this man, this is what he said to me, this is what he did.

Throughout the book, the women work toward material as well emotional security. Ruth gleans to provide food for herself and Naomi, while Naomi advises Ruth so that she obtains a worthy husband. Eventually Naomi instructs Ruth thus: 'Wash therefore and anoint yourself, and put on your best clothes, and go down to the threshing floor' (3.3). Ruth responds, 'I will do everything you tell me' (3.5). Perhaps here we see mother–daughter behavior at its best: perfect trust by each woman in the judgment of the other, perfect willingness by each to gamble for long-term material security for both of them and for the chance of a son who would continue the lineage.

Indeed, some scholars argue that the entire purpose of the scroll *is* the end: the birth of the son. The lineage established is full of strange quirks, however, including two foreign women. The scroll details the actions of one of these foreign women and has the elders explicitly remind Boaz and us of the actions of the other: 'And may your house be like the house of Perez whom Tamar bore to Judah' (4.12). Both Tamar and Ruth were childless widows, and Tamar plays the harlot and Ruth visits Boaz alone at night in order to force the male relative (redeemer) to give her the necessary son. In the scroll of Ruth, even the biblical tradition of the necessity for the 'right' mother for the 'right' son is ignored. As Exum writes,

> Abraham's wife Sarah, not his concubine Hagar, must be the mother of the rightful heir; Isaac and Jacob may not marry Canaanite—that is, 'foreign'—wives (Gen. 24.3; 27.46; 28.1). Not only must the 'right' woman be the mother of the chosen people, but the 'right' son must be the bearer of the promise: of Abraham's sons, Isaac and not Ishmael; of Isaac's sons, Jacob and not Esau.[28]

28. J. Cheryl Exum, 'The Mothers of Israel: The Patriarchal Narratives from a Feminist Perspective', *BR* 2 (1986), pp. 60-67 (63).

Boaz has married a foreign woman (a Moabite) who bears the son, Obed, named by a chorus of women as the rightful heir and progenitor of the line of David:

> Blessed be the Lord, who has not withheld a redeemer from you today! May his name be perpetuated in Israel! He will renew your life and sustain your old age; for he is born of your daughter-in-law, who loves you and is better to you than seven sons (Ruth 4.14-15).

It is the love of Ruth and Naomi that provides the lineage of King David. It is they, not the men of the story, who shape the hope of the nation of Israel out of the hopelessness of their own situation; it is they who draw sweetness out of bitterness and the agent of this transformation is love rather than jealousy, inclusion rather than exclusion. The pattern set by the matriarchs in Genesis is remade by love in Ruth.

There is a long and honored tradition of viewing the story of Ruth and Naomi as a book about women working to re-establish the line of their dead husbands—not as a book about two women caring for one another. This is indeed an element of the narrative throughout the scroll, and indeed the final four verses of the scroll are given over to a genealogy that does not mention the women. Yet coupled with the scroll's concern for husbands and sons is a story of love between women that is not only the love of friends but also the love of mother and daughter. The narrative of the scroll of Ruth may provide insight into the situation of foreign women and childless women among the Israelites. It may say something about women and economic pragmatism and the family. It does say a lot about the relationship between God and his people and about the collective life of the nation. But embedded in all of that is the story of a particular relationship between individuals—specifically the cross-generational relationship between two women—which closes with the strongest articulation of the love of a daughter for her mother and of a mother for her daughter that appears in the Bible: 'he is born of your daughter-in-law, who loves you and means more to you than seven sons' (4.15).[29] This is a very direct observation on the love between Ruth and Naomi, and one that harks back to their initial condition—before Naomi's sons died, before Ruth married Boaz, for it must be noted that Ruth's

---

29. Compare the words of Elkanah to his barren wife Hannah: 'Am I not better, do I not mean [*tôb*] more to you than ten sons?' (1 Sam. 1.8). See Edward F. Campbell, Jr, *Ruth* (AB, 7; Garden City, NY: Doubleday, 1975), p. 164 n. 15, on the uses of *tôb* in the book of Ruth to emphasize 'not only Ruth's quality of person but also her prime importance to Naomi's well-being'.

second marriage does not officially make Naomi either her mother or her mother-in-law but rather a relative by marriage. It indirectly suggests that their initial relationship has become fixed, as if it were written in blood, in love and loyalty.

The *ḥesed* (lovingkindness) that characterizes the relationship between Ruth and Naomi spills over into the other relationships of the book. Boaz is not one who simply fulfilled the legal requirements of levirate marriage—he has acted out of kindness beyond duty. The willingness of both members of this couple to accept obligations not incumbent upon them by law or custom makes them paragons of righteousness, living embodiments of *ḥesed*. If there were more mother–daughter relationships in the Bible, we could test a theory that the absence of the mother augurs a daughter endangered, at the mercy of the evil men may wish to do to her (e.g. Tamar, Dinah, Jephthah's daughter, the Levite's concubine), while the presence of the mother equals a daughter protected from danger (e.g. Naomi and Ruth, Bethuel's wife and Rebekah). The only other place in the Bible to test this theory is the Song of Songs.

The Songs of Songs comprises a number of love poems that dramatize an emotionally rather than narratively coherent story of the love between a young girl and her lover. They perform a duet in which the woman usually leads, her lover answers, and various anonymous voices join in from time to time. Some poems generalize about love while others praise the physical beauty of the lovers, speak of the difficulties and the ecstasies of their love, or envision the marriage rites of King Solomon. Over the ages, this book has been approached most often either as an allegory of the love of God for his people (partly in order to justify the inclusion of love poetry in the biblical canon) or (especially in modern times) as a sequence of erotic poetry celebrating the love of a man and a woman.

I want to focus, however, on the surprising importance in the Song of Songs of the woman's relationship to her mother and her brothers, and on how their relations correspond to as well as differ from patterns set up elsewhere in the Bible. Ariel Bloch and Chana Bloch, in their commentary on their translation of the scroll, lay out her embeddedness in the family:

> The Shulamite is her mother's favorite (6.9); when she speaks of her brothers, she calls them, in the Hebrew, 'my mother's sons' (1.6); she wishes her lover were as close to her as a brother 'who nursed at [her] mother's breast' (8.1). She brings her lover home to her 'mother's house', perhaps to signify a more binding relationship (3.4; 8.2). She declares that she awakened her lover in the very place where his

mother conceived and gave birth to him (8.5). Even King Solomon's mother appears in the poem, crowning her son on his wedding day (3.11)… The brothers [1.6; 2.15; 8.8-10] and the watchmen [3.3; 5.7] provide whatever friction there is in the poem. From the beginning, the Shulamite's brothers are watching her; as one would expect in a biblical text, they are their sister's keepers.[30]

We find here the same configuration of characters as in the story of Naomi, Ruth and Boaz—a mother, her daughter, the daughter's lover, and no father for the daughter—with the notable addition of the daughter's brothers. We find as well a variation on the configurations of characters found in the stories of Rebekah, Tamar and Dinah: Tamar and Dinah's stories never mention their mothers and center on the relations among the lover/rapist, father and full brothers; Rebekah's story mentions her father Bethuel once but centers on the negotiations of her future husband's representatives and her full brother Laban and (unnamed) mother. Every story has a different configuration of the family, and every story has the family act and react differently to the relationship between the daughter and her suitor. The stories of Dinah and Tamar are the tragic ones, and this is in part, as I have argued, because the mothers are missing from the stories of Dinah and Tamar. For both, there is no voice of loving kindness; for both, there is no refuge in the mother's house.

The noun phrase 'mother's house' appears twice in the Song of Songs. In both cases the daughter is talking to her lover: 'I held him fast, I would not let him go / Till I brought him to my mother's house, / To the chamber of her who conceived me' (3.4); 'I would lead you, I would bring you / To the house of my mother, / Of her who taught me' (8.2).[31] The daughter may simply be eager to designate him as her official lover by introducing him to her mother,[32] but the language surrounding the term indicates as well, I think, that the daughter regards her mother's house as a place where love can and does reside, and that she believes she is honoring their love by bringing him home. Clearly, she expects acceptance from her mother, even if

---

30. Ariel Bloch and Chana Bloch, *The Song of Songs: A New Translation with an Introduction and Commentary* (New York: Random House, 1995), p. 6.

31. The association of the mother and the mother's house with learning appears as well in Ruth (who learns from Naomi) and in Proverbs (Woman Wisdom, chs. 1–9; praise of woman, 31.10-31; and *passim*).

32. For this reading and the wide range of allegorical as well as sociological interpretations that the term 'mother's house' has received, see M.H. Pope, *Song of Songs* (AB, 7C; Garden City, NY: Doubleday, 1977), pp. 421-22.

her mother's sons are not so accommodating ('My brothers were angry with me, / they made me guard the vineyards. / I have not guarded my own' [1.6]; 'What shall we do for our sister / when suitors besiege her? / If she is a wall, we will build / a silver turret upon her. / If she is a door, we will bolt her / with beams of cedar wood' [8.8-9][33]).

The term 'mother's house' appears in only two other places in the Bible—in the stories of Ruth and Rebekah—where it is again linked to love, wisdom, women's agency and marriage.[34] As we saw above, Naomi tells Orpah and Ruth, 'Turn back, each of you to her mother's house' (Ruth 1.8). It is not clear what associations Naomi has with the mother's house—whether she thinks of it as a place that will take in these bereft daughters-in-law in grudgingly or as a place where they will be welcomed. Given the tone of the rest of this scroll, surely Naomi hopes that she is sending them to a place like the mother's house in the Song of Songs. In the story of Rebekah and Isaac, we find that 'The girl ran to her mother's house and told them what had happened' (Gen. 24.27). Shortly thereafter, her mother and her brother agree to her marriage with a stranger, but the Bible records their strong reluctance to part with Rebekah: 'Let the maiden remain with us some ten days, then you may go' (Gen. 24.55), they plead with the messenger. This courtship story ends in the tent of the lover: 'Isaac brought her into the tent [house] of his mother Sarah, and he took Rebekah as his wife. Isaac loved her, and thus found comfort after his mother's death' (Gen. 24.67). These mother's houses in Genesis are clearly like those in the Song of Songs. In sum, although the term 'mother's house' appears only four times in the Bible, in every case the daughter seems to be cherished.

In addition to the two appearances of 'mother's house', the word 'mother' appears in the Song of Songs five times—a high proportion

---

33. Trans. Bloch and Bloch, *The Song of Songs*.

34. See the article by Carol Meyers addressing the sociological implications of this term and drawing out the similarities of its context, ' "To Her Mother's House": Considering a Counterpart to the Israelite Bêt 'āb', in David Jobling, Peggy L. Day and Gerald T. Sheppard (eds.), *The Bible and the Politics of Exegesis* (Cleveland: Pilgrim Press, 1991), pp. 39-51. Meyers also discusses the history of emendation that tends to regard 'mother's house' as a textual corruption. See as well Pope, *Song of Songs*, pp. 421-22; Carol Meyers, 'Returning Home: Ruth 1.8 and the Gendering of the Book of Ruth', in A. Brenner (ed.), *A Feminist Companion to Ruth* (Feminist Companion to the Bible, 3; Sheffield: Sheffield Academic Press, 1993), pp. 85-114.

for any book of the Bible[35]—while the words 'father' and 'father's house' do not appear at all in this scroll. Twice we hear of the mother of the daughter's brothers, twice of the mother of a male lover, and three times of the mother of the daughter. Altogether, 'mother' is used once by the lover, once by an anonymous speaker and five times by the daughter. It is the daughter who twice speaks of 'my mother's house', who twice identifies her brothers as 'my mother's sons' (1.6; 8.1), and who imagines her lover's conception thus: 'It was there your mother conceived you, / There she who bore you conceived you' (8.5). Clearly, if the mother is in this scroll, she is there through the agency of the daughter. Just as in the scroll of Ruth, it is the daughter to forces us to pay attention to the mother.

The similarities between Ruth and the Song of Songs do not end here, however. Just as the extraordinarily loving relationship between Ruth and Naomi seems to spill over into all of the relationships in the scroll of Ruth, the excess of love in the Song of Songs permeates every relationship. The daughter clearly cherishes her mother and the mother of her lover; and even though she may begin by describing her bothers as dictatorial—'My mother's sons were angry with me, / They made me watch the vineyards' (1.6)—she later tells her lover that they could kiss in the street 'If only it could be as with a brother, / As if you had nursed at my mother's breast' (8.1). Here and in 8.8-9 the brothers come across as zealous yet cherishing guardians with whom she does not always agree. In another section of the scroll, an anonymous speaker tells the maidens of Zion to 'go forth / And gaze upon King Solomon / Wearing the crown that his mother / Gave him on his wedding day' (3.11)—even the king appears in this scroll primarily as a lover and as the son of his mother.

It is left to the male lover, however, to tell of the relationship between the daughter and her mother and between the daughter and other women:

> The only one of her mother,
> The choice one of her who bore her.
> Maidens see and acclaim her;
> Queens and concubines, and praise her (6.9).

Throughout the Song of Songs, the lover praises the daughter extravagantly. He makes comparisons to flora that we now find commonplace as well as architectural comparisons and faunal metaphors

---

35. 'Mother' appears 209 times in the Hebrew Bible, 'mother-in-law' 11 times (10 in Ruth, 1 in Micah; see also Deut. 27.23).

that we now find odd.[36] In the context of the Bible, his praise in 6.9 is just as startling as such figures as 'your neck is like the tower of David' or 'your hair is as a flock of goats' (4.4), because he speaks of the preciousness of the daughter to her mother.[37] The Bible does not prepare us for such a mother–daughter relationship. The mother in the Song of Songs has sons as well as this daughter, but the idiom indicates not only that she prizes the daughter but also that she treasures the daughter *over* the sons. Ariel and Chana Bloch point out that 'one she is to her mother' (6.9) shows 'a child's unique beloved-ness or preciousness', but it is worth emphasizing that it is only in the Song of Songs that this idiom is applied to a daughter.[38]

Conclusion

The mother–daughter relationships visible in the Bible are scattered across thousands of years: from the early patriarchal period (Rebekah) to the time of Judges (Ruth) to after the Babylonian exile (Song of Songs). Discussion of the dates of composition and redaction of these works is not within the ambit of this essay, yet I think this historical range is worth pointing out. So many mother–daughter relationships are missing from the Bible; yet, when they become visible, they are unexpectedly and movingly positive. They form a continuum with the imagery of God as the caring mother of Israel in exilic Isaiah. Over the ages, biblical exegesis has looked at Rebekah not as daughter but as matriarch, has tended to allegorize the Song of Songs and has focused on the genealogical aspects of the book of Ruth. In so doing, it overlooked and thus obscured what traces of the mother–daughter relationship were written into the Bible. The biblical narrative usually constructs women in accordance with a patriarchal vision; yet as I have tried to show in this essay, the Bible does provide some positive portrayals of the mother–daughter relationship. Focusing on these

36. Particularly good on the latter is Carol Meyers, 'Gender Imagery in the Song of Songs', *HAR* 10 (1986), pp. 209-23 (repr. in A. Brenner [ed.], *A Feminist Companion to the Song of Songs* [Feminist Companion to the Bible, 1; Sheffield: Sheffield Academic Press, 1993], pp. 197-212).

37. Naming a daughter 'Hephzibah', which means 'my delight is in her', indicates a warm feeling for the daughter, but the Bible does not provide substantiating details; see 2 Kgs 21.1 (the wife of Hezekiah and the mother of Manasseh, king of Judah) and Isa. 62.4 (a name for Jerusalem restored). The description of the warmth among women here in the Song of Songs is as unique as the warmth between the mother and daughter.

38. Compare Gen. 22.2 and Prov. 4.3. See Bloch and Bloch, *Song of Songs*, p. 190.

traces of mother and daughter in the Bible forces us to remember that women must have played far more varied and significant roles in the public and private life of ancient Israel than the textual evidence encourages us to believe.[39] There are many gaps in our knowledge about ancient women, but not everything about their lives is missing. The biblical mother–daughter relationship, as I hope I have shown, is an enduring element in the Bible well worth recovering. When the mother appears along with the daughter, love appears as well.

39. J. Cheryl Exum, *Fragmented Women: Feminist (Sub)versions of Biblical Narratives* (Valley Forge, PA: Trinity Press International, 1993), p. 136.

BLACK MOTHER WOMEN[1] AND DAUGHTERS: SIGNIFYING
FEMALE–DIVINE RELATIONSHIPS IN THE HEBREW BIBLE
AND AFRICAN-AMERICAN MOTHER–DAUGHTER SHORT STORIES

Cheryl A. Kirk-Duggan

> *Oh, you sassy mother-daughter women*
> *Your dynamism burns*
> *The fabric of your souls*
> *And then some.*
> *You electrify the wind as it whistles past*
> *Making some angry, some jealous*
> *Some puzzled and mystified.*
> *Who are you?*

Introduction

Women bond with women and with their daughters, within family, within extended family and within society. Such familial relationships resemble patterned, colorful gardens of diversity. The vibrancy and life force of these gardens exist in living stories and written texts. Mother–daughter poems and stories by African-American writers in *Memory of Kin*,[2] edited by Mary Helen Washington, provide a lens for reading the stories of Esther and Ruth. Both biblical protagonists shift between the roles of mother to daughter midst the metaphors of famine, רעב and feast, משתה. In the biblical and contemporary short stories mother–daughter dyads reckon with the dynamics of identity, sexuality, anger, awareness, abundance, racism, creativity, boundaries and the pain of the mothers and their woman—like girl children. This essay uses the mother–daughter short stories from Washington's *Memory of Kin* as the context for a womanist treatment of female

---

1.   Audre Lorde, 'Black Mother Woman', in Mary Helen Washington (ed.), *Memory of Kin: Stories about Family by Black Writers* (New York: Anchor/Double-day, 1991), p. 98.

2.   Mary Helen Washington (ed.), *Memory of Kin: Stories about Family by Black Writers* (New York: Anchor; Garden City, NY: Doubleday, 1991).

relationships resonating from the intriguing theology of Ruth and Esther. That is, several elements present in these two biblical texts make them both engaging and enigmatic. These elements are: (1) both stories are the only two texts named for women in the Hebrew Bible; (2) theologically, a faithful Moabite protagonist symbolizes a universal יהוה in Ruth, while the explicit name and voice of יהוה are absent in Esther; (3) both stories concern a shift in the power status of women: in Ruth, a politics of displacement, where Ruth moves from fullness to emptiness, and the reverse dynamic occurs for Naomi; and in Esther, a politics of empowerment where Esther goes from being 'an orphan' to queen and her people move from being fair game for Haman, to being triumphant over their adversaries. These topics of women's roles, God's activity on behalf of 'the outsider' and the notion of power brokerage make these two books excellent texts for a womanist reading.

'*Womanist*',[3] a term coined by Alice Walker, comes from the Black folk expression, 'you acting womanish'; it means to act 'grown up, responsible and in charge', in a way that is 'outrageous, audacious, courageous, willful', and one who loves everyone; a feminist of color. Womanist theory particularly explores racism, sexism, classism, towards a theory and praxis of wholeness. Naomi learns wholeness from Ruth. Esther enables Israel's, her extended family's, salvation. I review the dynamics of five biblical and contemporary short stories under the rubrics of משתה and רעב. Under the thematic epithets of (1) the evocation of sensory perception, (2) the politics of seduction and (3) the compassion of silence, I set up the dialogue between the mother–daughter familial short stories in Washington's volume and the biblical 'short stories' of Ruth and Esther. This discourse affords an examination of several motifs: the self and community midst difference; paradigms of meaning and conflict; mother–daughter social location, theology and spirituality; and mother–daughter notions of hope midst oppression. I use the terms משתה and רעב in both a metaphorical and an actual sense.

Esther and Ruth are kinship stories where משתה and רעב form the bass voice to the counterpoint of relational differences, catastrophes, celebration and irony. Esther, a story that initially places the protagonist in the roles of daughter and later of queen–mother (which I delineate below) begins with the opulence and splendor of multiple משתה, hosted separately by King Ahasuerus and Queen Vashti. This

---

3. Alice Walker, *In Search of our Mothers' Gardens: Womanist Prose* (New York: Harcourt Brace Jovanich, 1983 [1967]), p. xi.

wealth stands in opposition to Esther's metaphorical experience of
רעב in the loss of her parents. After Ahasuerus deposes Vashti from
her throne for disobeying his direct order to parade before his guests,
he chooses Esther to be queen. If Vashti were allowed to disobey
without reprimand, the other women of Persia and Media would no
longer acquiesce and be under the total control of their husbands
(Est. 1.10-22). That is, these women would subvert male dominance;
despise and disrespect their husbands; deny these men total control
over their lives, and hold them in contempt (1.17-18). For the king and
his noble wise men, his advisors, such willful behavior would not be
viewed as an invitation toward mutuality, but was viewed as unacceptable chaos. Thus when Memucan, one of the nobles, proposed
that the king issue an edict that would assure that all women would
honor their husbands, this pleased the royal court, and a letter of the
same was sent to all provinces (1.22). When Esther ascends to the
throne, she engages in political intrigue to attain the king's favor via a
משתה in her quarters; yet she symbolically confronts רעב in the threat
to the lives of her guardian and her people, her 'children'. Esther, at
the coaching of her cousin and guardian Mordecai, has not yet
revealed she is Hebrew, like her subjects (2.10, 20). She had not yet
made public that these were 'her people, her kin'. One can either posit
that the text here signifies a closeness and sense of responsibility, or a
matter of ethnic identity. If one pursues the former sense of related-
ness, then Esther's later attitude makes a case for the persona of
queen–mother, as the texts seem to support a reading of strong
maternal authority. For instance, when Esther tells the Jews to fast for
her, when she must intercede on their behalf (4.16) and, again, when
she asks the king for the lives of her people (7.3). Further, Esther was
distressed and alarmed (4.4) after learning of Mordecai's mourning
and grief over the impending doom of the Jews (4.1-3), because of the
edict to destroy them (3.7-11). Her concern for Mordecai and for the
other Jews, in the context of her socio-political location as queen, supports the notion of Esther as queen–mother. Her ultimate maternal
success culminates in the elevation of Mordecai (8.2), the overthrow of
Haman's projected pogrom—that is, the return of the documents to
carry out Haman's plan to destroy the Jews (8.7-8), and the celebration
of this triumph with the משתה of Purim (9.19, 22).

Was יהוה the providential force in the wings behind the drama on
stage? In Esther, the answer to this question concerns one's reading of
4.14. Mordecai reminds Esther that if she does not speak up, deliverance will emerge from 'another place'. Her initial hesitancy occurred
because all of the king's subjects knew that any individual who

entered the court without the king's summons would be executed. Mordecai encourages Esther to act as a participant in accomplishing God's purpose. While the book of Esther seems to lack religiosity, and the Septuagint and rabbinical traditions attempt to remedy this lack by adding religious elements, the text seems to imply that יהוה stands within and behind history to act on the part of God's people.[4]

In contrast, Ruth's maternal experience vaporizes. After Ruth gives birth to a son, Naomi takes him in her lap and becomes his nurse. The neighbor women, meanwhile, call the child the son of Naomi, disavowing Ruth's maternity (Ruth 4.16-17).

Ruth, a short story of faith and family loyalties, opens with a double רעב: the lack of food and the symbolic רעב through the loss of husbands and sons, the locus of ancient women's identity. That loss or figurative רעב creates emptiness for 'mother' Naomi. 'Daughter' Ruth avoids her own emptiness and loss, supported by יהוה, to bring Naomi back toward an encounter of fullness, of illustrative, realized משתה: the shift from Naomi's emptiness (which Naomi later signifies in her expression of bitterness, 'call me Mara', 1.20) to fullness is embodied in Ruth's proclamation, 'where you go, I go; where you lodge, I lodge...' (1.16-17) and in all that Ruth does for Naomi (Ruth 2.11). A sense of existential and spiritual רעב sets the context and impetus at the beginning of the story. Elimelech and his family leave Bethlehem for Moab, a country linked (1) to hostility toward Israel (Moab either fears or tries to capture Israel—Num. 22–24; Judg. 3.12-30); (2) to sexual perversity (incestuous relations facilitate the origins of the Moabites—Gen. 19.30-38); (3) to a place that used food for the feast of local gods (Num. 25.1-5); and (4) to the practice of encouraging Israel to commit idolatry (Deut. 23.3-6).[5] Amidst three events and

---

4.   Sidnie Ann White, 'Esther', in Carol A. Newsom and Sharon H. Ringe (eds.), *The Women's Bible Commentary* (Louisville, KY: Westminster/John Knox Press, 1992), pp. 124-29 (125). Many unresolved questions remain concerning the Esther text. Most scholars posit that this story is an early Jewish novella made up of three separate tales: one about Esther also known as Hadassah; another story about Mordecai and court situations that threaten the destruction of the Jews in Susa; and a story about Vashti. The story was probably included in the Hebrew Bible because of its relation to Purim, a popular festival for Jews in the Diaspora later accepted in Judah, although the Purim material seems to be an addition. The only tie between the story and the festival is the use of *pūr*, or lot[s] by Haman when he seeks to determine the day for the massacre of the Jews.

5.   Amy-Jill Levine, 'Ruth', in Carol Newsom and Sharon H. Ringe (eds.), *The Women's Bible Commentary* (Louisville, KY: Westminster/John Knox Press, 1992), pp. 78-84 (79).

processes, Ruth experiences fullness: an air of seduction (ch. 3); Boaz's negotiation with the elders about property (ch. 4); and an allusion to the levirate obligation.

Boaz speaks with ten elders and says to Naomi's closest relative, her 'redeemer', that Naomi has to sell the land that belonged to Elimelech. Since Elimelech is dead, the land would ordinarily go to his eldest son. According to the levirate code, if a man dies without leaving an heir, his wife is to have sexual intercourse with his next oldest brother and the child of that union belongs to the lineage of the dead brother (Deut. 25.1-10). The text does not mention the existence of a brother for Elimelech. Although Elimelech did have two sons by Naomi, both of them are dead. While the levirate code is an obligation to be acted on by men, the text has Boaz ask *Naomi's* relative if he will redeem the land, hence the condition of the levirate (4.5). The text creates a reversal as it turns a tradition on its head by asking of a woman a question that should be asked of a man and by implying the levirate obligation. Ruth stealthily uncovers Boaz's feet and lies down during the middle of the night, at the advice of Naomi (3.4-5, 7, 19). Boaz negotiates and alludes to levirate marriage as he offers Elimelech's (and de facto his dead sons') property, including daughter-in-law Ruth, to restore the names of the dead. After Naomi's relative, the redeemer, rejects the offer, Boaz purchases all that belonged to Elimelech and his sons Chilion and Mahlon (4.1-10). Though Boaz's negotiations are not the exact specifications of levirate marriage, an allusion to that legality exists, although more so in 1.11-13 than in ch. 4. While one can argue for or against the presence of, or allusion to, levirate obligation in Ruth, one of the goals of the levirate—producing a son, a male heir, so that the name of the dead will live on—is certainly at stake in Ruth.

The second goal or social institution embodied in levirate obligation is a commitment to provide for a husbandless woman.[6] While Ruth is under no obligation to marry Boaz, the text does tie marriage to Ruth with attaining possession of Elimelech's land (4.1-12). The text reflects that marriage to Boaz was an experience of fullness. But this short-

---

6.   Jack M. Sasson, *Ruth: A New Translation with a Philological Commentary and a Formalist-Folklorist Interpretation* (The Johns Hopkins Near Eastern Studies, 11; Baltimore: The Johns Hopkins University Press, 1979), pp. 128-33. Thus the two goals of perpetuating the name of the dead and providing for husbandless women become merged into levirate obligation. A husbandless woman is one whose husband is dead, but she can still rely on his brothers and his father. A separate institution concerns a woman whose husband is dead, where she must produce a son as heir for the dead husband and a provider must be secured for her.

lived fullness dissipates again into a symbolic רעב. The neighbor women and the text name Naomi as the mother of the child that Ruth has conceived. Ruth never receives permission to grieve her loss or to bond with her child. Despite that loss, Naomi no longer needs Ruth, and Ruth's name and voice disappear from the text. For all that Ruth gave, was too much taken away?

> *You be strong, powerful, courageous, contemplative*
> *Humorous, joyful, mischievous, sad*
> *Lonely, alone, together, tough,*
> *Close to omnipotent females of African descent.*
> *Problem is—*
> *The beingness of needing to be omnipotent*
> *May blind if not kill you.*

What are the ramifications in the biblical text? That no positive mother–daughter relations exist? Those mother–daughter relations that do exist (e.g. the mother and daughter in Moses' birth story, Exod. 2), concern the well-being of a male child (Moses), or concern idolatry (Jezebel) or other forms of violence (Athaliah, Jael). Does the mother-in-law/daughter-in-law story of Naomi and Ruth effect a reversal? That is, instead of the 'mother' giving up everything for her family, especially for her husband and son(s), here the 'mother's' fullness subverts the daughter's well-being. Ultimately, the biblical text provides no referent for ancient, balanced, loving 'mother–daughter' stories.

The mother–daughter contemporary short stories focus on their bonding, midst משתה and רעב, to create harmony, rupture and ambiguity.

> *We are daughters, too.*
> *Excited, vulnerable,*
> *Needing love and guidance*
> *Not ridicule, not false expectations.*
> *Our lives, a paradox of survival, of being self, but oppressed*
> *Strains the very sinews of our*
> *Mother-woman-daughter connection*
> *An ever-present umbilical cord*
> *Hidden, yet there, midst ambiguity*
> *Of being, of becoming, of beneficence.*

'Mother', by Andrea Lee,[7] concerns the 'paradoxes of privilege'[8] of a Black elite family in suburban Philadelphia. The daughter's

7. Andrea Lee, 'Mother', in Washington (ed.), *Memory of Kin*, pp. 99-108.
8. Washington, 'Commentary on Andrea Lee', in *Memory of Kin*, p. 109.

heightened senses and the mother–daughter 'chaotic מִשְׁתֶּה of imagination'[9] that celebrate their experiences of smell, place, physicality,
language, empathy, pain, playfulness and humor, all converge in
sumptuous culinary ecstasy, from dawn to eventide. 'Circling Hand',
by Jamaica Kincaid,[10] juxtaposes numerous examples of a symbolic
mother–daughter מִשְׁתֶּה involving secret, prepubescent, intimate rituals over against a rupturing metaphorical רָעָב, as the mother emotionally and physically abandons the daughter because she resents
and fears her daughter's emerging sexuality. 'Getting the Facts of
Life', by Paulette White,[11] dramatizes the metaphorical רָעָב experienced by mother and daughter, as they deal with the harsh and awe-
some realities of poverty and womanhood in their ritual walk and
visit to the welfare office. Each of these Black mother women and
their daughters and their daughter's daughters, like their grand-
mothers before them, have an awareness of self and environments
that, in the apt circumstances, propels them toward an aesthetic of
evocative sensuality.

The Evocation of Sensory Perception

In 'Mother', Grace Renfrew Philips and her daughter Sarah daily
create symphonies of sounds and smells, appreciating the fragrances
of 'magnificent azaleas', 'hot clean clothes', 'odors of frying scrapple
or codfish'; and the resonances of parents talking, doors closing, pots
clanging, cloaked in secrecy and mystery, order and abundance
(p. 99). Sarah discovers these special moments on summer mornings,
via her mother's creations, while her minister-father visits parish-
ioners and brother Matthew plays. Sarah voraciously reads and
reflects during her 'chaotic מִשְׁתֶּה of the imagination' as she idolizes
her mother, a strong, athletic woman, teacher and housekeeper,
adored by children for her 'touch of barbarism' and her attraction to
the bizarre (pp. 99-100). The bizarre, the chaotic, the barbaric, the sen-
suous set a tone for reading Esther.

> *Who says you must be that powerful?*
> *Slavery? Yes.*
> *Male friends and foes? Yes!*

9.   Washington, 'Commentary', p. 109.
10.   Jamaica Kincaid, 'The Circling Hand' (1985), in Washington (ed.), *Memory
of Kin*, pp. 111-24.
11.   Paulette White, 'Getting the Facts of Life', in Washington (ed.), *Memory of
Kin*, pp. 129-39.

Other folk that don't look like,
feel like, think like you? Yes.
Are you mammy, matriarch, welfare prone?
Maybe Yes, Maybe No!
No, says the Black Mother Woman.

Ahasuerus has one extended משתה, and another week-long משתה before Esther enters the scene: 180 days of pomp, splendor and drink for his most influential constituency, and a 7-day משתה for local people (Est. 1.3-5). Vashti has a משתה for the king's palace women (1.9). The eating and drinking make for a story steeped in suspense, fear, hatred, hope, irony, humor, satire and twoness: two loyalties, two edicts about Jews (3.8-13; 8.8-12), and two days of Purim that involve conflict and victory (8.17; 9.22, 25, 26, 29) midst human ingenuity, and ends with a משתה (9.22; 27–28; 31–32).[12] Just as Grace Philip's 'love of food embraced every aspect' of her culinary enterprise (pp. 99-108), משתה embraces pivotal moments in Esther. An inebriated king orders Vashti to flaunt her beauty during a משתה. The king commands Vashti to parade before a drunken crowd, wearing her crown (1.11-12). The textual omission of other attire, coupled with the eunuchs as messengers of this command, may imply the king's desire to flaunt Vashti's *naked* beauty. Her refusal to be objectified angers and embarrasses him, and implies that husbands cannot control wives. Consequently, Vashti can no longer come into the presence of Ahasuerus and her royal position will be given to another (v. 19). Both Ahasuerus and Grace are people who have positions of authority and power. While Ahasuerus rules, with the advice of seven royal princes (vv. 13-15), Grace rules her own domestic scene.

Grace's artistry and agility as she moves about her kitchen, her laboratory, while fashioning 'works in progress' acknowledges her own 'kingdom', where no one can tell her not to enter. Her children even learn their ancestry via foods and the notion of משתה. Lacking Grace's assurance, Ahasuerus's behavior typifies dominance and dysfunctionality. Esther's rise to the throne, while keeping her ethnicity secret at Mordecai's request (Est. 2.10, 20), also ties into objectification and משתה. After twelve months of beautifying along with her family of other virgins in his harem (2.12-13), the king chooses Esther to be

---

12. Angel Manuel Rodriguez, *Esther: A Theological Approach* (Berrien Springs, MI: Andrews University Press, 1995), pp. 1-3, 11; Janet L. Larson, 'The Battle of Biblical Books in Esther's Narrative', *Nineteenth Century Fiction* 38 (1983), pp. 131-60 (141-42).

queen and gives a מִשְׁתֶּה in her honor (v. 18). This kind of objectification forces a kind of 'body-identified identity',[13] where women's
identities are defined primarily through their relationships with their
bodies. A Western vision of beauty means many women cannot attain
this artificial sense of beauty, and they overlook the beautiful *imago
dei* within. Because Black women, mothers and daughters live in a
world where most women are devalued, healthy extended families
often help mothers and daughters celebrate their beauty of personhood.

In this world of Black mother-women and their daughters accepted
beauty norms distort reality and can become demonic in the pain
exacted via racial, sexual and classist oppression and humiliation. The
fact is that Black women come in an array of colors, from browns and
pinks to whites and blacks. Black women's bodies, especially larger,
rounded women also come under attack and are challenged concerning self-image, which has resulted in a chronicle of ambivalence about
body type and size that involves paradoxes, loves and troubles amidst
African-American female bodies in America. Alice Walker names
these self-destructive adversities and suggests a development of 'self-
constructed inner resources' toward living a life shaped by 'an ethic of
love and resistance' that helps one experience hope and wholeness.[14]
A womanist prescriptive hermeneutic for dealing with Black women's
concepts of beauty, and how they relate to their own skin color, hair
textures and size involve liberation theology and ethic that let Black
women help generate a beloved community. Such a paradigm enables
Black women to transcend the pettiness and the pain of ugly/pretty,
fat/slim dichotomies that nurture and perpetuate self-hatred and the
idolatry of Whiteness. With transformed values generated by such a
womanist love ethic, Black women can celebrate life and, creatively

13. Barbara Trepagnier, 'The Politics of White and Black Bodies', *Feminism* 4
(1994), pp. 199-205 (199).
14. Cheryl Townsend Gilkes, 'The "Loves" and "Troubles" of African-American Women's Bodies': The Womanist Challenge to Cultural Humiliation and Community Ambivalence', in Emilie Townes (ed.), *A Troubling in my Soul: Womanist
Perspectives on Evil and Suffering* (Maryknoll, NY: Orbis Books, 1993), pp. 232-49
(232-34). Both Mary Church Terrell and Alice Walker noted that Black African-
American women come from a 'flower garden' full of 'universal' potential with
families having skin hues ranging from 'brown, pink, yellow, and our cousins are
white, beige and black'. Thus, Black people experience multifaceted differences,
not from a locus of White privilege, but are challenged in ways (a composite of
race, sex, class) many women of Eurocentric origin will never face.

and aesthetically, love struggle, roundness, folk and food.[15] Such celebrations and the accompanying soul משׁתה are important for Black families. From the times of US antebellum slavery to the present day, Black folk could make a משׁתה out of leftovers and scraps. When there was so little to share, mealtimes were the one place where Black folk could make people feel welcome. In present-day private or public celebrations, food remains a central focus in the affirmation of יהוה, self and life by African-Americans. Thus 'soul food' feeds one physically, spiritually, aesthetically, culturally; and allows the time to come together as the one and the many, as extended family, as community.

> I am of the Great I am.
> I am[16] Delores, Katie, Cheryl, Kellie,
> Jackie, Karen, Marcia, Bernice, Valerie
> Barbara, Alice, Toni, Bebe
> Leontyne, Lena, Ella, and Etta
> Esther, Ruth, Deborah, Naomi;
> And all female others born
> Midst the soils of Africa,
> The bowels of slavery
> The complexities of America.

African-American families celebrate strong kinship bonds; strong achievement motivation; flexibility and adaptability; strong religious and spiritual orientation; and a strong work ethic. They value the group and group survival over individuals and individualism; cooperation over competition, dominance and power; oral sensibilities over visual–written language; holistic human condition over body/ mind dualism.[17] These families tend to build extended kinship groupings that involve both biological ties and friendships of attraction within the community. The community focuses on nurturing

15. Church Terrell and Alice Walker in Townes (ed.), *A Troubling in my Soul*, pp. 238-40.

16. The listing of 'I am's' include the following womanist scholars and Black female writers and entertainers, as well as four biblical female characters: theologians, ethicists, sociologists of religion and biblical scholars—Delores Williams, Katie Cannon, Cheryl Gilkes, Kellie Brown Douglas, Jacquelyn Grant, Karen Baker-Fletcher, Marcia Riggs and Valerie Bridgeman Davis; writers—Barbara Christian, Alice Walker, Toni Morrison, Bebe Moore Campbell; singers—Leontyne Price, Lena Horne, Ella Fitzgerald and Etta James.

17. Beverly Greene, 'What Has Gone before: The Legacy of Racism and Sexism in the Lives of Black Mothers and Daughters', *Women and Therapy* 9 (1990), pp. 207-30 (209); Barbara Haile and Audreye Johnson, 'Teaching and Learning about Black Women: The Anatomy of a Course', *SAGE: A Scholarly Journal on Black Women* 6 (1989), pp. 69-73 (69).

individuals, but in a communal context: the many and the one. Ahasuerus values his own ego and power. Esther values community. Her activity on its behalf places her in the role of mother. After being made queen, Esther had not yet made known her connection with the Jews (Est. 2.20), signifying a closeness and sense of responsibility. Esther learns about the initial edict against the Jews and hears of Mordecai's mournful state, as he has adorned himself with sackcloth and ashes. Then, with maternal authority, she tells the king's eunuchs to tell all the Jews in Susa to fast for three days (4.16). Esther asks the king if she has found favor, then for the lives of *her* people (7.3). Both Ruth and Naomi mother each other between emptiness and fullness. African-Americans tend to feel their mothers' special place is sacred and cannot be modified. At the same time, it is imperative that Black mother women not be so glorified that no one hears their pain, no one says 'thank you', or believes that Black women ought to be super-strong machines.[18]

> *Mother-woman status*
> *Means I am daughter*
> *I am mother, grandmother, other mother*
> *I am wife, partner*
> *I am sister-friend, aunt, cousin*
> *to persons, communities, ideas.*
> *Yes, I am strong, but frail*
> *And definitely not God.*
> *Yes, I'm full of love*
> *But I need love, too.*
> *When I am not well,*
> *I hurt and maim.*

Esther, as mother, confronts the Western norm of mother and family. The monolithic ideal of a nuclear, conjugal patriarchal grouping of mother, father and children, where tasks are divided according to sexuality, is not and has never been the American form of family.[19] Biblical families, often including simultaneous multiple wives and concubines, do not depict the alleged ideal nuclear family of father, mother and children. In an extended family setting, both the self and the community have an opportunity to grow and differentiate while being interrelated but separate beings: family as friends, and friends

18. Andrea Alonzo, 'My Extended Family', in Nan Maglin and Nancy Schniedewind (eds.), *Women and Stepfamilies: Voices of Anger and Love* (Philadelphia: Temple University Press, 1989), pp. 38-43 (42-43).

19. Bette Dickerson, *African American Single Mothers: Understanding their Lives and Families* (London: Sage, 1995), pp. x, xi.

as family.[20] Healthy families afford suitable environments for healthy, joyous, sensory discovery. That discovery of the self and of the other often leads to the discovery of the divine, who works behind the scenes in Esther—if we assent to an implied יהוה in Mordecai's comment that, if Esther does not aid the Jews, there is another who will. An awareness of the other can also lead to the conflict about the nature of boundaries and the politics of seduction.

> *I am a person*
> *Not what I do, or who I know*
> *I am person with female relational status*
> *Due to choice, circumstance, or chance.*
> *I have power; I am political*
> *Trample not on me.*

The Politics of Seduction

In 'The Circling Hand' author Jamaica Kincaid weaves together the lives of Annie John, her Momma and father, in tropical Antigua, through a maze of intimate rituals that portray a politics of seduction between mother and daughter. The politics of seduction involves a conscious and unconscious artistic strategy of manipulation that feigns endearment on some level; yet the actions of Momma, the more powerful party, places Annie, the weaker party, in a potentially compromising position. Afraid of losing her control over Annie, Momma assumes that a conspiracy exists. Momma posits that the other women in father's life want to hurt Annie, and uses this apparent harm to Annie to justify retaining control over Annie. Annie is always included in her Momma's day. Many of their activities are endearing, like their communion rites of opening the trunk containing items that tell a story about Annie. Annie revels in the knowledge of

---

20. 'Family'—ancestors, kinfolk, parents, siblings, children—signifies a social, cultural, often religious group in society, which includes those related by blood and those related by choice and circumstance, who share goals and values, have long-term commitments to one another and usually reside in the same dwelling place. A healthy family is the living laboratory where we learn who we are, where we are loved and nurtured and protected; where we learn the meaning of YES/NO, where we must deal with the complexities and demands of relationships. Friends, close companions, buddies, are people with whom we can share special and private thoughts; those who will be by our side; whom we know, like and trust. A friend is one who supports or sympathizes with us. Some friends are closer than family. Yet a healthy understanding of friend and family means family can be our friends, and friends can be part of our extended family. Thus, in many ways, the two are one and the same.

how lucky she is and how awful it must be to not love, or be loved. Annie loves both her parents; she finds her mother beautiful and describes her intimately in sensual terms. Inappropriately, Momma still bathes with Annie as she approaches puberty. What started as bonding shifts to the seduction of Annie by Momma, and becomes an incestuous end in itself. The dialectical strategy of seduction between mother and daughter often involves direct and indirect exhortations, orders, and advice. Sometimes mothers see their daughters as extensions of themselves, which can impede the shift in socialization from dependence to independence. Our culture encourages male independence but sanctions and encourages continued dependence of girls on their mothers.[21] The intimacy and seductive artistry question motive and appropriate boundaries: Has the behavior between Momma and Annie bordered on incest? Ought Esther to use her femininity and Ahaseurus's weakness toward her to aid her people? Did the neighbor women and Naomi overstep their boundaries and, ultimately, betray Ruth?

> Mother-woman status
> Means I am daughter
> I am mother, grandmother, other mother
> I am wife, partner
> I am sister-friend, aunt, cousin
> to persons, communities, ideas.

While scholars differ as to whether these boundaries are fluid or static, mothers and daughters struggle for subjectivity about their bodies and sexualities. Holistic health requires that women be aware of all facets of the self, their aggressive and autonomous nature, and not deny the context of the self amidst social relations. The summer Annie turns 12 her mother abruptly detaches from her, blaming it on Annie's menses, 'that young lady business'. Prior to this time, Annie and Momma went everywhere and did everything together, dressed alike and re-enacted rituals of bonding as they repeatedly examined and admired the mementos of Annie's life that Momma kept in a chest beneath the bed. In her twelfth year, all public and private displays of affection stopped. This blatant abandonment, without prior

---

21. Ruth Wodak and Muriel Schulz, *The Language of Love and Guilt: Mother–Daughter Relationships from a Cross-Cultural Perspective* (Amsterdam: John Benjamins, 1986), pp. 4, 1-2. The daughter, even as an adult or if married, is still the child who needs supervision and still belongs to her mother. Mothers often probe while daughters evade—communicative rituals that occur between children and parents and characterize their interactions.

warning or communication, leaves Annie in existential רעב, wracked
with bitterness and hatred (p. 120). Momma purposely lets Annie see
her in bed with her father, rubbing the small of his back in a circular
motion with her hand, as she smothers her husband with kisses. Sensory perception and seduction merge to flaunt intimacy of persons
and place, privacy of bedroom and bathroom, personal cleanliness
over against a trifling conscience. The wrenching pushes Annie away.
Annie finds love with Gwen, a schoolmate.

In the politics of seduction Esther, unlike Annie, wins her lover's
favor. Esther moves from bondage to a Cinderella-like rise in social
amenities and station. She moves from desolation to deontology as
she leaves the tutelage of Mordecai for her place in her lover–king's
Ahasuerus's court, and a משתה is given in her honor (Est. 2.5-17). In
support of her people she seduces the king, critiques Persia's socio-
legal practices, rejects social control, condemns human pride and
arrogance and mocks authority (5.1-8; 7.1-6).[22] When she entertains
the king and Haman in order to gain the king's favor and ultimately
win her people's freedom, she does so at a משתה (5.5; 7.1). Completely
taken by Esther, Ahasuerus condemns Haman to death, elevates
Mordecai and grants the Jews freedom (7.5-10). Esther's distance from
the king is less than the politics of distance between Annie and
Momma, where Annie's innocence and her mother's fear of change
create havoc.

Ruth's politics of seduction pales by comparison, yet has a major
impact on her life. With Naomi's initiative, according to the beginning
of Ruth 3, Ruth seduces Boaz. Boaz handles the land purchase
(couched in allusions of 'levirate' obligation, though again, not a 'levirate marriage' in a legal sense) frees Elimelech's land and frees Ruth
to marry Boaz. The down side finds a reverse on her locus as mother:
after Ruth gives birth, the community women name Naomi as Obed's
mother, usurping Ruth's place and function as mother, moving her
back from fullness to emptiness in a society that places value on
motherhood. Ruth and Boaz disappear from the text. Shifts in power
and place can have harsh results.

> *Don't put me on a pedestal and sanctify me;*
> *Pedestals get ignored and collect dust.*
> *Besides, you expect me to work,*
> *And porcelain and bone china don't do dishes.*

---

22. Larson, *Battle of Biblical Books*, p. 143; Rodriguez, 'Esther: A Theological
Approach', p. 11.

The products of the seductions in these stories play like bad economics. With Annie, a daughter's inability to detach from her mother
causes disruption and pain. Her beloved mother does not communi-
cate about sexuality either as a guide or as a protector but simply,
abandons her. Esther, a daughter to Mordecai, herself becomes a
mother to her daughter Israel. Amid irony and surprise, Esther uses a
משתה as both delaying tactic and device to set up Haman's fall. At the
second משתה for the king and Haman, Esther both identifies with her
people and names Haman as a conspirator. Thus, Esther uses her wisdom about the king's sensibilities and his character to make her
appeal and, ultimately, effect Haman's death and her people's liberation.[23] If one accepts Tucker's notion of including the additions (the
six additions found in the Codex Vaticanus that do not appear in the
Masoretic Hebrew text) to Esther in the textual study, then the key
human virtues are humility and piety, not shrewdness or power.
Those verses then make the text a religious story about divine will
and piety. Then this text may indicate how genuine religion affects a
people's salvation.[24] If we question Esther's tactics regarding her
duplicity in Haman's death in light of Tucker's notion, we must
acknowledge that given her *Sitz im Leben* as a queen who wants to
overcome the death edict on her people within a patriarchal kingdom,
she does what she must. Esther saves her people and obtains a position of authority with little damage to her self-esteem; and, in a reversal, the Jews get to do to others what Haman wanted to do to them (8,
9). Yet Esther's characterization cannot be subsumed under piety, and
one must be cautious in stipulating gross divine activity in the book.
At any rate, at the close of Esther the queen–mother and her children
do know fullness. Conversely, Ruth's seductive liaison ends with
famine: her 'daughter' Naomi, whom she brings to fullness, completely usurps her reality.[25]

Role transitions result from exercising a politics of seduction. When
a self can no longer differentiate from other selves and disappears,
several possibilities obtain: (1) poetic license; (2) annihilation of

23.   Mervin Breneman, *Ezra, Nehemiah, Esther: The New American Commentary; an
Exegetical and Theological Exposition of Holy Scripture*, X (n.p.: Broadman & Holman,
1993), pp. 338, 348; White, *Esther*, p. 128.

24.   Gene M. Tucker, 'The Book of Esther', in Bruce M. Metzger and Michael
Coogan (eds.), *The Oxford Companion to the Bible* (New York: Oxford University
Press, 1993), pp. 198-201 (200-201).

25.   Wodak and Schulz, *The Language of Love and Guilt*, p. 148; Greer Litton Fox,
'Patterns and Outcomes of Mother–Daughter Communications about Sexuality',
Journal of Social Issues 36 (1980), pp. 7-29 (25-26).

personhood and a breach of familial ethics; or (3) the missing character becomes the scapegoat, which allows a culture or a society to continue without destroying itself. Whichever choice a self makes, that choice can be the catalyst to create relationships through passions shared. Sometimes, amid change, the resulting differences are so profound that one can only respond with a moment of silence, of blessed quietness.

> Black mother-womanhood connotes community
> Not a function of male powerlessness
> Black mother-womanhood exists in extended family,
> With two parent, single parent, mother-child groupings;
> Choices made, passions shared,
> Oh do I marvel in quietude.

The Compassion of Silence

'Getting the Facts of Life'[26] connects us with the Blue family, a welfare family in the industrial North. This is a family that hit on hard times, a family from the wrong side of the track, a family that experiences existential רעב—the loss of the father's job and an attack on their security and well-being. This story takes place on the day Mrs Blue, accompanied by her daughter Minerva, goes to the welfare office. The irony—the word 'welfare' means 'good', but has become stigmatized—is not lost on Mrs Blue. The Blues are one of those families allegedly causing the US deficit. The Blues symbolize all those we name as *other*; those who, many of us would pretend, do not exist. But within Mrs Blue's struggle to maintain her family there are moments when the compassion of silence, a moment of meaningful unspoken communication, reinvigorates mother and daughter. Their walk to the welfare office is filled with companionable silence and intermittent monologues by Minerva. Mrs Blue instinctively appreciates Minerva's company and talks to her about life in a way that rehearses the 'vibrancy and richness in the South' (p. 140). The potency of silence implies absence.

Ruth's silence heralds the absence of Ruth and Boaz (Ruth 4.14-22): after the neighbor women name Naomi as Obed's mother and Naomi nurses him, the narrative text does not mention Ruth or Boaz again. We do not know what happens to them. The story ends with a genealogy that links the descendants of Perez with Obed and yokes Obed

---

26. White, 'Getting the Facts of Life', in Washington (ed.), *Memory of Kin*, pp. 129-39.

with his grandson David (4.18-22). Haman's silence affirms his demise (Est. 8-10): Haman, an instigator and anti-Semite, pushed the king toward a pogrom, but, after Esther's plea, the king orders Haman hanged (7.10). With poetic justice, Haman is hung on the same gallows he has constructed for Mordecai. With Haman's death, the king's anger subsides. Though Haman is dead, his name appears again in the text. In order to create a historical context, the text identifies Haman as the Jews' enemy (8.1; 9.24); as former owner of the signet ring and of the house to be given to Mordecai (8.2, 7); as the father of ten sons who will be hanged (9.1-10, 13, 14). Ahasuerus's silence confirms his absent power over Esther: after the death edict has been rescinded, his name serves to identify provinces (9.2, 12, 16, 20), as Mordecai and Esther exercise more and more power (9.4; 16); and, like Ahasuerus who remains king. Grace Phillips and her daughter Sarah share a compassion of silence in the short story 'Mothers'. Sarah

> felt her hands against my back, that was enough. There are moments when the sympathy between mother and child becomes again almost what it was at the very first… It was an excitement [about discerning her mother]… While my mother pushed me in the swing, it seemed as if we were conducting, without words, a troubling yet oddly exhilarating dialogue about pain and loss (p. 107).

The year Sarah was six the Phillips had visited the Barber family home, where a particular silence symbolized the absence of Judge Barber: the previous winter the judge had committed suicide, thus was silenced by his own hand. Mrs Barber and her daughter Phyllis continued to live in that house, which 'itself seemed to be mourning' (p. 106). The profound silence in the air when Annie watched her parents in bed, with her mother seeing her and not speaking, is the profound absence of life, the way it was and the way it will never be and, in part, should never have been. Mrs Blue's silence is a silence that knows her plight but refuses to be a victim. She only goes to the welfare office because her husband has been laid off and she needs food and clothes for the children. She is not lazy. Mrs Blue, like most Black women, sees work as a valuable and important dimension of Black motherhood, not as opposition or incompatibility.[27]

The visit to the welfare office was not compassionate, but there were moments when Mrs Blue maintained silence under the scrutiny of the case worker. The case worker took a most patronizing attitude in handling the Blue family's case. At one point Minerva's feet were

27. Patricia Hill Collins, *Black Feminist Thought: Knowledge, Consciousness, and the Politics of Empowerment* (London: Routledge, 1990), p. 124.

numb, she felt bodiless. In her imagination she could make all of her body disappear, except her face. Like Toni Morrison's Pecola in *The Bluest Eye*,[28] Minerva wanted the absence that accompanies silence. As her mother's answers grew softer and softer, Minerva wanted to escape the embarrassment of needing to be there. Mr Blue existed in the absence of silence, because for his family to get Aid to Dependent Children (ADC), he could not live with them; he had not been able to get a job since the railroad moved. As Minerva and Mrs Blue leave the office to walk home, the earlier companionable silence turns to conversation. Time is suspended and they absent themselves from reality as they talk about Mrs Blue's childhood years in Alabama. As they talk about having babies and Minerva becoming a woman, Minerva feels like 'a suffocating rose': repressed beauty, silenced life. For Minerva, neither silence nor 'the facts of life' hold any further mystery (p. 140).

> *We are daughters, too.*
> *Excited, vulnerable,*
> *Needing love and guidance*
> *Not ridicule, not false expectations*

Esther and Ruth and Annie and Sarah and Minerva are Black mother–daughter women: they experience incredible power, yet weakness; as they realize, with Ntozake Shange, that, for colored girls, the rainbow is not enough.[29] These women are all daughters and have been or will be mothers, via biology and/or service.

The story of Esther involves sexual and ethnic oppression; ultimately, these do not impede her relationship with Israel as the powerful mother. Her womanist-ness is celebrated to the present day in the משתה of Purim. Ruth explores issues of race, class, gender differences and roles in addressing Jewish exclusivism, levirate customs of land ownership and Naomi's locus as Obed's mother. Ruth ends where Naomi began, in רעב. Esther implicitly assumes יהוה: a providential, quiet presence; Ruth explicitly assumes יהוה: an active, universal יהוה of history, a resounding presence.

These biblical short stories, Ruth and Esther; and these Black mother-daughter short stories, Andrea Lee's 'Mother', Jamaica Kincaid's 'The Circling Hand' and Paulette Childress White's 'Getting the Facts of Life' teach that healthy relationships require mutuality,

---

28. Toni Morrison, *The Bluest Eye* (with a new afterword by the author; New York: PLUME, 1970; London: Penguin Books, 1993).

29. Ntozake Shange, *for colored girls who have considered suicide/when the rainbow is enuf: a choreopoem* (New York: Macmillan, 1977).

reciprocity and accountability. Pain, annihilation and fracturing occurs if mother and daughter engage in manipulation and repression of emotions. When mothers try to recreate themselves in their daughters, the results are limited and unhealthy and foster youthful rebellion.[30] Because mothers have been daughters, it is important for them to remember and to be open. Esther teaches an awareness of responsibility undergirded by the divine. Ruth teaches how that same level of responsibility can end with annihilation of the self. The mother–daughter stories, often told by the daughters, remind us of how quickly girls become women, and the complexities of separating themselves from being mere extensions of their mothers.

> *Black mother woman*
> *Sing blue, sing true*
> *Let not your anger burn you up*
> *Be not a doormat.*
> *Sing gentle, sing electric, sing true.*

---

30. Lisa S. Babinec, 'Cyclical Patterns of Domination and Manipulation in Flannery O'Connor's Mother–Daughter Relationships', *Flannery O'Connor Bulletin* 19 (1990), pp. 9-29 (9, 26-27).

Part III

ESTHER

LOTS OF WRITING*

Mieke Bal

Introduction

Esther's dramatic second banquet, one out of many mentioned in the story, has understandably attracted painters; drama is, after all, a visually representable form of narrative.[1] Rembrandt's 1660 painting *Esther's Banquet*, in the Pushkin Museum, Moscow, is my favorite painting on this subject, but precisely because it does not enhance the scene's narrativity or its dramatic tension (Fig. 1). The three figures who, in the biblical story, are engaged in the most dramatic interactions with one another are each rendered here as if cocooned within an invisible veil, self-absorbed, silent, and isolated from the others.[2] Moreover, Haman, who is facing Esther, seems to be blind.

Another painting by Rembrandt, *Haman's Downfall*, dated 1665 and currently in the Hermitage, St Petersburg, represents the next episode in the Esther story, the downfall of the plotter (Fig. 2). Haman is strangely represented as almost literally falling forward, about to topple toward the viewer as he quits the scene; and here there is no doubt about his being blind.[3] In this work, the scene is even more strikingly drained of its narrativity; with Esther absent and Mordecai

*   I would like to thank Daniel Boyarin for having suggested the idea for this paper, and Fokkelien van Dijk Hemmes, Athalya Brenner and Ophira Shapiro for their help with the Hebrew text. An earlier version of this paper was published in *Semeia* 54 (1991), pp. 77-102. Reprinted by permission of SBL.
1.   See Sandra Beth Berg, *The Book of Esther: Motifs, Themes and Structure* (Missoula, MT: Scholars Press, 1979), pp. 31-58, for an analysis of banquets and fasts, and their relationship to Purim.
2.   For an analysis of such self-absorption in paintings, as opposed to 'theatricality', or interaction between characters and viewer, see Michael Fried, *Absorption and Theatricality: Painting and Beholder in the Age of Diderot* (Berkeley: University of California Press, 1980).
3.   The question of whether Rembrandt intended to represent these episodes or whether the works received their titles later is as irrelevant to my perspective here, as the question of whether 'Esther' really instituted Purim or was a fictional representation of/justification for the festival.

present, it is not the narrative event itself, but rather its proleptic meaning—Haman's displacement by Mordecai—that is represented.

Fig. 1 Esther's Banquet by Rembrandt van Rijn (1660).
Courtesy of Pushkin Museum, Moscow

Rembrandt is generally considered a narrative painter, exceptionally so for a Dutch artist,[4] but here, in representing a lively, highly dramatic scene, he has eliminated movement from the image. In this still medium, the figures are emphatically arrested, as if to represent the stillness of visual art itself. And once self-reflexion becomes a mode of reading these paintings, another, more complex type of reflexivity is activated, one which courts paradox. On the one hand, due to its representation in a wordless medium, the scene's emphasis is on speechlessness, the lack of communication between the figures mirroring the non-linguistic quality of a painting. In the text, on the other hand, direct discourse—speech—is used to dramatize climactic confrontations. In this respect and in contrast to each other, both works are self-reflexive, articulating the truth of their medium at

4. Svetlana Alpers, *The Art of Describing: Dutch Art in the Seventeenth Century* (Chicago: University of Chicago Press, 1985).

Fig. 2 *Haman's Downfall* by Rembrandt van Rijn (1665). Courtesy of the Hermitage, St Petersburg

the moment of diegetic truth. Neither work appears to make any use of food, the pretext for the banquet. But there is more.

The episode of Haman's downfall, following Esther's masterly plotted denunciation, offers a different, negative relationship to the respective media, a systematic inversion or counter-mirroring. In the visual text (i.e. Fig. 2), blindness acquires a particular status that challenges the very visuality on which it is based, a status paralleled by the description of this scene in the New English Bible: 'At that Haman was dumbfounded' (Est. 7.6).[5] Where sight falls in the visual work, words fail in the verbal one.

5.   *The New English Bible with the Apocrypha* (Oxford Studies edn, 1976). The

The failure of both sight and speech is reflected in the following, remarkable statement: 'The word left his [the king's, MB] mouth, and they covered Haman's face' (7.8).[6] The king verbalizes what he sees, and his word causes Haman's face to be covered. To paraphrase J.L. Austin,[7] words are things that do things here. Words are the principal agents of this narrative. In causing Haman's face to be covered, words blind him. The inability to see thus enters the verbal scene, just as in *Esther's Banquet* (Fig. 1), the visualized figures are unable to speak. Hence, Rembrandt foregrounds only what is already in the text, and the neat distinction between speech and vision falls flat. Rembrandt's paintings enable us better to read the text by demonstrating how it has already been read.[8]

I shall use these paintings as a gloss on the book of Esther, approaching the text from the perspective of Rembrandt's interpretations of it. Assuming that the realm of visual representation has its own devices for supporting interpretive claims, I shall endorse its heuristic power and accept that it has something to add that verbal argumentation might well, so to speak, fail to see. What, then, is Esther's feast? As we shall see, it is a feast of writing, and its relation to Purim lies in its expression of the tension between writing and randomness, between agency and luck, or lot.

Writing is precisely the mediator between sight and speech. Using the representational system of language as its code, writing requires sight in order to be processed, that is, for what Roman Jakobson called its phatic function. The Esther scroll is a celebration of writing and, as

less striking Hebrew phrase translates simply as 'And Haman was scared'. I have chosen to draw upon a modern, popularized version of the biblical text because I am not really focusing on an accurate reading of the 'original' (whatever that may be), but rather on the cultural vitality of the text as it has increasingly resonated over time.

6.   Here, the Hebrew remains ambiguous. Hebrew scholars have suggested 'and Haman's face [was] clouded', or 'Haman's face fell, became bland'. I have allowed myself to play with these possibilities, but obviously my argument does not depend on these particular words. What matters is the power of words to defeat, even kill, and, conversely, the visual impotence expressed in the ambiguity of seeing as an epistemological and a perceptual act.

7.   J.L. Austin, *How to Do Things with Words* (Cambridge, MA: Harvard University Press, 1975).

8.   I shall not go into the vast number of existing interpretations, even by way of translation. Although any reconstruction of the 'original' meaning is, in my view, doomed to failure, attempting a closer reading would, of course, require an analysis of the canonical Hebrew text, which, again, is not pertinent to my argument.

the climax of the story, so is Esther's banquet. A lot of writing takes place in Esther, and writing is where words and images, the visual and the verbal, converge; where, specifically in Esther, fate and agency, randomness and history, Providence and plotting dovetail. Writing is also, of course, the medium that produced the book of Esther.

In Esther writing both partakes of and struggles against the lots that allegedly gave Purim its name. For, as is often the case in biblical literature, the celebration is a working through of the ambivalence associated with what is being celebrated. And there are plenty of reasons to feel ambivalent about writing. While it is commonplace in cultural anthropology to consider the invention of writing the inaugurator and index of civilization, what has also been acknowledged is that the careful political management of literacy has contributed to oppression and to the centralization of state power.[9] Writing has been a tool of the elite, a means of enforcing inequity and exploitation, of promulgating ideology through religion, and of generalizing laws; it has definitively impressed upon its practitioners a particular view of history that rendered collective memory futile and undermined the participation of the masses in oral history—all of which can be thematized in a political reading of Esther.[10]

9.   See T. Lemaire, 'Antropologie en schrift: Aanzetten tot cen ideologickritick van het schrift', in T. Lemaire (ed.), *Antropologie en ideologie* (Groningen: Konstapel, 1984), pp. 103-26.

For the connection between religion and the economy of the state as supported by writing, see R.Mc.C. Adams, *The Evolution of Urban Society: Early Mesopotamia and Prehistoric Mexico* (Chicago: Aldine, 1966). Diamond (S. Diamond, *In Search of the Primitive* [New Brunswick: Transaction Books, 1974]) argues against evolutionism in this domain. Jack Goody (*The Domestication of the Savage Mind* [Cambridge: Cambridge University Press, 1977] and Goody [ed.], *Literacy in Traditional Societies* [Cambridge: Cambridge University Press, 1968]) offered the now-classic critique of the repression of orality by writing; and Lévi-Strauss's classic text (*Tristes Tropiques* [Paris: Plon, 1955]), Rousseauistic in its nostalgia, is 'The Writing Lesson'. Precisely because of the Romantic residue in the orality/literacy debate, I should point out that I use the term 'writing' here in the limited sense of script, not in the extended sense ascribed to it by Derrida (Jacques Derrida, *Of Grammatology: Translated and Introduced by Gayatri Chakravorty Spivak* [Baltimore: The Johns Hopkins University Press, 1976]). I do not, however, view innocence and non-violence or, indeed, a state of culture-without-writing as the opposite of literacy. On the contrary, the tensions that I perceive in the role of writing in the plot of Esther demonstrate the fragility of just such an opposition. I do not consider the Derridean view of writing to be intrinsically incompatible with the political critique of writing's complicity in domination.

10.   While it is widely assumed that literacy was relatively widespread in Israel

In political terms, the pronounced central role of writing and the efficiency of the Persian postal system corresponded to the king's rule over many peoples, that is, to both the appropriation of power and the abuse of power for the (attempted) destruction of a particular people and their culture. Writing was the instrument of a real, historical threat (Haman's first decree). In epistemological terms, Plato described (in the *Phaedrus*) the destructive effect of writing on memory, which was usually associated with the breakdown of archaic, small-scale 'democracies'. As it happens, in Esther the displacement of memory by writing also occurs, in the chronicle of Mordecai's deed, but it is enacted by Ahasuerus, the very ruler whose centralized and autocratic power extended 'from India to Ethiopia'. His failing memory should not be too hastily ridiculed—a ridicule that cannot avoid the charge of anachronism, if not arrogant evolutionism,[11] as it is so often based on a contemptuous presumption of little psychological depth or realistic plausibility in ancient texts. Instead, the king's poor memory should be seen as a reflexion of the inevitable but ambivalent shift toward the predominance of writing staged by the text. If Esther is about writing, however, it is also about itself.

Given the central position of writing in the book of Esther, self-reflexion seems a relevant concept with which to approach the text,

from the eighth century on, oral history, at one time the only form of history, has never totally disappeared from cultural life in Israel or anywhere else.

11. See, e.g., Jack Sasson ('Esther', in Robert Alter and Frank Kermode [eds.], *The Literary Guide to the Bible* [Cambridge, MA: Harvard University Press, 1987], pp. 335-42 [337, 341]): 'Yet the events of barely a fortnight earlier are so hazy in his memory'; and 'dim-witted monarchs'. Sasson's approach to Esther seems to reflect the hidden evolutionistic ideology of many works that are characterized as 'literary' approaches to the Bible. The view that the chronicle episode is implausible is widely held (see, e.g., Berg, *Esther*, p. 63). Sasson applies such anachronistic criteria as psychological plausibility in order to present the text as a typical, comically cute piece of ancient literature, by which Sasson means all pre-modern literature, from Hellenistic romance through medieval fabliau, up to Voltaire's *contes philoso-phiques*. My own view is that Ahasuerus should not be judged on his intelligence, but rather considered as a necessary agent of the plot, which is, by another reflexive turn, about plotting. Measuring the biblical story by standards derived from the modern psychological-realist novel is almost universal in commentaries; see, for example, Carey Moore (*Esther* [AB, 7B; Garden City, NY: Doubleday, 1971], pp. liii, liv), who finds the characters lacking in depth and compares Haman with Oedipus, to whom he fails to match up. One wonders about the unstated gender ideology in Moore's approach, where a realist bias also seems evident (see, e.g., the description of Mordecai as 'the greater hero...who supplied the brains while Esther simply followed his directions' [p. liil]). To my mind, it is the critic who lacks depth here.

and the two Rembrandt paintings indicate that this text's reflexivity may be highly complicated. In reflecting upon the possible uses of self-reflexion here, I shall therefore propose that it yields a perspective on Esther that extends beyond the question of the historical connection between 'lots' and Purim.

Self-Reflexion

Self-reflexion is too fashionable a concept to be endorsed unreflectively. If the Esther scroll centers on writing, then it may be considered a self-reflexive text; and if, as I shall argue, Esther reflects the uncertain status of writing and the ways in which writing produces reality—the reality of the threat to and the salvation of the Jews—it may represent a case of postmodernism *avant la lettre*.[12] Is this pushing anachronism too far? This question can only be answered in connection with the very core of self-reflexion, for I will argue that the concept's appeal for contemporary criticism is precisely its ambiguity, which frees representation from its ties to the psychological realism of nineteenth-century Western fiction.

Notions of self-reflexion are not only popular in literary criticism, due to the impact of postmodern literature and deconstructionist writing; they have also begun to circulate in art criticism, particularly with respect to the visual arts. Foucault's remarks at the end of his chapter on Velázquez's *Las Meninas* in *The Order of Things* beautifully expresses this mode of reading:

> Representation undertakes to represent itself here in all its elements, with its images, the eyes to which it is offered, the faces it makes visible, the gestures it calls into being... Representation, freed finally from the relation that was impending it, can offer itself as representation in its purest form.[13]

The specific relevance of visual art to a discussion of self-reflexion stems from the representational imposition of the *subject*: while literature can be about *itself*, enabling critics to ignore the reader, self-reflexive visual art imprisons the *viewer*. This distinction invites a

---

12. Both self-reflexivity and ontological uncertainty are considered characteristic of postmodernism (see Linda Hutcheon, *A Poetics of Postmodernism: History, Theory, Fiction* [London: Routledge, 1988]; Brian McHale, *Postmodernist Fiction* [London: Methuen, 1987]; and Ernst van Alphen, *Francis Bacon and the Loss of Self* [London: Reaktion Books; Cambridge, MA: Harvard University Press, 1992]).

13. Michel Foucault, '*Las Meninas*', in *The Order of Things* (trans. Alan Sheridan; New York: Vintage Books, 1973), pp. 3-16 (16).

more complex interrogation of the concept and enables us to historicize it, too. For transposed to the literary text, within the framework of a reading-oriented theory of texts, self-reflexive reading entails a complication: Whose/Which self is being reflected? The identity between the work and its subject—between work as labor and work as product—is not unified; it is fragmented by the intrusion of the reader, whose position is inherently paradoxical: Is she or he part of the self that is being reflected or reflected upon? If so, then the self-reflexive mode of reading, in which the reader is subsumed by the work, would not encourage reader reflexivity. The self would remain whole, while only the reflexion became fractured; if the reader were not part of the self being reflected (upon), then the self would be disrupted from the start, and again, reader reflexivity would not be encouraged. I contend that this obliteration of the reader dehistoricizes the critical endeavor even if, or precisely when, its overt aim is historical reconstruction.

This mode of reading is made double-edged by its relationship to narcissism. As an effectively antirealistic strategy, it is a means of reading for the work itself or, to use Linda Hutcheon's term, for the 'narcissism' in the work.[14] Resonating with its mythical, visual and psychoanalytic connotations, 'narcissism' also invokes the particular pictorial quality and the erotic near-gratification of self-reference. In the book of Esther, the reader is constantly reminded of the connection between visual beauty and power during the main character's adventures; once the instability of writing becomes the central theme for the self-reflexive reader, the power of beauty and the power of writing are enmeshed, and, as I shall argue, even the conventional gender division is destabilized.

The paradoxical entanglements contained by the concept of self-reflexion were particularly visible in the heated debate of 1980–81 that arose over Velázquez's *Las Meninas* between philosophers and art historians, which I have analyzed elsewhere.[15] As mentioned already, Foucault, a philosopher and hence a professional discursive self-reflector, opened his study of the classical age with a 13-page reflexion on this painting.[16] He saw the work as infused with the invisibility

14. Linda Hutcheon, *Narcissistic Narrative: The Metafictional Paradox* (New York: Methuen, 1982) and Hutcheon, *A Poetics of Post-Modernism*.

15. Mieke Bal, *Reading 'Rembrandt': Beyond the Word–Image Opposition* (Cambridge: Cambridge University Press, 1991).

16. Foucault, *'Las Meninas'*, pp. 3-16. Critics who took up the challenge of Foucault's self-confident *placing* of the work within his own argument made little of the specific intertextual relationship between the painting and the philosophical

of the viewer, whose place is taken by the royals—a view that to me suggests an unexpected symmetry between the seventeenth-century Spanish painting and the ancient Hebrew text, where the royal position is taken over by the outsider, Esther the Jewess. John Searle,[17] a philosopher of, significantly, language and therefore of discourse, saw the work as typically paradoxical precisely because the viewer could *not* be (yet *must* be) in the same place as the royal couple. The use of the term 'paradox' upset two critics[18] and amused others, thus provoking a series of responses, both to Searle's interpretation and to the painting itself.

These responses focus on the position of the viewer in relation to the mirrored image of the king and queen at the center of the work. The debate itself forms an appropriate intertext for self-reflexion

argument, a relationship that was inverted in the subsequent critical debate. Foucault's intention was not to say anything special about *Las Meninas*, but to make *Las Meninas* say precisely what he had to say about the classical age. It seems to me that this alleged use of a 'masterpiece' as a mere example was partly responsible for the emotional responses that Foucault's piece provoked. But there is no such thing as a mere example in Foucault's writing. *Las Meninas* provided the philosopher with the discourse that he needed: a visual one. This appropriation was quite strategic: it enabled him to evade the charge of simplification (which, ironically, is precisely what he was charged with). The Foucauldian view relativizes visuality by its strong emphasis on the irreducible difference between words and images: 'But the relation of language to painting is an infinite relation. It is not that words are imperfect, or that, confronted by the visible, they prove insuperably inadequate. Neither can be reduced to the other's terms: it is in vain that we say what we see; what we see never resides in what we say. And it is in vain that we attempt to show, by the use of images, metaphors, or similes, what we are saying; the space where they achieve their splendor is not that deployed by our eyes, but that defined by the sequential elements of syntax' (p. 9). This attitude toward the relationship between discourse and visual image also holds for my heuristic use of the two Rembrandt paintings here.

17. John Searle, '*Las Meninas* and the Paradoxes of Pictorial Representation', *Critical Inquiry* 6 (1980), pp. 477-88.

18. See Joel Snyder and Ted Cohen ('Reflexions on *Las Meninas*: Paradox Lost', *Critical Inquiry* 7 [1981], pp. 429-47), whose dismay seems to stem from the well-known discomfort engendered by interdisciplinary discourse. In one of their many defensive reactions to the language Searle uses, they refer to another critic as being 'in the Foucault–Searle line', and to his use of the term 'ambiguity' as 'a less exotic logical crux' than 'paradox' would entail. Indeed, Snyder and Cohen seem to be reacting primarily to the use of philosophical terminology. Their irony is just a little too heavy-handed for the context, and their scare quotes, intended to undermine the terms they frame, seem merely sarcastic. The focus of the irony, however, is not only the alien discourse, but also, precisely, the threat resulting from seeing the painting in terms of 'the Foucault–Searle line'.

because, at least in the articles by Searle and by Snyder and Cohen, there is a striking discrepancy between the positions that these critics espouse in their discursive reflexions and those that they reflect—mirror—in their discourse. This discrepancy points to the argumentational 'other', the connotative rhetoric of the texts. In other words, the critical texts lend themselves to the kind of specular and speculative reflexive reading that makes self-reflective reading genuinely relevant to critique. Such a reading strategy might also lead to a complacent sense of triumph, however, a self-congratulatory pleasure in discovery. In other words, once self-reflexion becomes common practice, reading for 'narcissism' is at risk of becoming narcissistic itself. What gets lost is a perspective on the historical position of self-reflexion, and that is, indeed, a powerful argument against this mode of reading, to which we will have to return.[19]

As I have suggested, self-reflexivity is a mode of reading that seems paradoxical because it leads the interpreter to submit to a position ostensibly determined by the work. As in a Hegelian master–slave dialectic, the reader is so overwhelmed by an apparently triumphant 'discovery' of self-reflexivity that they tend to abandon their own position for the self-reflexive one that the work seems to propose, thereby forfeiting the self-reflexion of the viewing or reading subject. But if reflexion of/on the work entails reflexion of/on the viewer's position, then any submissive response is paradoxically non-submissive: it refuses to obey the command of reflexion. In other words, an order of non-submission can be neither obeyed nor disobeyed. This paradox mirrors Esther's position at the moment in the narrative when she is ordered to disobey (Est. 4.8-17).[20] The question of obedience as a paradox, not as a neat opposition between the 'good' obedient queen and her 'bad' disobedient predecessor, is thematized

19. See the introduction to Hutcheon, *Narcissistic Narrative*, for a discussion of this criticism.

20. Ernst van Alphen (*Bij wijze lezen: Verleidinng enverzet van Willem Brakmans lezer* [Muiderberg: Coutinho, 1988], p. 59) addresses this paradox by differentiating between the reading attitudes proposed by the text and those adopted by the reader. He distinguishes four possible attitudes in relation to the corpus he discusses: (1) the realistic text read realistically; (2) the postmodern text read postmodernistically; (3) the postmodern text read realistically; and (4) the realistic text read postmodernistically. A realistic text, then, is a work which is not entirely realistic, but which both fits the conventions of realism and has elements that enable, or even encourage, a 'postmodern', self-reflexive reading attitude. In the book of Esther, which is neither realistic nor, of course, postmodern, the problem of obedience is thematized on the level of the narrative.

throughout the narrative. Bound to obey both her relative and her husband, Esther is forced to disobey both men in order to obey, thereby emancipating herself from the power of the two men and of their writing. Reading the book of Esther self-reflexively elicits a comparable compromise, that is, one must read the text anachronistically (say, postmodernistically) in order to gain a perspective on history— on Esther as neither realistic nor postmodern, but as the historical 'other'.

The paradoxes and possible confusions presented by the concept of self-reflexion are produced by the ambiguity of *both* parts of the term: self and reflexion. The former requires the reader to consider which self is reflected, that of the work or (and?) that of the reader. Assuming that self-reflexion risks the reader's entanglement within the work, it must endorse the reflexion of/on *both* selves. This is suggested by the ambiguity of the word 'reflexion', meaning both (visual) mirroring and (discursive) thinking.[21] Self-reflection as mirroring suggests the Lacanian mirror-stage as an early, visually based construction of the self in self-alienation, while discursive self-reflection/reflexion invokes self-critique.

The two ambiguities of the word 'reflection', coupled with the corresponding pair of selves to be reflected, yield four possible positions, which together comprise a useful typology of self-reflection/reflexion. The mirroring and the analytical, discursive forms of reflexivity differentiate between an unreflective, possibly unconscious, doubling of the work and a conscious position toward the work that problematizes representation. In the first case, there are again two possibilities, depending on the meaning of 'self ' involved.

1. *The fantasmatic position.* Here, the critic responds to the self of the work only, viewing it as radically other and leaving him or herself safely out of reach—or dangerously unconscious. This is Haman's mistake when (in Est. 3.6) he fantasmatically projects his rage at Mordecai over a purely personal insult onto the Jews at large, generalizing Mordecai's insult as Jewish insubordination. Seeing Mordecai as the mirror of his people, Haman fails to see the mirroring relationship between himself and Mordecai, that is, the reversibility of their relative positions. This failure to see (himself) is Haman's *lot*, his

---

21. The different spellings—'self-reflexion' for mirroring, 'self-reflection' for thinking—are not consistently applied and do not hold in French, where the same word carries the same ambiguity. If we have two different words, at least they are homonyms, close enough semantically to be confused in practice.

pûr, which will foil his plot because it undermines his autonomy as an agent.

2. *The narcissistic position*. If, by contrast, the two selves are conflated in the mirroring, while the reflection remains non-reflexive (i.e. non-analytical, nondiscursive), the result will be symptoms of primary narcissism, as described by Lacan.[22] This mode of self-reflexion can be read in the self-absorbed isolation of the three figures in each of the Rembrandt paintings. It is obviously also operating in Haman's childish dream of grandeur, in which he can imagine only himself as the object of the king's honoring (Est. 6.6-8). This is why Rembrandt's Haman is blind: already curbed in the first painting (Fig. 1), he loses his balance and falls down in/out of the second (Fig. 2). The discursive mode of self-reflexion, which requires that one take an explicit position on the reflexive qualities of the work and the self, can likewise assume two distinct forms.

3. *The theoretical position*. If reflexivity is limited to the self of the work, the work will be viewed as a theoretical statement about representation. The text or painting thus becomes a theory, as *Las Meninas* becomes a theory of classical representation. The letters in Esther become statements about writing and its prevailing relationship to reality (e.g. Est. 1.1g). The critic who observes that 'conveniently, Esther seems to know nothing of the irrevocability of Persian law'[23] endorses this self-reflexion unreflectively; for him, apparently, writing reflects reality, and everything else is subsumed by this certainty.

4. *The metacritical position*. The second form of discursive reflexivity (and the fourth mode of self-reflexive reading) is one in which discursive, reflexive reading involves both the self of the work—the way in which it problematizes itself as representation—and the self of the critic, whose position as, say, an art historian or a philosopher is also subject to reflexivity. This type of self-reflection/reflexion requires that the splitting of the agency of writing staged in the narrative be viewed as a representation of the critic's position. In this mode of self-reflection/reflexion, our model is not the blind Haman but the (in)sight(ful) Esther, whom Rembrandt represents as fully aware of her isolated position, yet who accepts her split subjectivity, adopting Mordecai's position and risking death to save the lives of her people.

---

22. Jacques Lacan, *The Four Fundamental Concepts of Psycho-Analysis* (ed. J.A. Miller; trans. A. Sheridan; London: Hogarth Press and the Institute of Psycho-Analysis, 1979).

23. Roland E. Murphy, *Wisdom Literature: Job, Proverbs, Ruth, Canticles, Ecclesiastes, Esther* (Grand Rapids: Eerdmans, 1981), p. 167.

reflection　　　　self	self excluded	self included
visual mirroring	1 fantasma (3.6)	2 primary narcissism (6.6-8)
discursive reflection	3 text = theory (1.19)	4 metacriticism (8.5)

Fig. 3 Reading Reflexivity in the Book of Esther

Reading Haman's decree 'properly' as not only a reflection of reality, but also an opportunity for intervention, given writing's inscription of delay (see below), while also recognizing the embeddedness of subject positions, Esther sees that she must rewrite the fate of the Jews (Est. 8.5). Hers is the position that the critic would do best to mirror (see Fig. 3).

This mode of reading has two major problems, one of which, its generality, may be countered by specifying self-reflexion according to this systematic analysis. The second problem, its lack of historical awareness, is more difficult to remedy. I would contend, however, that this approach to the book of Esther is historical in two ways. First, by committing this blatant anachronism, the historical position of the critic is at least foregrounded, which is precisely what does not occur in less overtly anachronistic readings (see n. 11). The unity between text and critic that is the basis of most criticism is, therefore, disrupted, leaving room for historical awareness, including awareness of the impossibility of historical reconstruction. Secondly, it is impossible to identify writing as a major theme of the narrative without acknowledging writing's relationship to power, and so acknowledging the anthropological view of writing as the beginning of history. In other words, any analysis of writing will be necessarily reflexive, or self-historicizing, hence the product of the fourth mode of self-reflexive reading: the mirroring of history in criticism. This mode requires discursive reflexivity, which posits the historical positions of text and reader in relation to each other.

The historical position of the reader relative to the text that I would advocate is less committed to (illusory) reconstructions of the past than to an awareness of difference in similarity. Along these lines, I have argued elsewhere[24] that the unstable beginning of patriarchy (as represented in Gen. 2–3) is visible from the vantage point of the equally unstable end of patriarchy that we are currently witnessing. Similarly, the emphasis on writing in Esther betrays its unmarked status there, a status that is shifting today as writing becomes marked, or visible, again. Today, writing is no longer considered self-evident, no longer 'taken as read'. The exercise of power through writing, as (em)plotted in Esther, becomes visible and can be more readily problematized in an age of letter bombs, when the reach of the sender, hence of the power holder, is manifested in and extended by an information technology revolution. Our faith in the irrevocable nature of writing has been destabilized by computer technologies that enable us to alter or even delete what is written, to falsify records, to do what Esther does: to overrule in practice what was irrevocable in theory, using similarity for difference (cf. Est. 3.12-15; 8.9-11). Self-reflexion thus dictates, for the ancient author as for the modern critic, that writing (the book of) Esther is to (con)textualize Esther writing.

Esther Writing Esther's Writing

Lots, laws, banquets and letters: these are the devices deployed in the plot of Esther. All are inversions (or perversions) of their standard functions, which enable them to become agents, controlling the characters who (mis)handle them. Lots are perverted by plots, laws target the individual instead of regulating the general, banquets function as fasts instead of feasts and letters are disenfranchised from their senders. All four devices relate to writing: Haman's own lot is cast when his casting of lots leads to the writing of the decree, thus organizing lot randomness into plot system; laws are certainly written, but the power inherent to their status as written is seriously weakened by their lack of enforcement; banquets are occasions for the writing of decrees; and letters, of course, constitute the very embodiment of writing. But letters are also manifestations of writing's problematic status as a speech act: in fixing the ephemeral flow of speech, writing delays (hence undermines) its efficacy. I contend that Esther can be read as a reflexion on/of precisely these aspects of writing.

With respect to the two central letters, then, it is obvious that the second one reverses the first, which had been explicitly declared

---

24. Mieke Bal, *Lethal Love: Literary Feminist Readings of Biblical Love Stories* (Bloomington: Indiana University Press, 1987).

irrevocable (Est. 1.19). Ahasuerus's/Haman's letter decreeing the extermination of the Jews is annulled or erased by Ahasuerus's/ Mordecai's letter decreeing the extermination of the king's enemies. At first reading, these two letters seem almost identical, mirroring each other with an elegant symmetry. But this mirroring is only an effect of their being paraphrased; neither letter is actually quoted in the canonical text. When they are written out, as in the Apocryphal supplement, they are totally different, and, as it turns out, their symmetry is sacrificed to their inscription (see the Rest of Esther 3.13; 16.12). This is a first indication that mirroring may be an illusion, that reflection needs to be reflected upon. These letters are instances of mirroring as narrative plot elements, not mirroring as texts. And if we read the letters as distinct supplements to the canonical text, encrypted by the excursion to the Apocrypha, it turns out that the second letter is not just a reversal of the first. A people is thereby supplemented ('and also for the Jews in their own script and language' [8.9]) as well as an action ('unite and defend themselves' [8.11]). And so is the diffusion of the subject of writing enhanced.

Plot and counterplot prove asymmetrical on yet another score: one is initiated by lot, the other by reading (the first letter). The lot is a random 'text' read by Haman and blindly obeyed, while the decree is a plotted text that is disobeyed. The response to Haman's decree can be read as a reflection on reading, offering an alternative to blind submission. Reading is a response, a reader-response. The letter/ counter-letter confrontation constitutes a reader-response theory, proposing that reading is neither fixed by nor independent of the text. Obedience to the text (of Haman's decree) would have entailed killing; disobedience to the text, in the sense of ignoring or bracketing it, would also have entailed killing. The danger of this binary opposition—between overestimating and underestimating the power of writing—is represented in the narrative by the split between Haman's fall/Esther and Mordecai's elevation, on the one hand, and the necessity of writing the second decree, on the other: that is, the second decree is not rendered superfluous by Esther and Mordecai's victory. What is needed, both to save the Jews and to preserve reading as a historically meaningful act, is an adequate reading by a competent and committed subject who possesses autonomous agency.[25] There

25. See Jane P. Tompkins, 'The Reader in History: The Changing Shape of Literary Response', in Tompkins (ed.), *Reader-Response Criticism: From Formalism to Post-Structuralism* (Baltimore: The Johns Hopkins University Press, 1980), pp. 201-31, for a relevant view of the historical significance of reading.

cannot be an exact mirroring, for there is no more symmetry between oppressor and oppressed, between attack and defense, between letter and reply than there is between subject and mirror image. With the engagement of speech in narrative, in the plot, writing can alter only what is already there.

What, then, does the written narrative of the book of Esther teach us about writing? How can it make us more self-conscious about the writing we do about the writing it presents about writing—of letters as communicative action, of decrees as prescriptive behavior, of chronicles as delayed participation in history, of writing as mirroring the text of Esther?

Writing serves social functions, as described by anthropological critique; it is also related to narrativity and has semiotic functions. As it happens, in Esther the social functions of writing are exemplified by its narrative and semiotic functions. The act of writing is plotted in such a way as to undermine the standard social functions of writing, as conceptualized in the orality–literacy debate, thereby inviting reflection on the politics of writing and reading.

The primary writer is (or should be in a true autocracy) the king, who uses it to exercise his authority. But even in his first letter condemning Vashti, the only one that he could conceivably have written himself, the king's exercise of power goes awry on three levels of increasing seriousness. First, on his own initiative, Ahasuerus's authority is diminished by the agency of his 'wise men', who effectively undermine the authenticity of the king's writing by dictating its contents (Est. 1.19-20). Secondly, and as a consequence, his superior status is reduced by the elaboration of his personal humiliation at the hands of the disobedient Vashti as an insult to all men ('Queen Vashti has done wrong, and not to the king alone' [1.16]) that must be countered by a law to reinforce the authority of 'all husbands, high and low alike' (1.20).[26] And thirdly, Ahasuerus's authority as a male, thus revealed to be the real issue, is further undermined when Esther ends up organizing the writing (in the plot) and even doing some writing herself.[27] Hence, as if to emphasize the ambivalence of writing's

26. Murphy (*Wisdom Literature*, p. 59) mentions this elaboration of event into law as a wisdom motif in Esther, recalling Prov. 31.10-31 and Sir. 9.2. For a claim that Esther belongs to wisdom literature, see also S. Talmon, ' "Wisdom" in the Book of Esther', *VT* 13 (1963), pp. 419-55.

27. Against many commentators who emphasize Esther's obedience, it must be stressed that she is more like Vashti than they care to admit. Each is guilty of disobedience in terms of approaching the king, hence of taking control over her relationship with her husband. John Otwell (*And Sarah Laughed: The Status of*

complicity in the use and abuse of power, state, class and gender are respectively undermined by writing. This is the statement on the *social* function of writing that can be read in the self-reflexivity of writing in Esther.

The *narrative* function of writing in the scroll further undermines the presumed but illusory certainties of writing. The three decrees that structure the plot stage the ambivalence of writing insightfully and in detail. The first decree, deposing Vashti, was meant to forever ensure the obedience of wives, hence ensuring male power over women in private and in public. However, its excessiveness and fearful defensiveness, possibly parodic,[28] ensure nothing but the decree's own failure, which is played out in the rest of the story. The submission of women cannot be guaranteed in or by writing, the story teaches us. Esther's initiatives embody her agency, her exercise of power against the royal rule that has stipulated the absoluteness of her powerlessness: namely, the interdiction against her being, or even *approaching*, the king. Vashti's punishment, the law of the first decree, is thus negated by Esther's symmetrical transgression.

The second decree, Haman's (p)lot, which is even less Ahasuerus's doing than the first, is equally irrevocable, and proves to be equally futile. Haman's decree is less ambitious, more limited in scope, stipulating the submission—albeit absolute through the extermination of only a marginal segment of the population: one people instead of all wives. It is more circumspectly grounded not in 'wisdom', that is, human opinion, but in Haman's version of Providence: the lot cast in his presence (Est. 3.7) to set the date for fulfilling the terms of the decree. Writing alone, this casting of lots seems to say, is too shaky a ground on which to build. But the rule of lot is countered by the Providence that Mordecai suggests to Esther (4.14). Writing, intended to fix, does not fix well enough.

Again, the narrative mode itself, constructed on the basis of temporal sequentiality, is mirrored by, and mirrors, the incidental 'rests' of writing. For in the narrative, writing is used to produce danger, but not defeat; what separates the two is the temporal space of delay or deferral that, inherent to writing, undermines precisely the fixation it aims for. This delay is a crucial feature of writing, its negative feedback loop, here exploited to represent the revocability of the

Women in the Old Testament [Philadelphia: Westminster Press, 1977], p. 69), for example, sees Esther as merely 'the primary Old Testament example of an obedient daughter' (*sic*).

28. Murphy, *Wisdom Literature*, p. 159.

irrevocable. It is what makes identification among the relevant parties—writer, reader and object—impossible, as recently argued so well in the critique of anthropology.[29] Writing's fixation entails a 'not yet' that calls for a sequel and that mirrors narrative's pursuit of an ending.[30] The narrative play of letter-writing foregrounds the unwarranted pretence of writing-as-power, of what-is-written as 'never to be revoked'.

So crucial is this feature of delay in writing that its staging in Esther becomes almost comical in one of the episodes considered 'implausible' by realist standards and as signifying the king's limited intelligence by psychological standards.[31] In addition to the letter, a communicative mode of writing, and the decree, an authoritarian mode, a third type of writing, the chronicle, is used in the narrative. In a 'historical' narrative, this is the self-reflexive genre par excellence, as it is incorporated in another chronicle. The events narrated in Est. 2.21-23—how Mordecai saves the king—encapsulate those narrated by the Esther story as a whole—how Esther and Mordecai save the Jews, thus also saving the king's integrity. Both 'third-person narratives' and historical reports, the chronicle and the scroll of which it is a part, represent something outside themselves. The chronicle is in this sense a *mise en abyme*.[32] It is therefore significant that this chronicle, necessarily written after the event, is not read, not integrated as

29. Johannes Fabian, *Time and the Other: How Anthropology Makes its Object* (New York: Columbia University Press, 1983). *Time and the Other* closely examines the impossibility of what Johannes Fabian calls 'coevalness', or the simultaneity of the anthropologist's observation/participation and writing. This impossibility by definition renders the anthropological endeavor itself illusory.

30. Peter Brooks, *Reading for the Plot: Design and Intention in Narrative* (New York: Knopf, 1984).

31. See David J.A. Clines (*Ezra, Nehemiah, Esther* [New Century Bible Commentary; London: Marshall, Morgan & Scott, 1984], p. 259), among many others, for an example of the realist bias; see Sasson ('Esther') for an example of the psychological bias. As I argued above, these anachronistic standards are generally harmful, as they obscure other issues and the narrative motivations that might illuminate them. Their limited perspective on the text does not, therefore, do justice to its historical-literary specificity and thereby leads to a tacit complicity in ethnocentrism or rather, as I like to call it, 'parontocentrism'.

32. A *mise en abyme* is a sign that represents the work as a whole and that is itself incorporated in the work. This term, by now quite well known, was introduced by André Gide and extensively studied by Lucien Dällenbach in his 1977 work, *Le Récit spéculaire*. I have commented on and elaborated Dällenbach's use of the term (M. Bal, *Femmes imaginaires: L'Ancien Testament au risque d'une narratologie critique* [Utrecht: Hes; Paris: Nizet; Montreal: HMH, 1986], pp. 166-80).

history, not acted upon until much later. In that sense, too, the chronicle is a *mise en abyme* of this story about the delayed effects of writing.

Obviously, this chronicle-story also demonstrates the negative effects of writing on memory (Plato's warning), since Ahasuerus thinks of rewarding Mordecai only when he *reads* about the event, not when it actually occurs. But rather than interpreting this connection between writing and memory anachronistically as proof of the king's dimwittedness, what I see here is another instance of self-reflexion. For the delay in writing exemplified by the king's forgetfulness is utterly indispensable to the narrative plot, which is in turn indispensable to saving the Jews from the dangers of writing, which is in turn indispensable to instituting Purim. Such is the lot of writing: what's discursive is recursive.

Ahasuerus's real power lies in his identity as the reader of the chronicle, and in the adequacy of his reading; his memory fails in order to motivate his real function. The written text, which was impotent before the king read it, acquires in the reading the power to force the king to act: justice must be done/served by the writing. This self-reflexion also applies to us: as delayed readers, we are likewise called upon to see that good deeds (such as Mordecai's, which, in fact, consisted of conserving knowledge and using it to avert danger) do not go unrewarded, that people do not get destroyed.

Finally, the *semiotic* function of writing is also foregrounded in the book of Esther. If we take the Peircean typology of signs as a model not of truth, but, like the Rembrandt paintings, as a reading approach or strategy, we can view the writing in Esther as at once symbolic, indexical and iconic, with the very fact that it fits all three categories signifying its crucial role in the text. Writing's tripartite role is also, as I hope to show, precisely what binds all the elements of the plot together.

First, writing is *symbolic*, as the first, most ambitious decree demonstrates. It is deployed in law-making even while it embodies the law itself. This occurs in three stages, each more expansive than the last, which turn an event into a sign, making it meaningful via repetition: (1) generalization, (2) publication and (3) multiplication.

1. The generalization of Vashti's disobedience as a crime punishable by law makes a violation the grounds for a rule and turns a random occurrence into a precedent. Vashti's crime was thus to have *signified*, to have made possible this semiotization of her act. The ambivalence of writing immediately becomes visible again; it is part of the package, so to speak: for although the act is criminalized out of fear that it will become widespread, its being written into law actually promul-

gates it by publicizing the crime's meaning. Thus, fear of contagion inflates a domestic disagreement into the sign of a generalized battle of the sexes. What is reflected (upon) here, in my view, is the danger of generalization, which conjures up enemies and turns a disagreement into a war.

2. Its being written into law publicizes the event, literally—for such publication would have had much the same effect as a newspaper would today. The publication of the event is meant to make an impact on each and every household. Like the newspaper delivered to the door, the letter about Vashti would have reached all men and changed their relationships with women (Est. 1.22). Publication is the semiotic consequence of generalization and is what makes it irrevocable.

3. With publication, the writing is multiplied, sent 'to every province in its own script and to every people in their own language' (Est. 1.22; 3.12; 8.9). This third stage, expansion by multiple translation, further emphasizes the semiotic nature of the ideological act of generalization. But it is also here that writing acts against itself. Thanks to the multiplication of Haman's decree, Mordecai learns of the projected pogrom and is able to counteract it, by writing back.

Secondly, writing is also represented in Esther as *indexical*. It is emphatically materialist, with its materiality signified by the king's signet ring. This ring, meant to produce 'pure' indices—wax impressions of the seal—becomes the means by which indexicality is perverted. On the one hand, the king's letters can be copied, but only from an original issued personally by—from the person of—the king. On the other hand, the copies are processed via the signet, shifted from the king's finger to Haman's (Est. 3.12). The king's mistake is precisely his removing the ring from his body, thus severing the contiguity on which indexicality is based. This is a mistake that the king later corrects: although he entrusts the recovered signet to Mordecai, he seems to monitor what is written in his name (8.8) and, in any event, no conflicts arise between what the king desires and what is written in this later episode.

By thus emphasizing the materiality of writing, the text also establishes the continuity between writing and (other forms of) body language. Dress becomes a form of communication whenever it attains semiotic status by indexical signification, such as the royal regalia worn by Mordecai during his honorary tour through the city. Haman, the writer of the plot-letter, devises this indexical code himself, when he adds to 'royal robes' the emphatic index 'which the king himself' (Est. 6.8). The signet ring, which gave him royal power, is not enough for Haman, who wants to *be* the king, and the index is the most appropriate sign of this impossible conflation that would render signs superfluous. Thus he stipulates that iconic signification—robes that *look* royal—is not enough.

Another instance of indexical 'body-writing' is the (conventional, hence symbolic) sign of royal favor expressed by touch. This index is doubly coded: the king holds the scepter, thus extending his body as the (symbolic) sign of his power, and the scepter touches Esther. It may be sheer coincidence that this tool by which the king enacts his connection to his subject bears an iconic relation to the phallus, likewise coded as power, but, in any case, the scepter also resembles the writing tool, the use of which will later be granted to Esther.

Thirdly, writing is *iconically* meaningful in this text. With its publication, the decree is displayed, a display foreshadowed by the demonstration of wealth as power at the first banquet. As a means of controlling the future, by decree, and of preserving the past, in the chronicle, writing also iconically signifies fate: Providence as opposed to chance. In the case of both writing and fate, certainty is dependent on some agency. What is written can be annulled by a timely intervention (thanks to the delay inherent to writing in general and to narrative in particular), just as the lots cast can be counteracted by plotting, and Providence aided by courage and wit. These iconic meanings of writing, then, strengthen the connections among the different plot elements already produced by symbolic and indexical signification. The semiotic functions of writing help us to read Esther as a meaningful, relevant statement about writing's interactive nature: just as writing requires reading, so does the book of Esther require readers.

But if the self-reflexive text thus encourages (discursive) reflection on the act of reading, the resulting self-reflexion entails reflecting on the agent, or subject, of that act. It seems meaningful that the writer of the story's last letter is the one whose very existence as a subject needed to be written first: Esther, touched by the royal scepter, ends this narrative of writing with an act of writing-as-power: 'And Queen Esther and Mordecai the Jew wrote, giving full authority and confirming this second letter about Purim' (9.29). The narrative has accomplished its remarkable movement from the king whose authority has already been undermined to the powerful woman who began this narrative in a state of utter powerlessness, as orphan, woman, commoner, foreigner. This narrative also moves from the randomness of lots to the organization of Purim by writing, lot's counteraction. But it took the entire narrative to reveal Esther as a fully realized agent, or subect. For subjectivity is by no means self-evident.

The Subject of Writing

Foucault's remarks on *Las Meninas* provoked the question: Whose self is reflected in self-reflexion? As it turns out, the book of Esther adds a new dimension to this question, for, to begin with, it stages the question's unanswerability. The male subject is represented as dispensable, shifting and unstable, with writing as the locus of this representation. The female subject, on the other hand, blatantly dispensable at first, is also the one to re-emerge, strengthened, and ultimately to take over, albeit as a result of the instability of subjectivity.

In order to comprehend the view of subjectivity entailed by this self-reflexive text, it is necessary to reject the realist and psychological readings to which Esther has been traditionally subjected. I propose to avoid the temptation of seeing the characters in terms of psychological plausibility by foregrounding their functional status. It then becomes obvious that, as narrative agents, the characters are both unstable and interchangeable. Vashti, for example, is integral to the production of Esther. The plot requires the elimination of Vashti in order to open up a space for Esther to fill. But there is more to the narrative function of the first queen. As an agent of ideological reflexion she must be eliminated for the sake of the ideology of male dominance. But Vashti is eliminated only to be restored as Esther, who takes her place and avenges her by reformulating disobedience as achieving power. Vashti's refusal to be an object of display is in a sense a refusal to be objectivized, hence to be robbed of her subjectivity. Esther's insistence on appearing before the king and using the tools of display to do so ('On the third day, Esther put on her royal robes' [5.1]) is the positive version of Vashti's negative act; Esther appears not for show but for action, not as mere possession but as self-possessed subject; finally, to drive this continuity between Esther and Vashti home, it is Esther who then makes the king appear at her banquet.[33]

33. The occasionally made assertion (totally groundless) that Vashti was asked to appear naked before the king does point to this incident's impression of objectifying display and to its gendered quality. Although Ahasuerus is criticized by some for his 'male chauvinistic behavior' (Clines, *Ezra, Nehemiah, Esther*, p. 257), Vashti's refusal, which would be justified in light of that view, is often criticized nonetheless, with the inconsistency typical of unreflective gender ideology. Identifying with ancient patriarchy, some critics tend to endorse, fully to underwrite, the sexism in the event while remaining blind to the shakiness of male power that the episode also underscores. Rabbi Meir Zlotowitz (*The Megillah: The Book of Esther*

Similarly, Haman, in all his wickedness, is necessary to the pro-
duction/motivation of Mordecal and his counterplot. Although he
seems to come out of nowhere in Est. 3.1, without Haman and his
(p)lot we would have no narrative, hence no Purim. It is highly
appropriate, then, that the name of the festival is derived from his
initial act. Haman's introduction as a newcomer rather than as one of
the established characters can be seen as a narrative stratagem to
avoid too much monitoring of Esther's behavior by the enraged wise
men (Est. 1.16-22).

Esther and Mordecai serve to produce and motivate each other:
without Esther, Mordecai would have no access to the court; without
her cousin, Esther would have no access to news from the city. Both
sources of information are necessary to make up for the defects of
writing. The narrative production of characters makes a psychological
reading both futile and mystifying. Such a reading obscures the very
issue that is foregrounded by this narrative: the instability of subjectivity.

With this in mind, it is easy to see that writing is the semiotic act
par excellence where the subject is destabilized, and, again, Esther
exploits that destabilization for its plot. Indeed, the awareness of
historical discrepancy helps us to reflect on the historicity of the very
notion of subjectivity. As Derrida reminds us, the notion of writing as
expression of the self is a modern one, emerging with the pre-Roman-
tic individualism of Rousseau, and may itself be symptomatic of the
loss of the self in writing. It seems to be a nicety of history that this
same Rousseau used himself as a weapon against the law which
decreed a *prise de corps* (!) against him. And, as Peggy Kamuf recalls, it
is in and through the signature, considered indexically contiguous to
the body of the writer, that the illusory stability of the subject/writer
is signified. The need for the signature is the need for indexicality.

But the Esther narrative severs the tie between signature and subject. The shifting of the signet ring from body to body is the narrative
representation of the subjective instability that writing promotes.
Kamuf rightly emphasizes the *evenemential* status of the signature, its

[New York: Mesorah Publications, 1976], pp. 46-51) exemplifies this tendency. After
quoting from ancient commentaries which deny Vashti any honorable motivation
and conclude that she deserved death, Zlotowitz states not only that she was
indeed killed, but also that Ahasuerus had Vashti killed. Interestingly, at the very
moment when this critic provides an imaginary murderer/subject to carry out this
imaginary murder, he neglects to specify the subject of his own text, thus endors-
ing the ancient commentators' view and allowing himself to be unreflectively
reflected in ancient ideology.

narrativity, when she observes that 'signature occurs in a difference from itself and an address to the other'.[34] The writings in Esther dramatize this mobility of the subject/writer. The chronicle (2.23), for example, has no subject. Lacking a represented self—a chronicle is a 'third person' narrative in which the thematic subject, the agent of events, is what's written about in a so-called objective presentation— the chronicle also lacks a signature: it is written in the presence of, not by, the king. The subject of the chronicle is, however, otherwise inscribed, notably, in the structure of address, here dramatized by the delayed reading.

For writing to fulfill its destiny, it is not enough that it be written in the presence of its intended reader; it must actually be read in order fully to achieve its deployment as writing. Without being realized by reading, writing remains a dead letter. In other words, the reader is the ultimate subject of writing, responsible for its consequences, for the actualization of the reality it proposes. By rewarding Mordecai, Ahasuerus shows himself to be a competent subject in this specific sense, with his apparently defective memory used as a narrative ploy to drive the point of reading home.

The description of the apparatus of royal administration and of the postal system (Est. 3.12), to give another example, while plausibly read as a demonstration of power or as circumstantial evidence of the text's historicity, can also be seen in light of the shifting subject of writing. The act of writing is broken down into its various aspects, each performed by an unidentified agent, or subject: the secretaries are summoned (by whom?); the writ is issued (by whom?);[35] it is drawn up in the king's name, which specifically means not by him but for him by someone else; and it is sealed with the king's signet, which is no longer on his finger. The stamp intended to validate the identity of the writer becomes instead the index of anonymous writing.

Again, writing emblematizes a feature that is displayed by the narrative in other ways as well. Subjectivity is placed in question generally, and the plot is built on that questioning. The irony of Est. 6.4-6 provides one example among many. Haman must decide the honor that is destined to be Mordecai's, but he mistakes the subject who is to be honored. The king mistakes Haman for a reliable adviser; hence the name of the subject to be honored is irrelevant. Because

34. Peggy Kamuf, *Signature Pieces: On the Institution of Authorship* (Ithaca, NY: Cornell University Press, 1988).
35. By Haman, obviously, but this is not stated.

Haman wishes to use his power to merge his subjectivity with the king's, he does not identify the people who are to be destroyed, which might have saved his enterprise. Thus the plot turns on subjectivity by default.

As if to foreground the intimate complicity of language in this plot of mistaken identities, Haman's use of language is doubly defective when (6.7-9) he mistakes the identity of the man to be honored; when Haman misreads the king's speech, he utters an anacoluthon, producing 'bad' language, and he misfires, producing a 'bad' speech act. Hence, the same speech act demonstrates the failure of both 'writer' and 'reader' due to unwarranted assumptions about subjectivity.

If we read the text from the perspective suggested by the Rembrandt paintings, as reflections of and on the vexed relationship between text and subject, the problematic of the subject of writing encapsulates the entire narrative: its language, its plot and its characters. And the reader is not excluded from this perspective, but merely delayed by writing, with his or her response on hold. Haman's blindness in the Rembrandt painting (Fig. 2) threatens to infect the viewer/reader, toward whom his body is emphatically directed; the icon of blind eyes is dangerously indexical as body language.

Conclusion

At this juncture, a critical question must be addressed: What have we gained by applying this willfully anachronistic contemporary concept to this ancient text? While it will be for others to say what, if anything, has been gained, I can suggest a few possibilities. I wish to make no claim about the historical meaning of the text, let alone about authorial intention or the origins of Purim, but I do think that I have made a case against the nineteenth-century model of reading predominant in many interpretations that do claim historical validity. While the enigma of Purim's origins and the meaning of its name are not, cannot be, resolved, I have opened up a space for an interpretation of the meaning of *purim* that is relevant to the contemporary reader, while also illuminating aspects of the text whose pertinence can hardly be denied.

Guided by an oddity in the two Rembrandt paintings, I have tried to draw a few lines that break up the text even as they pull its various elements together, not to yield a deceptive coherence but to problematize unity. By looking into the various meanings of self-reflexion and the ways in which these meanings appear to be dramatized in Esther, I have developed a view on the ancient text that affects the subject of criticism. For if reading is the only way to breathe life into the dead letter of the text, and if, moreover, reading is a matter of historical importance, then Esther herself becomes a mirror for the contemporary critic. If engaged, like her, in exposing the abuse of power, the danger of writing, and the instability of subjectivity, the critic will escape neither responsibility for her activity nor the encapsulation of that activity in historically diverse, subjectless writing.

Thus, writing criticism in accordance with Esther entails not obscuring either its predecessors or its opponents, not denying either its complicity or its agency. The book of Esther demonstrates that writing is not necessarily either a deadly weapon or an innocent toy; closer to the time bomb than to anything else, however, it can be countered by virtue of its delayed effect. Hence, when involved in the act of reading—the deferred completion of writing—critics should be aware of both their (overt or covert) allegiances (reading is an act in which subjectivity is dispersed) and their own inevitable contributions to this act (it is an act).

In terms of allegiances, one cannot but reflect on the question of where the 'rest' of one's subjectivity lies: that is, with Ahasuerus's 'wise men' and their battle or with Esther and Mordecai and their collaboration. Should one endorse/reject the generalization of Vashti as 'all women'/the individualization of Esther as different from Vashti? This question of implicit allegiances to ideological positions is less obvious than it seems precisely because obvious positions are offered as a lure. It is only too easy to disavow Haman's genocidal impulse, but the mirror also reflects more insidious generalizations from a single individual to an entire people, more subtle expressions of hatred for the Other, whoever he or she might be. Those positions and their similarity to the obvious ones should be brought to awareness by a reflexivity that extends to the critic him/herself. By insisting on the complex functioning of writing and the instability of its subjects, the book of Esther shows that critics are no more autonomous or stable than any other readers/writers; hence, their network of unconscious allegiances is both inevitable and dangerous.

In order to draw all readers in, *pûrîm* must be a form of plurality. Haman's downfall warns the viewer not to be blind to the mirroring power of the text, which extends beyond any immediate or simple historical veracity into the realm of historical agency. Had Mordecai and Esther been as blind as Haman, they would not have been able to read the writing on the wall. Seeking the historical origins of Purim in a forlorn past, safely out of reach, the critic may forfeit her or his own

pûrîm. For when the lots have been cast, and another people imper-
iled, the critic reading Esther cannot passively submit to the dictate of
lots: obedience has been revealed as the wrong attitude. It would be
an ironic misreading of the mirror of Esther to see the scroll as reflecting only the history of the Jews and one of their festivals. By reading it
as a text about reading/writing, however, one is invited to reflect
upon all the issues implicated in it: upon gender, power and the state;
genocide and otherness; submission and agency—in short, upon
history.

ESTHER: A NEW INTERPRETATION OF THE JOSEPH STORY IN THE FIGHT AGAINST ANTI-SEMITISM AND SEXISM[*]

Klara Butting

Joseph Is Created Anew

The book of Esther tells of Jewesses and Jews in exile. The scene is set at the Shushan Palace of the Persian king. Here Esther and Mordecai, the two Jewish protagonists of the story, appear. A dangerous fight for survival of the Jewish diaspora threatened by state-organized persecution takes place. To tell this story of Esther and Mordecai at the Persian court, the narrators of the book of Esther refer to words and motives of the Joseph story (Gen. 37–50).

Many motives and narrations here are similar to those of the Joseph story. There is as well a number of linguistic correspondences.[1] I will outline a few examples only for this claim here.

Mordecai refuses to prostrate himself before Haman and demonstrates that there is a limit to the assimilation of the Jewesses and Jews to the king's power (Est. 3.1-5). As far as structure and choice of words are concerned, this part follows the story that tells how Joseph refuses to have sex with Potiphar's wife (Gen. 39.7). While this results in a prison sentence for Joseph (39.20), for Mordecai it may mean annihilation of himself as well as his people. In spite of this danger, however, Mordecai rises at the court of the foreign king—just as

*   This article, translated by Ursula Petruschke, is a summary of my studies on the book of Esther as outlined in my dissertation: Klara Butting, *Die Buchstaben werden sich noch wundern: Innerbiblische Kritik als Wegweisung feministischer Hermeneutik* (Alektor-Hochschulschriften; Berlin: Alektor-Verlag, 1994), pp. 49-86; 172-76.

1.   Cf. L.A. Rosenthal, 'Die Josephsgeschichte mit den Büchern Esther und Daniel verglichen', *ZAW* 15 (1895), pp. 278-84; Arndt Meinhold, 'Die Gattung der Josephsgeschichte und des Estherbuches: Diasporanovelle, I', *ZAW* 87 (1975), pp. 306-24; *idem*, 'Die Gattung der Josephsgeschichte und des Estherbuches: Diasporanovelle, II', *ZAW* 88 (1976), pp. 72-93; Sandra Beth Berg, *The Book of Esther: Motifs, Themes and Structure* (Missoula, MT: Scholars Press, 1979), pp. 123, 165.

Joseph did—and becomes the second in command in the state (Est. 10.3; Gen. 41.43). Like Joseph in Egypt, Mordecai is honoured publicly (Est. 6.11; Gen. 41.42b, 43) and is given the king's signet ring (Est. 8.2; Gen. 41.42). Esther's story also reminds one of Joseph in Egypt. Their beauty is described with almost the same words (Est. 2.7; Gen. 39.6) and both are endangered because of their beauty. Esther is caught by the king's agents and brought into the king's harem. Joseph is molested by Potiphar's wife and thrown into prison. Imprisoned in the king's harem, Esther experiences signs of favour and grace just like Joseph in his captivity (Est. 2; 9.15/Gen. 39.4; Est. 2.17/Gen. 39.21). Finally, Esther is raised to become queen of Persia. She, too, becomes the second to the king in a foreign country as did Joseph in Egypt. And just as Joseph uses his position to save his people from a famine, Esther as queen of Persia succeeds in saving her people from impending persecution.

These similarities can best be explained by the assumption that the story of Joseph was the model for the book of Esther. The book of Esther presents a new interpretation of Joseph's story. The decisive character, Joseph himself, is recreated anew in two persons, Esther and Mordecai.[2] Obviously, the narrators of the book of Esther did not find it sufficient just to read and retell the Joseph tales in their context. Joseph's story had to be told anew. Insights into the social context that this revision requires are given by the authors in the first chapter of their book. Before Esther and Mordecai appear their place of future action, the court of the Persian king in Shushan, is described. Most probably, this location of the story is historically not quite accurate. We do not know anything about the impending persecution of the Jewish people in the Mediterranean area during the period of Persian hegemony (about 550–331 BCE); rather, events such as happened under Hellenistic rule (about 332–141 BCE) are reflected in the book.[3] We know, for example, that towards the end of the Hellenistic predominance Antiochus IV Epiphanes tried to destroy the Jewish religion. But even if the place and date of the book's origin remain uncertain, in the end the context of the Esther story is presented to us in its main essentials. The first chapter outlines the milieu in which Esther and Mordecai have to operate.

2.   Butting, *Die Buchstaben*, pp. 67-77.
3.   Berg, *Esther*, pp. 169-73.

The Social Background

The story starts with a demonstration of power. The ruler of the Persian empire, King Ahasuerus, is sitting on his throne—Ahasuerus is the Hebrew imitation of the Persian manner of writing Xerxes (Xerxes I is probably the king referred to). His reign is undisputed and order in his empire unflagging. The king demonstrates his stability and power by celebrating. In a celebration of 180 days, he *shows his wealth and power* to the representatives of his state (1.4). Then there is a banquet for all the men of Sushan. Now Queen Vashti is to appear to crown this banquet. The king wishes *to show her* to everybody (1.11).The sight of this queen he owns as part of his power shall make all men aware of their own power as men in the social hierarchy of the empire. This way the unshakeable order of the empire is to be demonstrated once again.[4]

'But Queen Vashti refused' (1.12). At the moment of her refusal, her title is put before her name (and cf. 1.9-11). Thus, it is emphasized that she refuses as queen. Vashti defends her personal and political independence against the king.

The council of the wise men regard this refusal as an attack on their whole system of government. This represents the viewpoint of the ancient world, namely, that the power a man exercises in the state corresponds to the power he exercises at home.[5] This opinion leads the wise men to believe that female resistance endangers the whole state. In particular, they fear that Vashti's refusal will induce other women to do the same. They will despise their husbands and start talking about Vashti's attitude (1.17-18). Thus, the council suggests to set an example and to repudiate Vashti. They hope women throughout the country will be reminded that they have to pay their respects to their husbands. Last but not least, a decree is published for the whole country in which the social status quo is described and fixed: 'Every men should rule his home and speak his local language' (1.22). The man should assert his authority and so represent in his home the king and his superiors. Much as these authorities send letters in local languages (1.22), at home men should not use the official language—Aramaic—but their own people's tongue. The danger that, through a

4.   Cf. Timothy K. Beal, 'Tracing Esther's Beginnings', in Athalya Brenner (ed.), *A Feminist Companion to Esther, Judith and Susanna* (Feminist Companion to the Bible, 7; Sheffield: Sheffield Academic Press, 1995), pp. 87-110.

5.   Michael Foucault, *Der Gebrauch der Lüste: Sexualität und Wahrheit* (3 vols.; Frankfurt: Suhrkamp Verlag, 1991), II, p. 195.

precedent, women might aquire their own language and learn to speak, is thus met and removed. With the everyday language, masculine domination shall penetrate everybody's thoughts and determine the images and ideas of men and women.

Totalitarian and sexist structures are given in this first chapter of Esther as the social context. An empire extending over many peoples and languages strengthens its power by trying to gain control over everybody's feelings thoughts by masculine rule. Vashti's opposition and the panic-like resistance of the wise men show that this is *not* a natural order, but an order established again and again by force. The protest of women can undermine the powerful system based on masculine arbitrariness.

Predecessors of Feminist Bible Reading

The notes regarding the social context of the story reveal the initial motives for the revision of the Joseph story as found in the book of Esther. The authors included the relationship between the sexes, attribution of sexist roles and the prevailing subordination of women in their social analysis. They have obviously reached the conclusion that a masculine inclination alone is of little help in view of all this violence. Their story focuses on the resistance of Esther who, following in Joseph's footsteps, saves her people. With their analysis and criticism concerning sexist role patterns, the Esther authors intervene in the historiography of Israel. The declared intent of the royal council meeting to deprive the women of the empire of an antecedent and to avoid a discussion of rebellious female history seems to reflect how the authors of Esther have interpreted the silence concerning the suffering and fate of women in large parts of the biblical record. In any case, the book bearing the name of Esther reveals protest against the breaking and silencing of female power, together with the understanding that women need antecessors or precursors to help them find their own language.

We thus become aware of antecessors in feminist Bible reading. In fact, I think it is quite in order to assume that women took part in reading Joseph's story and in writing the book of Esther. On the one hand, the relentless disclosure of the relationship between men and women as one of violence leads us to believe that women took part in writing the book. On the other hand, Esther is presented as a woman who is able to write and does write. The instructions for inaugurating the Feast of Purim are written by her (9.29). Besides, it is mentioned that her words and instructions were written in the book (9.32).

The text signals that women were involved verbally and in writing. These authors have read the Bible, within the context of sexist violence, with love and criticism. They use Joseph's story to tell about God's faithfulness to his people in oppression and away from home. At the same time, they also analyse the prevailing suppression of women in their own tradition. Androcentric structures in Israel's historiography are rejected, and the old story is told anew as a story of a woman. The authors testify with their procedure that the Bible wants to be an interlocutor, not an authority. They recognize the deity witnessed therein as a deity that invites examination of all transmitted texts, in order to determine whether their God talk legitimizes and reassures the suppression of women and men. In this dispute over biblical texts, the book of Esther is interesting for feminist hermeneutics. Feminists, in their discussion of the Bible, can go on from here. We are encouraged to find evidence of the liberating deity in biblical texts and, at the same time, stimulated to testify to this deity by telling the story anew and after a critical analysis of the existing record.

Anti-Semitism and Sexism

As the story continues, it becomes obvious that the handed-down promises given to the Jewish people are told anew, albeit with criticism and with revision of previous tradition.

In the beginning Esther and Mordecai are confronted with the totalitarian, sexist power of the empire. When the whole machinery of absolute rule is set into action in order to catch and register all the beautiful girls in the empire, so as to find a new queen for the king, Esther also comes into the harem. At first Esther and Mordecai adjust. Esther even marries a non-Jewish man and conceals her Jewish identity. However, this silence anticipates a forthcoming conflict. From the very beginning potential anti-Semitism smoulders, being noticable only because of Esther's and Mordecai's fear of such an attitude. The conflict breaks out when the king reorganizes his officials after a plot (2.21-23), and Haman is appointed prime minister (3.1). The narrators characterize Haman's political way of thinking by calling him 'the Agagite'. Agag was king of Amalek (1 Sam. 15). The biblical Amalek stands for the absolute hostility against Israel and Israel's history of liberation (Exod. 17.8-16; Deut. 25.17-19). Amalek is personified anti-Semitism. The political submission to this leader, as demanded, marks the limit of possible assimilation for Mordecai. He refuses to bow in deep reverence before Haman. His colleagues report that Mordecai adopts this attitude because he is a Jew (3.4). When Haman learns that

Mordecai is a Jew, he plans to destroy all the Jews throughout the kingdom. A propitious time for this action is determined, a day when by state persecution the Jewish population of the empire is to be annihilated.

This conflict between Haman and Mordecai, and the planned action of the Persian ruling power against Jewesses and Jews, is described in the book of Esther in such manner that different details remind us of Vashti's refusal and the state-ordered submission of women. Twice we see how the wounded arbitrariness and resulting fury of a man become an affair of state (1.12; 3.5). First, the refusal to submit to absolute power gives an excuse officially to organize the submission of women. Then it gives licence for the extermination of Jewesses and Jews. A whole group is identified with a single resistant person. Since Vashti is a woman her refusal has, according to Memucan, not wronged the king *only* (1.16); since Mordecai is a Jew, according to Haman it is not enough to eliminate him *only* (3.6). The state persecution is aimed at *all women* (1.16-20) and *all Jews* (3.6). The powerful feel threatened by all those who are different, for example the 'other' sex and the 'other' people. Both decrees are finally published throughout the kingdom (1.20; 3.13) in the written and spoken languages of the various provinces and countries (1.20; 3.12), giving totalitarian thinking a well-defined form.

These observations are not meant to obscure the differences between the two powers of violence, violence against women and violence against Jews. The women are to be declassed, whereas the hatred against the Jewish people means extinction. In view of this unique basic threat of extinction, it is so much more astonishing that the authors describe the extinction plans in analogy to the submission plans. They establish connections between the basic threat of anti-Semitism for Jewesses and Jews, and the discrimination of women because of their sex. They reveal that the spirit is the same in both cases. This connection links the solution of the question of women's rights inseparably to the deliverance of the Jewish people from the threat of the other nations. A radical dispute about masculine complicity in totalitarian power becomes obvious. The authors reveal structures of violence that have to be fought against. In the house of each man, where submission and dominion are practised, a totalitarian structure of thinking and acting is acquired, a structure that shows its deadly dimension in the hatred against the Jewish people. So, in the submission and mutilation of the history of women, the threat of anti-Semitism to the existence of the Jewish people is transmitted. In this reflection we find a further motive for the authors' intervention in Israel's historiography, and for their telling that Esther saves her people by following in Joseph's footsteps. In the background we find the insight that the rise of women against supremacy and oppression is essential in order to avoid situations whereby generation after generation produce the same pattern of violence which finds, in the long run, a suitable field of action in anti-Semitism. A revision of the own-tradition is essential in hoping for salvation and liberation.

Reconstruction of Women's History in Hearing the Biblical Promise

Finally, with Esther's resistance against the order and the rule of the king, it is described how the fight against sexist power and for the liberation of Jewish people from anti-Semitic threat are linked together. When Mordecai asks Esther to go to the king and to help her people, her social place as a woman in the Persian society is described (4.10-11). She lives without resistant hopes and perspectives. She sees no chance to do anything for the liberation of her people. She only sees the power of the king she is subjected to. The king decides who may come to him and who may not. It is forbidden on pain of death to come near him without being summoned. And Esther herself has not been called for 30 days. In this situation, Vashti's refusal and her repudiation, a repudiation with which the king publicly demonstrated his power of disposal over all people around him, come to mind. Esther describes the situation in the harem as absolutely dependent on the king's laws, laws authorized by the power to kill. She is formed by Vashti's failed resistance and moulded by her own experience of being dependent and handled.

This balance of power in which Esther finds herself collapses because of Mordecai's reply (4.13-14). He says that the Persian king and his officials have no power over her life and death. Life and death are decided by participation in the history of the Jewish people. If Esther lets her people down in this danger she will not live, her name and that of her relatives will be wiped out from history. The political powers are challenged in matters of controlling life and death (cf. Mk 8.35-36). The God of Israel gives life and cuts off from life. In this conviction Mordecai expresses the hope that Jewesses and Jews will find 'room to breathe and salvation' (4.14), and assesses Esther's sufferings and her being raised up as queen as a sign that she can accomplish the deliverance of her people.

In this conversation between Esther and Mordecai, the promises handed down to the Jewish peole have liberating strength. Although no change of the political power Esther has been subjected to is effected at this point, this conversation makes her able to act. This becomes obvious when, at the end of the conversation, Esther is the one to tell Mordecai what has to be done (4.17). She re-establishes the communion between herself and her people with a communal period of fasting and, as part of the community, confronts herself with death (4.16). At the same time, she is able to analyse her situation anew, having realized that the powerful who reign with the aid of death cannot decide over *her* life and death. Vashti's broken-off resistance is no longer the booty of these men. Vashti's story is no longer a landmark in the history of women's oppression. Esther learns to hope by listening to the tradition of her people: the present time is not determined by the victors in history, but by the expectation of threatened and defeated women and men. She learns to consider the story of a loser as her own. In the harem, the place of Esther's double alienation as a woman as well as a Jewess, women's history comes to life by listening to tradition. With this wonder starts the deliverance of the Jewish people.

Esther's Resistance

For Esther, Vashti's story becomes a living source from which she takes directives and plans for her own resistance. Esther breaks the king's law. She approaches the throne without having been asked. She puts on her royal robes, remembering that the king wanted to 'decorate himself' with a beautiful royal woman (1.11); and she stays alive. She chooses two festive occasions as the place of action (5.4-8) and stages the scenery which the king needs for the demonstration of his glory (1.3-5). Esther makes her plan, knowing that Vashti has been the demonstration object on such occasions. At first, she prepares a banquet *for him*, the king, and invites the king and Haman (5.4). During the banquet she announces a further banquet that she will prepare *for them*, the king and Haman, and invites both men (5.8). So, on her first banquet she honors Haman just as much as the king and sows the seed of mistrust and fear in the king. She begins to play the two men off against each other.

Esther's plan would not be conceivable without Vashti's refusal. The prevailing sexist balance of power has been made public by Vashti's resistance and makes an analysis possible. There is a power hidden in Vashti's broken-off story that is available to Esther when she fights for the survival of her people within the given structures.

The seed Esther has sown works in seclusion. Haman enjoys being honoured by his friend and his wife (5.9-14). However, the king whose wife is celebrating someone else has trouble sleeping that night.[6] He reads in the records of his kingdom, hoping to find a man he could use as an antagonist against Haman. He really finds one, Mordecai, who has exposed a plot to assassinate the king (6.1-14).

Finally, Esther's second banquet becomes a counterpart to the king's second banquet, during which Ahasuerus destroyed Queen Vashti (7.1-10). Esther uses the despotism that has become obvious in summoning Queen Vashti, for example, making women functional for glorifying men, as a wile to overthrow Haman. Esther, still not revealing that she is a Jewess, accuses Haman of planning to destroy her and her people (7.3-4). Esther accuses Haman, normally called 'the oppressor of the Jews' (3.10; 8.1; 9.10-24), of being 'the man, the oppressor and enemy' (7.6). She generalizes Haman's threat and suggests to the king that this threat is aimed at her, the queen, and insofar it goes also at him, the king, and at the empire. The plan works. The king feels threatened. Even when Haman goes down on his knees before Esther, begging for mercy, the king only sees a rival man. He misinterprets the scene as attempted rape (7.8) and has Haman hanged as a usurper.

An Exodus Is Still Pending

After Haman's downfall king Ahasuerus gives the estate of Haman, the Jews' enemy, to Queen Esther (8.1). This note shows a future where anti-Semitism ends and the liberation of women is present. Esther has gained her own wealth and the power of a house of her own. Her fight against Haman, the hater of Jews, has undermined the power of those who want to see a man rule over his home and to assert his authority (1.22). Outwardly the sexist pattern remains the same. Esther appoints Mordecai to be in charge of Haman' s estate and the king appoints him prime minister. Now Mordecai can act publicly. Therefore, the freedom that the authors of the book of Esther show in conversing with Joseph's story is essential when reading the book of Esther.[7]

6. Jonathan Magonet, 'The Liberal and the Lady: Esther Revisited', *Judaism* 29 (1980), pp. 167-76 (173).

7. Cf. Bea Wyler, who adds, with eleventh and twelfth chapters, a happy end to the book of Esther: B. Wyler, 'Esther: The Incomplete Emancipation of a Queen', in Brenner (ed.), *A Feminist Companion to Esther, Judith and Susanna*, pp. 111-35. Wyler's article is based on my work on Esther; however, for some reason she does not make reference to it.

Haman's downfall is *not* the end of anti-Semitism although Mordecai, with the king's ring, comes into power in the empire. Haman's order to destroy the Jewish population is irreversible, because it is an order bearing the king's seal (8.8). For the rescue of the Jewish people Esther and Mordecai get only the permission that the Jewish people may resist the attack of their enemies. The book of Esther is not another book of Exodus. Therefore, at the closing lines of Esther, the beginning of the book of Exodus is pointed out to us. With the lines, 'King Ahasuerus not only laid tribute upon the mainland but even of the islands of the sea' (10.1), we are reminded of the beginning of Israel's oppression in Egypt, where 'they laid tribute masters over them' (Exod. 1.11). The exodus from oppression is still missing at the end of the book of Esther. This goes for the whole Jewish diaspora that remains scattered, subjected to an inconstant and unpredictable king. This is the case also with Esther, who remains in the king's harem and is ignored by official historiography. The books of the Cronicles of the Kings of Media and Persia only mention Mordecai, 'his [Ahasuerus's] great deeds; also, the full account of Mordecai's greatness and the honors given him by the king, they are written in the book of Chronicles of the Kings of Media and Persia' (10.2). And also, within Israel in the second book of Maccabees, Purim is handed down as the 'Mordecai Feast' (2 Macc. 15.26). At the end of the book of Esther we are once again confronted with the social context of the story: royal politics and historiography's silence concerning power and women's history. The book of Esther takes its place in this patriarchal history and historiography—and participates in it. Still, this book bears the name of Esther and not of Mordecai. It tells history from the bottom. It revises biblical historiography in order to reconstruct the history of women and to recount a wonder: the Jewish people, scattered among other nations, can withstand impending persecution. The story is a breathing space in alienation and, as such, the story of Purim.

BIBLIOGRAPHY

Adams, R.McC., *The Evolution of Urban Society: Early Mesopotamia and Prehistoric Mexico* (Chicago: Aldine, 1966).

Ahmed, Leila, *Women and Gender in Islam* (New Haven: Yale University Press, 1992).

Alexander, Jonathan J.G., *Medieval Illuminators and their Methods of Work* (New Haven: Yale University Press, 1992).

Allen, S., and D.L. Barber, 'Sexual Division and Society', in D.L. Barber and S. Allen (eds.), *Sexual Divisions and Society: Process and Change* (Explorations in Sociology, 6; London: Tavistock, 1976), pp. 1-24.

Alonzo, Andrea, 'My Extended Family', in Nan Maglin and Nancy Schniedewind (eds.), *Women and Stepfamilies: Voices of Anger and Love* (Philadelphia: Temple University, 1989), pp. 38-43.

Alpers, Svetlana, *The Art of Describing: Dutch Art in the Seventeenth Century* (Chicago: University of Chicago Press, 1985).

Alphen, Ernst van, *Bij wijze lezen: Verleidinng enverzet van Willem Brakmans lezer* (Muiderberg: Coutinho, 1988).

—*Francis Bacon and the Loss of Self* (London: Reaktion Books; Cambridge, MA: Harvard University Press, 1992).

Anderson, Janice and Jeffrey Staley, 'Taking It Personally: Autobiographical Biblical Criticism', *Semeia* 72 (1995).

Andreasen, Niels-Erik A., 'The Role of the Queen Mother in Israelite Society', *CBQ* 45 (1983), pp. 179-94.

Austin, J.L., *How to Do Things with Words* (Cambridge, MA: Harvard University Press, 1975).

Baab, O.J., 'Woman', *IDB*, IV, pp. 864-67.

Babinec, Lisa S., 'Cyclical Patterns of Domination and Manipulation in Flannery O'Connor's Mother–Daughter Relationships', *The Flannery O'Connor Bulletin* 19 (1990), pp. 9-29.

Bailey, Randall C., 'They're Nothing but Incestuous Bastards: The Polemical Use of Sex and Sexuality in Hebrew Canon Narratives', in Fernando F. Segovia and Mary Ann Tolbert (eds.), *Reading from This Place. I. Social Location and Biblical Interpretation in the United States* (Philadelphia: Fortress Press, 1995), pp. 121-38.

Bal, Mieke, *Femmes imaginaires: L'Ancien Testament au risque d'une narratologie critique* (Utrecht: Hes; Paris: Nizet; Montreal: HMH, 1986).

—*Lethal Love: Literary Feminist Readings of Biblical Love Stories* (Bloomington: Indiana University Press, 1987).

—'Heroism and Proper Names, or the Fruits of Analogy', in Brenner (ed.), *A Feminist Companion to Ruth*, pp. 42-69.

—*Reading 'Rembrandt': Beyond the Word–Image Opposition* (Cambridge: Cambridge University Press, 1991).

Barré, Michael L., SS (ed.), *Wisdom, You Are my Sister: Studies in Honor of Roland E. Murphy, O.Carm., on the Occasion of his Eightieth Birthday* (CBQMS, 29; Washington: Catholic Biblical Association, 1997), pp. 216-33.

Beal, Timothy K., 'Tracing Esther's Beginnings', in Brenner (ed.), *A Feminist Companion to Esther, Judith and Susanna*, pp. 87-110.

Beit-Arié, Malachi, *The Makings of the Medieval Hebrew Book: Studies in Paleography and Codicology* (Jerusalem: Magnes Press; Hebrew University, 1993).

Belich, James, *The New Zealand Wars and the Victorian Interpretation of Racial Conflict* (Auckland: Auckland University Press, 1989).

Ben-Barak, Zafrira, 'The Status and Right of the G^ebîrâ', *JBL* 110 (1991), pp. 23-34.

Berg, Sandra Beth, *The Book of Esther: Motifs, Themes and Structure* (Missoula, MT: Scholars Press, 1979).

Berkhofer, Robert F., Jr, *The White Man's Indian: Images of the American Indian from Columbus to the Present* (New York: Random House, 1978).

Berlin, A., *Poetics and Interpretation of Biblical Narrative* (Winona Lake, IN: Eisenbrauns, 1994).

Bernstein, M.J., 'Two Multivalent Readings in the Ruth Narrative', *JSOT* 50 (1991), pp. 15-26.

Bird, P., 'Images of Women in the Old Testament', in R.R. Ruether (ed.), *Religion and Sexism: Images of Women in the Jewish and Christian Traditions* (New York: Simon & Schuster, 1974), pp. 41-88.

—'The Place of Women in the Israelite Cultus', in P.D. Miller, P.D. Hanson and S.D. McBride (eds.), *Ancient Israelite Religions: Essays in Honor of Frank Moore Cross* (Philadelphia: Fortress Press, 1987), pp. 397-420.

—'Women (Old Testament)', *ABD* (1992), VI, pp. 951-57.

Blaeser, Kimberly M., 'Pagans Rewriting the Bible: Heterodoxy and the Representation of Spirituality in Native American Literature', *Review of International English Literature* 25.1 (1994), pp. 12-31.

Bledstein, A.J., 'Female Companionships: If the Book of Ruth Were Written by a Woman', in Brenner (ed.), *A Feminist Companion to Ruth*, pp. 116-33.

Bloch, Ariel, and Chana Bloch, *The Song of Songs: A New Translation with an Introduction and Commentary* (New York: Random House, 1995).

Bohlen, R., 'Die Rutrolle', *TTZ* 101 (1992), pp. 1-19.

Bos, J.W.H., 'Out of the Shadows', *Semeia* 42 (1988), pp. 37-67.

Boer, R., *Novel Histories* (Sheffield: Sheffield Academic Press, 1997).

Braulik, G., 'Das Deuteronomium und die Bücher Job, Sprichwörter, Rut', in E. Zenger (ed.), *Die Tora als Kanon für Juden und Christen* (HBS, 10; Freiburg: Herder, 1996), pp. 61-138.

—*Deuteronomium II* (NEB.AT, 28; Würzburg: Echter Verlag, 1992).

Breneman, Mervin, *Ezra, Nehemiah, Esther: The New American Commentary; an Exegetical and Theological Exposition of Holy Scripture*, X (n.p.: Broadman & Holman, 1993).

Brenner, Athalya, 'Introduction', in Brenner (ed.), *A Feminist Companion to Ruth*, pp. 9-18.

—'Naomi and Ruth', in Brenner (ed.), *A Feminist Companion to Ruth*, pp. 70-84.

—'Naomi and Ruth: Further Reflections', in Brenner (ed.), *A Feminist Companion to Ruth*, pp. 140-45.

Brenner, Athalya (ed.), *A Feminist Companion to Esther, Judith and Susanna* (Feminist Companion to the Bible, 7; Sheffield: Sheffield Academic Press, 1995).

—*A Feminist Companion to Ruth* (Feminist Companion to the Bible, 3; Sheffield: Sheffield Academic Press, 1993).

Brenner, Athalya, and Carole R. Fontaine (eds.), *A Feminist Companion to Reading the Bible: Approaches, Methods and Strategies* (Sheffield: Sheffield Academic Press, 1997).

Brenner, A., and F. van Dijk-Hemmes, *On Gendering Texts: Female and Male Voices in the Hebrew Bible* (BIS, 1; Leiden: E.J. Brill, 1993).

Bridenthal, R., and C. Koontz (eds.), *Becoming Visible: Women in European History* (Boston: Houghton Mifflin, 1977 and 1987).

Bronner, Leila Leah, *From Eve to Esther: Rabbinic Reconstructions of Biblical Women* (Louisville, KY: Westminster/John Knox Press, 1994).

—'Gynomorphic Imagery in Exilic Isaiah (40–66)', *Dor leDor* 12 (1983–84), pp. 71-83.

—'A Thematic Approach to Ruth in Rabbinic Literature', in Brenner (ed.), *A Feminist Companion to Ruth*, pp. 146-69.

Brooks, Peter, *Reading for the Plot: Design and Intention in Narrative* (New York: Knopf, 1984).

Brown, Kathleen M., 'The Anglo-Algonquian Gender Frontier', in Nancy Shoemaker (ed.), *Negotiators of Change: Historical Perspectives on American Indian Women* (London: Routledge), pp. 26-48.

Brown, Michelle P., *Understanding Illuminated Manuscripts: A Guide to Technical Terms* (Malibu, CA: J. Paul Getty Museum, 1994).

Brubaker, Rogers, *Citizenship and Nationhood in France and Germany* (Cambridge, MA: Harvard University Press, 1992).

Butler, Judith, 'Kantians in Every Culture?', *Boston Review* 18 (1994), p. 18.

Butting, K., *Die Buchstaben werden sich noch wundern: Innerbiblische Kritik als Wegweisung feministischer Hermeneutik* (Alektor-Hochschulschriften; Berlin: Alektor-Verlag, 1994).

Campbell, Edward F., Jr, *Ruth* (AB, 7; Garden City, NY: Doubleday, 1975).

'Cat, Domestic', *Microsoft ® Encarta® 97 Encyclopedia* (Redmond, WA: Microsoft Corporation, 1993–96).

Chilsen, Liz, and Sheldon Rampton, *Friends in Deed: The Story of U.S.–Nicaraguan Sister Cities* (Madison: Wisconsin Co-ordinating Council on Nicaragua, 1988).

Clines, David J.A., *Ezra, Nehemiah, Esther* (New Century Bible Commentary; London: Marshall, Morgan & Scott, 1984).

Collins, Patricia Hill, *Black Feminist Thought: Knowledge, Consciousness, and the Politics of Empowerment* (London: Routledge, 1990).

Coxon, P.W., 'Was Naomi a Scold? A Response to Fewell and Gunn', *JSOT* 45 (1989), pp. 25-37.

Cronin, C., 'Illusion and Reality in Sicily', in A. Schlegel (ed.), *Sexual Stratification: A Cross-Cultural View* (New York: Columbia University Press, 1977), pp. 67-93.

Dangarengwa, Tsitsi, *Nervous Conditions* (Philadelphia: Fortress Press, 1989).

Darnton, Robert, *The Great Cat Massacre and Other Episodes in French Cultural History* (New York: Basic Books, 1984).

Darr, Kathryn Pfisterer, *Far More Precious than Jewels: Perspectives on Biblical Women* (Louisville, KY: Westminster/John Knox Press, 1991).

Das Buch Ruth (Beratungstelle für Gestaltung von Gottesdiensten and anderen Gemeindeveranstaltungen; Frankfurt, 1994).

Derrida, Jacques, *Glas* (Lincoln, NE: University of Nebraska Press, 1986).

—*Of Grammatology: Translated and Introduced by Gayatri Chakravorty Spivak* (Baltimore: The Johns Hopkins University Press, 1976).

—*Politics of Friendship* (trans. George Collins; London: Verso, 1997).

DeVaux, R., *Ancient Israel* (trans. J. McHugh; New York: McGraw–Hill, 1961).

Diamond, S., *In Search of the Primitive* (New Brunswick: Transaction Books, 1974).

Dickerson, Bette, *African American Single Mothers: Understanding their Lives and Families* (London: Sage, 1995).

Dijk-Hemmes, F. van, 'Ruth: A Product of Women's Culture?', in Brenner (ed.), *A Feminist Companion to Ruth*, pp. 134-39.

Ebach, J., 'Fremde in Moab—Fremde aus Moab', in J. Ebach and R. Faber (eds.), *Bibel und Literatur* (Munich: Fink, 1995), pp. 277-301.

Epstein, Louis M., *Sex Laws and Customs in Judaism* (New York: Ktav, rev. edn, 1967).

Evans, S.M., *Born for Liberty: A History of Women in America* (New York: Free Press; New York: Macmillan, 1989).

Even-Shoshan, A., *A New Concordance of the Old Testament* (Jerusalem: Kiryath Sepher, 1985).

Exum, J. Cheryl, *Fragmented Women: Feminist (Sub)versions of Biblical Narratives* (Valley Forge, PA: Trinity Press International, 1993).

—' "Mothers in Israel": A Familiar Story Reconsidered', in Letty M. Russell (ed.), *Feminist Interpretation of the Bible* (Philadelphia: Westminster Press, 1985), pp. 73-85.

—*Plotted, Shot, and Painted: Cultural Representations of Biblical Women* (JSOTSup, 215; Gender, Culture, Theory, 3; Sheffield: Sheffield Academic Press, 1996).

—'The Mothers of Israel: The Patriarchal Narratives from a Feminist Perspective', *BR* 2 (1986), pp. 60-67.

—' "You Shall Let Every Daughter Live": A Study of Exodus 1.8–2.10', *Semeia* 28 (1983), pp. 63-82.

Fabian, Johannes, *Time and the Other: How Anthropology Makes its Object* (New York: Columbia University Press, 1983).

Fander, Monika, 'Die Geschichte einer Freundschaft', in Meissner (ed.), *Und sie tanzen aus der Reihe*, pp. 94-104.

Fanon, Frantz, *A Dying Colonialism* (trans. Haakon Chevalier; New York: Grove Press, 1965).

Fewell, Danna Nolan, 'Joshua', in Newsom and Ringe (eds.), *The Women's Bible Commentary*, pp. 63-66.

—'Judges', in Newsom and Ringe (eds.), *The Women's Bible Commentary*, pp. 67-77.

Fewell, Danna Nolan, and David M. Gunn, ' "A Son Is Born to Naomi!": Literary Allusions and Interpretation in the Book of Ruth', *JSOT* 40 (1988), pp. 99-108.

—'Boaz, Pillar of Society: Measures of Worth in the Book of Ruth', *JSOT* 45 (1989), pp. 45-59.

—*Compromising Redemption: Relating Characters in the Book of Ruth* (Louisville, KY: Westminster/John Knox Press, 1990).

—'Is Coxon a Scold? On Responding to the Book of Ruth', *JSOT* 45 (1989), pp. 39-43.

Fisch, H., 'Ruth and the Structure of Covenant History', *VT* 32 (1982), pp. 425-37.

Fischer, I., 'Affidamento in einer patriarchalen Gesellschaft: Frauenbeziehungen im Buch Rut', in Grazer Interdisziplinäre Frauengruppe (ed.), *Paris-Milano-Graz* (Vienna: Wiener Frauenverlag, 1991), pp. 111-25.

—'Den Frauen der Kochtopf—den Männern die hohe Politik?', *CPB* 108 (1995), pp. 134-38.

—'Der Männerstammbaum im Frauenbuch', in R. Kessler *et al.* (eds.), *'Ihr Völker alle, klatscht in die Hände!': Festschrift für Erhard S. Gerstenberger zum 65 Geburtstag* (Exegese in unserer Zeit, 3; Münster: LIT-Verlag, 1997), pp. 195-213.

—*Die Erzeltern Israels* (BZAW, 222; Berlin: W. de Gruyter, 1994).

—'Eine Schwiegertochter—mehr wert als sieben Söhne! (Rut 4.15)', in H. Pissarek-Hudelist and L. Schottroff (eds.), *Mit allen Sinnen glauben: Für Elisabeth Moltmann-Wendel zum 65. Geburtstag* (GTBS, 532; Gütersloh: Gütersloher Verlagshaus, 1991), pp. 30-44.

—*Gottesstreiterinnen* (Stuttgart: W. Kohlhammer, 1995).

—'Rut—Das Frauenbuch der Hebräischen Bibel', *rhs* 39 (1996), pp. 1-6.

Fontaine, Carole R., 'More Queenly Proverb Performance: The Queen of Sheba in Targum Esther Sheni', in Michael L. Barré, SS (ed.), *Wisdom, You Are my Sister: Studies in Honor of Roland E. Murphy, O.Carm., on the Occasion of his Eightieth Birthday* (CBQMS, 29; Washington: Catholic Biblical Association, 1997), pp. 216-33.

Foucault, Michel, *Der Gebrauch der Lüste: Sexualität und Wahrheit* (3 vols.; Frankfurt: Suhrkamp Verlag, 1991).

—'Las Meninas', in *The Order of Things* (trans. Alan Sheridan; New York: Vintage Books, 1973), pp. 3-16.

Fox, Greer Litton, 'Patterns and Outcomes of Mother–Daughter Communications about Sexuality', *Journal of Social Issues* 36 (1980), pp. 7-29.

Freud, Sigmund, *The Standard Edition of the Complete Psychological Works of Sigmund Freud. XVIII. Beyond the Pleasure Principle* (ed. James Strachey; London: Hogarth Press, 1953–74).

—*Moses and Monotheism* (New York: Vintage Books, 1955).

Frick, F.S., 'Cities: An Overview', *OEANE*, II, pp. 14-19.

Fried, Michael, *Absorption and Theatricality: Painting and Beholder in the Age of Diderot* (Berkeley: University of California Press, 1980).

Friedl, E., 'The Position of Women: Appearance and Reality', *Anthropological Quarterly* 40 (1967), pp. 97-108.

Fritz, V., 'Cities of the Bronze and Iron Ages', *OEANE*, II, pp. 19-25.

Gerleman, G., *Ruth: Das Hohelied* (BK, 18; Neukirchen-Vluyn: Neukirchener Verlag, 1965).

Gilkes, Cheryl Townsend, 'The "Loves" and "Troubles" of African-American Women's Bodies: The Womanist Challenge to Cultural Humiliation and Community Ambivalence', in Emilie Townes (ed.), *A Troubling in my Soul: Womanist Perspectives on Evil and Suffering* (Maryknoll, NY: Orbis Books, 1993), pp. 232-49.

Goody, Jack, (ed.), *Literacy in Traditional Societies* (Cambridge: Cambridge University Press, 1968).

—*The Domestication of the Savage Mind* (Cambridge: Cambridge University Press, 1977).

Gottwald, N.K., *The Hebrew Bible: A Socio-Literary Introduction* (Philadelphia: Fortress Press, 1985).

—*Tribes of Yahweh* (Maryknoll, NY: Orbis Books, 1979).

Goulder, M.D., 'Ruth: A Homily on Deuteronomy 22–25?', in H.A. McKay and D.J.A. Clines (eds.), *Of Prophets' Visions and the Wisdom of Sages: Essays in Honour of R. Norman Whybray on his Seventieth Birthday* (JSOTSup, 162; Sheffield: Sheffield Academic Press, 1993), pp. 307-19.

Green, Rayna, 'The Pocahontas Perplex: The Image of Indian Women in American Culture', *Massachusetts Review* (autumn 1975), pp. 698-714.

Greene, Beverly, 'What Has Gone before: The Legacy of Racism and Sexism in the Lives of Black Mothers and Daughters', *Women and Therapy* 9 (1990), pp. 207-30.

Gunkel, Hermann, *What Remains of the Old Testament, and Other Essays* (trans. A.K. Dallas; New York: Macmillan, 1928).

Gunn, David Miller, *Compromising Redemption: Relating Characters in the Book of Ruth* (Louisville, KY: Westminster/John Knox Press, 1990).

Gutmann, Joseph, *Hebrew Manuscript Painting* (New York: George Braziller, 1978).

Hadley, Judith M., 'From Goddess to Literary Construct: The Transformation of Asherah into Hokma', in Athalya Brenner and Carole R. Fontaine (eds.), *A Feminist Companion to Reading the Bible: Approaches, Methods and Strategies* (Sheffield: Sheffield Academic Press, 1997), pp. 360-99.

Haile, Barbara and Audreye Johnson, 'Teaching and Learning about Black Women: The Anatomy of a Course', *SAGE: A Scholarly Journal on Black Women* 6 (1989), pp. 69-73.

Halbfas, Hubertus, 'Sakrament Brot', in Misereor (ed.), *Biblische Frauengestalten*.

Harris, Rivkah, 'Independent Women in Ancient Mesopotamia?', in Barbara S. Lesko (ed.), *Women's Earliest Records from Ancient Egypt and Western Asia* (Atlanta: Scholars Press, 1989), pp. 145-56.

Helly, D.O., and S. Reverby (eds.), *Gendered Domains: Rethinking Public and Private in Women's History* (Ithaca, NY: Cornell University Press, 1992).

Hendricks, Obery O., 'Guerilla Exegesis: A Post-Modern Proposal for Insurgent African-American Biblical Interpretation', *Koinonia* 7.1 (1995), pp. 1-19.

Hollifield, James, *Immigrants, Markets and States: The Political Economy of Postwar Europe* (Cambridge, MA: Harvard University Press, 1992).

Honig, Bonnie, *Democracy and Foreignness* (Princeton, NJ: Princeton University Press, forthcoming 1999/2000).

—'Immigrant America? How Foreignness "Solves" Democracy's Problems', in *Social Text* 56.16.3 (Fall 1998), pp. 1-27.

Horst-Warhaft, Gail, *Dangerous Voices: Women's Laments in Greek Literature* (London: Routledge, 1992).

Hubbard, R.L., *The Book of Ruth* (NICOT; Grand Rapids: Eerdmans, 1988).

Hutcheon, Linda, *A Poetics of Postmodernism: History, Theory, Fiction* (London: Routledge, 1988).

—*Narcissistic Narrative: The Metafictional Paradox* (New York: Methuen, 1982).

Irigaray, Luce, *Speculum of the Other Woman* (Ithaca, NY: Cornell University Press, 1985).

Jaffé, H.L.C., 'The Illustrations', in M. Spitzer (ed.), *The Bird's Head Haggada of the Bezalel National Art Museum in Jerusalem* (2 vols.; Jerusalem: Tarshish Books, 1965–67), I, pp. 31-88.

Jefferson, Thomas, *Notes on the State of Virginia* (ed. William Peden; New York: W.W. Norton, 1982).

—*The Writings of Thomas Jefferson* (ed. Albert Ellery Bergh; Washington, DC: The Thomas Jefferson Memorial Association of the United States, 1907).

Jobling, David, 'Ruth Finds a Home: Canon, Politics, Method', in J. Cheryl Exum and David J.A. Clines (eds.), *The New Literary Criticism and the Hebrew Bible* (JSOTSup, 143; Sheffield: Sheffield Academic Press, 1993), pp. 125-39.

Jost, R., *Freundin in der Fremde* (Stuttgart: Quell, 1992).

Kaiser, Barbara Bakke, 'Poet as "Female Impersonator": The Image of Daughter Zion as Speaker in Biblical Poems of Suffering', *Journal of Religion* 67 (1987), pp. 164-82.

Kamuf, Peggy, *Signature Pieces: On the Institution of Authorship* (Ithaca, NY: Cornell University Press, 1988).

Kaplan, Rosa Felsenburg, 'The Noah Syndrome', in Susanna Heschel (ed.), *On Being a Jewish Feminist* (New York: Schocken Books, 1983), pp. 167-70.

Kates, Judith A., 'Women at the Center: Ruth and Shavuoth', in Kates and Reimer (eds.), *Reading Ruth*.

Kates, Judith A., and Gail Twersky Reimer (eds.), *Reading Ruth: Contemporary Women Reclaim a Sacred Story* (New York: Ballantine, 1994).

Kessler, R., 'Zur israelitischen Löserinstitution', in M. Crüsemann and W. Schottroff (eds.), *Schuld und Schulden* (KT, 121; Munich: Kaiser, 1992), pp. 40-53.

Kincaid, Jamaica, 'The Circling Hand', in Washington (ed.), *Memory of Kin*, pp. 111-24.

Kristeva, Julia, *Nations without Nationalism* (trans. Leon S. Roudiez; New York: Columbia University Press, 1993).

—*Strangers to Ourselves* (trans. Leon S. Roudiez; New York: Columbia University Press, 1991).

Krüger, T., 'Genesis 38—ein "Lehrstück" alttestamentlicher Ethik', in R. Bartelmus et al. (eds.), *Konsequente Traditionsgeschichte: Festschrift für Klaus Baltzer zum 65 Geburtstag* (OBO, 126; Fribourg: Universitätsverlag, 1993).

Kwok, Pui Lan, *Discovering the Bible in the Non-Biblical World: The Bible and Liberation* (Maryknoll, NY: Orbis Books, 1995).

Labovitz, Priscilla, 'Immigration—Just the Facts', *New York Times*, 25 March 1996.

Lacan, Jacques, *The Four Fundamental Concepts of Psycho-Analysis* (ed. J.A. Miller; trans. A. Sheridan; London: Hogarth Press and the Institute of Psycho-Analysis, 1979).

LaCocque, A., *The Feminine Unconventional: Four Subversive Figures in Israel's Tradition* (Philadelphia: Fortress Press, 1990).

Lambert, C., 'Leadership in a New Key', *Harvard Magazine* 97 (1995), pp. 28-33.

Larkin, Katrina J.A., *Ruth and Esther* (Old Testament Guides; Sheffield: Sheffield Academic Press, 1996).

Larson, Janet L., 'The Battle of Biblical Books in Esther's Narrative', *Nineteenth Century Fiction* 38 (1983), pp. 131-60.

Lee, Andrea, 'Mother', in Washington (ed.), *Memory of Kin*, pp. 99-108.

Lemaire, T., 'Antropologie en schrift: Aanzetten tot cen ideologickritick van het schrift', in T. Lemaire (ed.), *Antropologie en ideologie* (Groningen: Konstapel, 1984), pp. 103-26.

—'Une inscription phénicienne découverte récemment et le mariage de Ruth la Moabite', *ErIs* 20 (1989), pp. 124*-29*.

Lenski, G., *Power and Privilege: A Theory of Social Stratification* (Chapel Hill: University of North Carolina Press, 1984).

Lesko, B., 'Women of Egypt and the Ancient Near East', in R. Bridenthal and C. Koonz (eds.), *Becoming Visible: Women in European History* (Boston: Houghton Mifflin, 1987), pp. 41-77.

Lévi-Strauss, Claude, *Tristes Tropiques* (Paris: Plon, 1955).

Levine, Amy-Jill, 'Ruth', in Newsom and Ringe (eds.), *The Women's Bible Commentary*, pp. 78-84.

Little, Ganse, '2 Samuel: Exposition', *IB*, II, pp. 1041-1176.

Loader, J.A., 'Of Barley, Bulls, Land and Levirate', in F. García Martínez *et al.* (eds.), *Studies in Deuteronomy: In Honour of C.J. Labuschagne on the Occasion of his 65th Birthday* (VTSup, 53; Leiden: E.J. Brill, 1994), pp. 132-38.

Lorde, Audre, 'Black Mother Woman', in Washington (ed.), *Memory of Kin*, p. 98.

Magonet, Jonathan, 'The Liberal and the Lady: Esther Revisited', *Judaism* 29 (1980), pp. 167-76.

Maher, V., 'Kins, Clients, and Accomplices: Relationships among Women in Morocco', in D.L. Barber and S. Allen (eds.), *Sexual Divisions and Society: Process and Change* (Explorations in Sociology, 6; London: Tavistock, 1976), pp. 52-75.

Maldonado, Robert D., 'Reading Malinche Reading Ruth: Towards a Hermeneutics of Betrayal', *Semeia* 72 (1995), pp. 91-109.

Mankiller, Wilma, with Michael Wallis, *Mankiller: A Chief and her People* (New York: St Martin's Press, 1984).

March, K.S., and R.L. Taqqu, *Women's Informal Associations in Developing Countries* (Women in Cross-Cultural Perspective; Boulder, CO: Westview Press, 1986).

Matthews, Victor H., and Don C. Benjamin, 'Introduction: Social Sciences and Biblical Studies', *Semeia* 68 (1994), pp. 7-21.

McClintock, Anne, 'The Angel of Progress: Pitfalls of the Term "Postcolonialism"', in Francis Barker, Peter Hulme and Margaret Iversen (eds.), *Colonial Discourse/Postcolonial Theory* (Manchester: Manchester University Press, 1994), pp. 253-66.

McHale, Brian, *Postmodernist Fiction* (London: Methuen, 1987).

Meehan, Bernard, *The Book of Kells: An Illustrated Introduction to the Manuscript in Trinity College Dublin* (London: Thames & Hudson, 1994).

Meinhold, Arndt, 'Die Gattung der Josephsgeschichte und des Estherbuches: Diasporanovelle, I', *ZAW* 87 (1975), pp. 306-24.

—'Die Gattung der Josephsgeschichte und des Estherbuches: Diasporanovelle, II', *ZAW* 88 (1976), pp. 72-93.

Meissner, Angelika, 'Hoffnung wider alle Hoffnungslosigkeit. Noomi', in Angelika Meissner (ed.), *Und sie tanzen aus der Reihe: Frauen im Alten Testament* (Stuttgart: Verlag Katholisches Bibelwerk, 1992), pp. 105-119.

Menchú, Rigoberta, *I, Rigoberta Menchú: An Indian Woman in Guatemala* (ed. Elisabeth Burgos-Debray; trans. Ann Wright; London: Verso, 1984).

Mesters, Carlos, *Rute: Una historia da Biblia* (Sao Paolo: Ediçoes Paulinas, 1985).

Metzger, Thérèse, and Mendel Metzger, *Jewish Life in the Middle Ages: Illuminated Hebrew Manuscripts of the Thirteenth to the Sixteenth Centuries* (New York: Alpine Fine Arts Collection, 1982).

Meyers, Carol L., 'Everyday Life: Women in the Period of the Hebrew Bible', in Newsom and Ringe (eds.), *The Women's Bible Commentary*, pp. 244-51 (expanded edn, 1997, pp. 251-59).

—'Gender Imagery in the Song of Songs', *HAR* 10 (1986), pp. 209-23.

—'Guilds and Gatherings: Women's Groups in Ancient Israel', in P.M. Williams, Jr, and T. Hiebert (eds.), *Realia Dei: Essays in Honor of Edward F. Campbell, Jr* (Scholars Press Bible and Archaeology Series; Atlanta: Scholars Press, forthcoming).

—'Midwife (Gen 35.17; 38.28)', in C. Meyers, T. Craven and R. Kraemer (eds.), *Women in Scripture: A Dictionary of the Named and Unnamed Women in the Hebrew Bible, Apocryphal/Deuterocanonical Books, and New Testament* (Boston: Houghton Mifflin, forthcoming).

—'Mother to Muse: An Ethnoarchaeological Study of Women's Performance in Ancient Israel', in A. Brenner and J.W. van Henten (eds.), *Recycling Biblical Figures: NOSTER Conference 1997* (Leiden: DEO, forthcoming).

—'Procreation, Production, and Protection: Male–Female Balance in Early Israel', *JAAR* 51 (1983), pp. 569-93.

—'Returning Home: Ruth 1.8 and the Gendering of the Book of Ruth', in Brenner (ed.), *A Feminist Companion to Ruth*, pp. 85-114.

—'The Family in Early Israel', in L. Perdue, C. Meyers, J. Blenkinsopp and J.J. Collins, *Families in Ancient Israel* (Family, Religion and Culture Series; Louisville, KY: Westminster/John Knox Press, 1997), pp. 1-47.

—' "To Her Mother's House": Considering a Counterpart to the Israelite Bêt 'āb', in David Jobling, Peggy L. Day and Gerald T. Sheppard (eds.), *The Bible and the Politics of Exegesis* (Cleveland: Pilgrim Press, 1991), pp. 39-51.

Miller, David, *On Nationality* (Oxford: Oxford University Press, 1996).

Miller, J. Hillis, *Topographies: Crossing Aesthetics* (Stanford, CA: Stanford University Press, 1995).

Milne, P.J., 'Toward Feminist Companionship: The Future of Feminist Biblical Studies and Feminism', in Brenner and Fontaine (eds.), *A Feminist Companion to Reading the Bible*, pp. 39-60.

Misereor, Bischoefliches Hilfswerk e.V. (ed.), *Das Misereor-Hungertuch: Biblische Frauengestalten—Wegweiser zum Reich Gottes* (Aachen: Misereor-Vertriebsgesellschaft; Reihe: Arbeitshefte zum Hungertuch, 1989).

Moore, Carey (ed. and trans.), *Esther* (AB, 7B; Garden City, NY: Doubleday, 1971).

Morrison, Toni, 'On the Backs of Blacks', in Nicolaus Mills (ed.), *Arguing Immigration* (New York: Simon & Schuster, 1994), pp. 97-100.

—*The Bluest Eye* (with a new afterword by the author; New York: PLUME, 1970; London: Penguin Books, 1993).

Moruzzi, Norma, 'A Problem with Headscarves: Contemporary Complexities of Political and Social Identity', *Political Theory* 22 (1994), pp. 653-72.

Murphy, Roland E., *Wisdom Literature: Job, Proverbs, Ruth, Canticles, Ecclesiastes, Esther* (Grand Rapids: Eerdmans, 1981).

Narkiss, Bezalel, *Illuminated Hebrew Manuscripts* (New York: Alpine Fine Arts Collection, 1983).

—'On Zoocephalic Phenomenon in Mediaeval Ashkenazi Manuscripts', in *Norms and Variations in Art: Essays in Honor of Moshe Barasch* (Jerusalem: Magnes Press; Hebrew University, 1983), pp. 49-62.

—*The Golden Haggadah* (Rohnert Park, CA: Pomegranate Art Books, 1997).

Newsom, Carol A., and Sharon H. Ringe (eds.), *The Women's Bible Commentary* (Louisville, KY: Westminster/John Knox Press, 1992).

Niditch, Susan, 'Genesis', in Newsom and Ringe (eds.), *The Women's Bible Commentary*, pp. 10-25.

Orange, Claudia, *The Treaty of Waitangi* (Wellington: Allen & Unwin New Zealand Ltd, 1987).

Otto, E., 'Biblische Altersversorgung im altorientalischen Rechtsvergleich', *Zeitschrift für altorientalische und biblische Rechtsgeschichte* 1 (1995), pp. 83-110.

Otwell, John H., *And Sarah Laughed: The Status of Woman in the Old Testament* (Philadelphia: Westminster Press, 1977).

Ozick, Cynthia, 'Ruth', in Kates and Reimer (eds.), *Reading Ruth*, pp. 211-32.

Pardes, I., 'Beyond Genesis 3: The Politics of Maternal Naming', in *idem, Countertraditions in the Bible: A Feminist Approach* (Cambridge, MA: Harvard University Press, 1992), pp. 39-59.

Patai, Raphael, *The Hebrew Goddess* (Detroit, MI: Wayne State University Press, 3rd edn, 1990).

Phipps, William E., *Assertive Biblical Women* (Contributions in Women's Studies, 128; Westport, CT: Greenwood Press, 1992).

Pope, M.H., *Song of Songs* (AB, 7C; Garden City, NY: Doubleday, 1977).

Pratt, Mary Louise, *Imperial Eyes: Travel Writing and Transculturation* (London: Routledge, 1992).

—'"Yo soy la malinche": Chicana Writers and the Poetics of Ethnonationalism', *Callaloo* 16 (1993), pp. 859-73.

Projektgruppe 'Ruth' (ed.), *Das Buch Ruth: Eine Weg-Beschreibung mit Texten, Liedern, Tänzen und Gebeten* (Frankfurt: Beratungsstelle für Gestaltung von Gottesdiensten und anderen Gemeindeveranstaltungen, 1994).

Quinn, N., 'Anthropological Studies on Women's Status', *Annual Review of Anthropology* 6 (1977), pp. 181-225.

Rashkow, I., 'Ruth: The Discourse of Power and the Power of Discourse', in Brenner (ed.), *A Feminist Companion to Ruth*, pp. 26-41.

Reimer, Gail Twersky, 'Her Mother's House', in Kates and Reimer (eds.), *Reading Ruth*, pp. 97-106.

Richler, Binyamin, *Hebrew Manuscripts: A Treasured Legacy* (Cleveland: Ofeq Institute, 1990).

Rodriguez, Angel Manuel, *Esther: A Theological Approach* (Berrien Springs, MI: Andrews University Press, 1995).

Rogers, S.C., 'Female Forms of Power and the Myth of Male Dominance: A Model of Female/Male Interaction in Peasant Society', *American Ethnologist* 2 (1975), pp. 741-54.

Rosaldo, M.Z., 'The Use and Abuse of Anthropology: Reflections on Feminism and Cross-cultural Understanding', *Signs* 5 (1980), pp. 389-417.

—'Women, Culture, and Society: A Theoretical Overview', in Rosaldo and Lamphere (eds.), *Women, Culture, and Society*, pp. 17-42.

Rosaldo, M.Z., and L. Lamphere (eds.), *Women, Culture, and Society* (Stanford, CA: Stanford University Press, 1974).

Rose, Wendy, *Going to War with All my Relations: New and Selected Poems* (Flagstaff, AZ: Entrada Books, 1993).

Rosenthal, L.A., 'Die Josephsgeschichte mit den Büchern Esther und Daniel verglichen', *ZAW* 15 (1985), pp. 278-84.

Rousseau, Jean-Jacques, '*On the Social Contract*', in *The Basic Political Writings* (trans. Donald A. Cress; Indianapolis, IN: Hackett, 1988).

Rudy, K., ' "Haven in a Heartless World": The Historical Roots of Gendered Theology', in *idem, Sex and the Church: Gender, Homosexuality, and the Transformation of Christian Ethics* (Boston: Beacon Press, 1997), pp. 15-44.

Sacks, Peter, *The English Elegy: Studies in Genre from Spenser to Yeats* (Baltimore: The Johns Hopkins University Press, 1985).

Sanday, P.R., 'Female Status in the Public Domain', in Rosaldo and Lamphere (eds.), *Women, Culture, and Society*, pp. 189-206.

Santner, Eric L., *Stranded Objects: Mourning, Memory and Film in Postwar Germany* (Ithaca, NY: Cornell University Press, 1990).

Sasson, Jack M., 'Esther', in Robert Alter and Frank Kermode (eds.), *The Literary Guide to the Bible* (Cambridge, MA: Harvard University Press, 1987), pp. 335-42.

—*Ruth: A New Translation with a Philological Commentary and a Formalist-Folklorist Interpretation* (The Johns Hopkins Near Eastern Studies, 11; Baltimore: The Johns Hopkins University Press, 1979; The Biblical Seminar, 10: Sheffield: JSOT Press, 2nd edn, 1989).

Schottroff, W., 'Die Armut der Witwen', in M. Crüsemann and W. Schottroff (eds.), *Schuld und Schulden* (KT, 121; Munich: Chr. Kaiser Verlag, 1992), pp. 54-89.

Schroer, Sylvia, ' "Under the Shadow of your Wings": The Metaphor of God's Wings in the Psalms, Exodus 19.4, Deuteronomy 32.11 and Malachi 3.20, as Seen through the Perspectives of Feminism and the History of Religion', in Athalya Brenner and Carole R. Fontaine (eds.), *Wisdom and Psalms: A Feminist Companion to the Bible (Second Series)* (The Feminist Companion to the Bible, 2; Sheffield: Sheffield Academic Press, 1998), pp. 264-82.

Schuller, Eileen, 'Women of the Exodus in Biblical Retellings of the Second Temple Period', in Peggy L. Day (ed.), *Gender and Difference in Ancient Israel* (Minneapolis: Fortress Press, 1989), pp. 178-94.

Schüssler Fiorenza, E., *Brot statt Steine* (Fribourg: Exodus-Verlag, 1988).

Scott, James C., *Domination and the Arts of Resistance: Hidden Transcripts* (New Haven: Yale University Press, 1990).

Searle, John, '*Las Meninas* and the Paradoxes of Pictorial Representation', *Critical Inquiry* 6 (1980), pp. 477-88.

Sed-Rajna, Gabrielle, *The Hebrew Bible in Medieval Illuminated Manuscripts* (trans. Josephine Bacon; New York: Rizzoli, 1987).

Seeligmann, I.L., 'Voraussetzungen der Midraschexegese', in *Congress Volume: Copenhagen 1953* (VTSup, 1; Leiden: E.J. Brill, 1953), pp. 150-81.

Sered, S.S., *Women as Ritual Experts: The Religious Lives of Elderly Jewish Women in Jerusalem* (New York: Oxford University Press, 1992).

Setel, Drorah O'Donnell, 'Exodus', in Newsom and Ringe (eds.), *The Women's Bible Commentary*, pp. 26-35.

Shange, Ntozake, *for colored girls who have considered suicide/when the rainbow is enuf: a choreopoem* (New York: Macmillan, 1977).

Shargent, Karla G., 'Living on the Edge: The Liminality of Daughters in Genesis to 2 Samuel', in A. Brenner (ed.), *A Feminist Companion to Samuel and Kings* (Feminist Companion to the Bible, 5; Sheffield: Sheffield Academic Press, 1994), pp. 26-42.

Sharistanian, J. (ed.), *Beyond the Public/Private Dichotomy: Contemporary Perspectives on Women's Public Lives* (Contributions to Women's Studies, 78; Westport, CT: Greenwood Press, 1987).

Small, M.F., *Female Choices: Sexual Behavior of Female Primates* (Ithaca, NY: Cornell University Press, 1993).

Snyder, Joel, and Ted Cohen, 'Reflexions on *Las Meninas*: Paradox Lost', *Critical Inquiry* 7 (1981), pp. 429-47.

Spiegelman, Art, *Maus II, a Survivor's Tale: And Here my Troubles Began* (New York: Pantheon Books, 1991).

Stager, L.E., 'The Archaeology of the Family in Ancient Israel', *BASOR* 260 (1985), pp. 1-36.

Steinberg, Leo, 'Velásquez' *Las Meninas*', *October* 19 (1981), pp. 45-54.

Stern, E., J. Berg, A. Gilboa, I. Sharon and J. Zorn, 'Tel Dor, 1994–95: Preliminary Stratigraphic Report', *IEJ* 47 (1997), pp. 29-56.

Strathern, M., *Women in between: Female Roles in a Male World* (Seminar Studies in Anthropology, 2; London: Seminar Press, 1972).

Takaki, Ronald, *A Different Mirror: A History of Multicultural America* (New York: Little, Brown & Co., 1993).

Talmon, S., '"Wisdom" in the Book of Esther', *VT* 13 (1963), pp. 419-55.

Thompson, D., and T. Thompson, 'Some Legal Problems in the Book of Ruth', *VT* 18 (1968), pp. 79-99.

Tinker, George E., *Missionary Conquest: The Gospel and Native American Cultural Genocide* (Philadelphia: Fortress Press, 1993).

Tompkins, Jane P., 'The Reader in History: The Changing Shape of Literary Response', in J.P. Tompkins (ed.), *Reader-Response Criticism: From Formalism to Post-Structuralism* (Baltimore: The Johns Hopkins University Press, 1980), pp. 201-31.

Tractenberg, Joshua, *The Devil and the Jews* (Philadelphia: Jewish Publication Society of America, 2nd edn, 1983).

Trenchard, Warren C., 'Woman as Daughter', in *idem, Ben Sira's View of Women: A Literary Analysis* (BJS, 38; Atlanta: Scholars Press, 1982), pp. 129-65.

Trepagnier, Barbara, 'The Politics of White and Black Bodies', *Feminism* 4 (1994), pp. 199-205.

Trible, Phyllis, *God and the Rhetoric of Sexuality* (Philadelphia: Fortress Press, 1978; in German, *Gott und Sexualität im Alten Testament* [GTBS, 539; Gütersloh: Gütersloher Verlagshaus, 1993]).

—*Texts of Terror: Literary-Feminist Readings of Biblical Narratives* (Philadelphia: Fortress Press, 1984).

Tucker, Gene M., 'The Book of Esther', in Bruce M. Metzger and Michael Coogan (eds.), *The Oxford Companion to the Bible* (New York: Oxford University Press, 1993), pp. 198-201.

Vesco, Jean-Luc, 'La date du livre de Ruth', *RB* 74 (1967), pp. 237-40.

Visvanathan, Shiv, 'From the Annals of the Laboratory State', *Alternatives: A Journal of World Policy* 12 (1987), pp. 37-59.

Vizenor, Gerald, *Manifest Manners: Postindian Warriors of Survivance* (London: Wesleyan University Press; University Press of New England, 1994).

Wacker, Marie-Theres, 'Biblisch-theologische Grundlegung. Ruth—Harmonie von Familie, Gesellschaft und Natur', in Misereor (ed.), *Das Misereor-Hungertuch*, pp. 37-38.

Walker, Alice, *In Search of our Mothers' Gardens: Womanist Prose* (New York: Harcourt Brace Jovanich, 1983 [1967]).

Washington, Mary Helen (ed.), *Memory of Kin: Stories about Family by Black Writers* (New York: Anchor; Garden City, NY: Doubleday, 1991).

Weems, Renita, *Just a Sister Away: A Womanist Vision of Women's Relationships in the Bible* (San Diego: Lura Media, 1988).

Weitzmann, K., 'The Question of the Influence of Jewish Pictorial Sources on Old Testament Illustration', in Herbert L. Kessler (ed.), *Studies in Classical and Byzantine Manuscript Illumination* (Chicago: University of Chicago Press, 1971), pp. 76-95.

West, R.F., *Ruth: A Retelling of Genesis 38?* (Ann Arbor: UMI, 1987).

Westbrook, R., *Property and the Family in Biblical Law* (JSOTSup, 113; Sheffield: Sheffield Academic Press, 1991).

White, Paulette, 'Getting the Facts of Life', in Washington (ed.), *Memory of Kin*, pp. 129-39.

White, Sidnie Ann, 'Esther', in Newsom and Ringe (eds.), *The Women's Bible Commentary*, pp. 124-29.

Wild, Ute, 'Das Buch Ruth: Denn wohin du gehst, will ich gehen', in Eva-Renate Schmidt *et al.* (eds.), *Feministisch gelesen* (2 vols.; Stuttgart: Kreuz Verlag, 1989), II, pp. 80-91.

Wilson, Elizabeth B., *Bibles and Bestiaries: A Guide to Illuminated Manuscripts* (New York: Farrar, Strauss & Giroux, 1994).

Winnicott, D.W., *Playing and Reality* (London: Tavistock, 1971).

Wodak, Ruth, and Muriel Schulz, *The Language of Love and Guilt: Mother–Daughter Relationships from a Cross-Cultural Perspective* (Amsterdam: John Benjamins, 1986).

Wolde, Ellen van, 'Texts in Dialogue with Texts: Intertextuality in the Ruth and Tamar Narratives', *Biblical Interpretation* 5.1 (1997), pp. 1-28.

Woodhull, Winnifred, *Transfigurations of the Maghreb: Feminism, Decolonization, and Literatures* (Minneapolis: University of Minnesota Press, 1993).

Wrangham, R.W., 'An Ecological Model of Female-Bonded Primate Groups', *Behaviour* 75 (1980), pp. 262-300.

Wyler, Bea, 'Esther: The Incomplete Emancipation of a Queen', in Brenner (ed.), *A Feminist Companion to Esther, Judith and Susanna*, pp. 111-35.

Young, Robert, *Analytical Concordance to the Bible* (Grand Rapids: Eerdmans, 1970).

Zelinsky, Wilbur, 'The Twinning of the World: Sister Cities in Geographical and Historical Perspective', *Annals of the Association of American Geographers* 81.1 (1991), pp. 1-31.

Zenger, Erich, *Das Buch Ruth* (ZBK, 8; Zürich: Theologischer Verlag, 1992 [1986]).

Zornberg, Avivah Gottlieb, *Genesis: The Beginning of Desire* (Philadelphia: Jewish Publication Society of America, 1995), pp. 225-29.

Zlotowitz, Rabbi Meir (trans. and comp.), *The Megillah: The Book of Esther. A New Translation with a Commentary Anthologized from Talmudic, Midrashic, and Rabbinic Sources* (New York: Mesorah Publications, 1976).

Zonabend, F., 'An Anthropological Perspective on Kinship and the Family', in A. Burghière, C. Klapisch-Zuber, M. Segalen and F. Zonabend (eds.), *A History of the Family*. I. *Distant Worlds, Ancient Worlds* (trans. S.H. Tenison, R. Morris and A. Wilson; Cambridge, MA: Harvard University Press, 1996), pp. 25-39.

INDEXES

INDEX OF REFERENCES

BIBLE

INDEX OF AUTHORS